# RIVERS OF FIRE

## *The Conflict over Water*
## *in*
## *the Middle East*

Arnon Soffer

Translated by
Murray Rosovsky and Nina Copaken

ROWMAN & LITTLEFIELD PUBLISHERS, INC.
*Lanham • Boulder • New York • Oxford*

ROWMAN & LITTLEFIELD PUBLISHERS, INC.

Published in the United States of America
by Rowman & Littlefield Publishers, Inc.
4720 Boston Way, Lanham, Maryland 20706

12 Hid's Copse Road
Cumnor Hill, Oxford OX2 9JJ, England

Copyright 1999 by Rowman & Littlefield Publishers, Inc.

British Library Cataloguing in Publication Information Available

**Library of Congress Cataloging-in-Publication Data**

Soffer, Arnon.
    [Neharot shel esh. English]
    Rivers of fire : the conflict over water in the Middle East /
Arnon Soffer : translated by Murry Rosovesky and Nina Copaken.
      p.  cm.
    Includes bibliographical references (p.  ) and index.
    ISBN 0-8476-8510-1 (hardcover : alk. paper).—ISBN 0-8476-8511-X
(pbk. : alk. paper)
    1. Water resources development—Middle East.  2. Water-supply—
Political aspects—Middle East.  3. Water rights—Middle East.
HD1698.M53S6413   1999
333.91'15'0956—dc21               98-25284
                                           CIP

Printed in the United States of America

# Contents

# Tables

# Maps and Figures

# Preface and Acknowledgments
# to the Hebrew Edition

Water use and its supply and demand are constant subjects in Middle Eastern geopolitics, and there is a great call for up-to-date information and additional knowledge on them. This book is intended to fill a gap on the issue, specifically for readers interested in the Middle East.

The book began as a report to the Israeli Foreign Ministry on water projects in the Middle East, prepared with my colleague Professor Nurit Kliot. Subsequently we worked together and individually to publish our conclusions.

Profound thanks are due to the staff of the Israeli Foreign Ministry, at whose initiative the report was written. I wish to thank Professor Nurit Kliot of the geography department at the University of Haifa for her enriching input, and my colleague Dr. M. Klein for his generous advice. I am grateful to my students at the various colleges for their support and their updated information, and to those who helped me bring the work to completion: S. Mansfeld, the cartographer; the staff at the University of Haifa Press; Atalia Zilber, for the editing; and my wife Mira, for her contributions all along the way.

# Preface and Acknowledgments
# to the English Edition

Since my book *Rivers of Fire* was first published in 1992, the Middle East has undergone some dramatic changes. The ideas of the Madrid Conference became real as Israel and the Palestinians signed the Declaration of Principles, Israel and Jordan signed a peace agreement, and intensive talks continue between Israel and Syria. The water issue is a notable topic in the talks and the agreement.

As a result of the new realities, Chapter 4 on the Jordan River has been rewritten entirely, and it covers events and interpretations up to July 1998. Since the first book was published, groundwater topics have become more problematic in the region, as have the complex relations along the Euphrates, the Tigris, and the Nile. All these developments are treated in the English edition.

Several books on water in the Middle East were published between 1992 and 1997. Many authors were enticed by the air of optimism that prevailed, and in some way forgot about the nature of the region under consideration. This book attempts to be more realistic, and does not as yet envisage a "New Middle East" or a new distribution of water.

I thank the cartographers S. Mansfeld and D. Binyamin for the new maps in the English version; Murray Rosovsky and Nina Copaken for their translation; Nurit Litvar for typing, organizing materials, and editing drafts; and my colleagues of the geography department at Portland State University, who provided me with a wonderful place to work and complete this English edition.

# Introduction

Water is a central issue on the national agendas of many countries owing to its multiple and varied uses: for drinking and irrigation, generation of electricity, sanitation, cooling, drainage, tourism and leisure activities, soil conservation, sailing, and fishing. Water may also cause natural disasters, which must be prevented or controlled. It is essential for the existence and security of certain countries, with its linkages to national interest, demography, agricultural and economic development, and sometimes even ideology (e.g., Israel). Indeed, it can shape domestic and foreign policies. In some countries water issues are not seen as particularly important, but in the Middle East they are of supreme significance, and matters related to water are treated as policy problems of utmost importance.

The severe droughts that struck various parts of the globe in the 1980s drew attention to the growing water shortage, which has become an almost worldwide phenomenon. The drought that hit the countries of the Sahel region in northwest Africa, as well as Ethiopia and Sudan, contributed to the grave famine there. In parts of the United States, especially California, a serious water shortage has developed following continuous years of drought. In 1990 the food stock of the United States dropped to the point where it became doubtful whether the United States and Canada could feed all those in need of their crops in both the developing and the developed world (*Time*, November 5, 1990, 35–40).

Nor have western European countries with rainy climates escaped drought and water shortage in the last decade. In Greece water rationing was imposed, and water shortage was felt in southern England, Italy, Spain, Hungary, and even Switzerland. In England the 1997 drought was the most severe for two centuries, and there is talk of importing water from Norway (*Yediot Aharonot*, May 16, 1997).

Yet it is not simply water shortage that causes concern, but primarily the serious lack of clean water for drinking and irrigation. Most rivers of the world have been polluted in ways that endanger those who use river water and who live on river banks (Biswas and Kindler, 1989: 225; Biswas, 1994: 186).

In the past 40 years the demand for water has risen as a consequence of high population growth, mostly in the developing world. In 1950 the world population was 2.5 billion. By 1996 the population of the world had more than doubled, reaching 5.77 billion. Every year an additional 100 million people are added, and in 2010 the world population will stand at 7.0 billion; 15 years later it should reach 8.2 billion (Population Reference Bureau, 1996). This population will need water for drinking, irrigation, industry, and leisure. Will it find enough water to provide for all its needs (Postel, 1992; Clark, 1993; Ohlsson, 1995: 26)?

The water shortage is aggravated not only by environmental pollution, natural disasters, and population growth; in most countries water management also is defective, and usually outdated. Water policy is also affected by geopolitical considerations, which prevent optimal exploitation. If the processes described above continue, crises and disasters are to be expected in extensive areas of the world, and they will strike with increasing frequency until economic and social order are imperiled (Homer-Dixon et al., 1993).

This book focuses on international rivers and groundwater in the Middle East. Nations in this region, locked in a never-ending battle to match population growth with food and energy production, have for the past few decades been frenziedly engaged in water resource development, including that of international rivers and groundwater, without considering each other's needs in the process. The inevitable result has been more frequent conflicts, the severity of which has grown increasingly serious (Gleick, 1993; Rogers and Lydon, 1994).

However, the collapse of the Soviet Union, leaving the United States the sole superpower, has led to a peace process between Israel and its neighbors. This peace process has involved the formation of various subcommittees to discuss regional issues in general, such as water, refugees, arms limitation, and ecology. Specific peace arrangements between Israel and Jordan also have been discussed (in October 1994 a peace accord was signed between the two states, including an extensive clause covering water distribution between them). Discussions are being conducted between Israel and the Palestinians, and an important clause in the Declaration of Principles signed in Oslo in 1993 is likewise devoted to the subject of water. The global geopolitical change, coupled with the various levels of water crisis already felt in the Middle East, may lead to the search for solutions.

The geopolitical changes in the Euphrates and Tigris basin and in the Nile basin might in the medium and long term produce rational solutions in those areas of the Middle East also. The peace processes between Israel and its neighbors are only beginning, be they between Israel and Jordan, Israel and the Palestinians, or Syria and Lebanon.

Meanwhile, the population of the area continues to grow apace and the extremist religious movements continue to claim victims in various countries and to threaten their regimes. There is also still tension among Turkey, Syria, and Iraq, and also among Egypt, Sudan, and Ethiopia.

In the 1990s the Middle East wavers between hope and despair over solutions to the water crises. The hope exists that with the help of the affluent countries in the world, and the assistance of the more thoughtful states and leaders in the region, the required water will be found for domestic and industrial needs, and agriculture will become less wasteful and more rational.

Yet a sense of despair stems from the feeling that the disinterest of the region's leaders in the looming crisis will grow ever greater causing additional catastrophe and greater suffering.

Academics and engineers alike ceaselessly offer logical solutions for the water crisis. Indeed, if we could disregard geopolitical considerations, personal ambitions, and ancient traditions, it would be possible to solve the problems of water in the Middle East.

I shall mention just a few of the optimistic proposals that have captured the attention of scholars, writers, and conference organizers. Hillel Shuval published, individually and together with Jewish and Palestinian colleagues, visions of the transfer of water from Turkey to the Near East and the import of other water to Israel and its independent neighbors (Shuval, 1992; Assaf et al., 1993).

The Israeli Foreign Ministry issued a series of proposals for giant desalination projects for Red Sea and Mediterranean Sea water, which would descend to the Dead Sea in impressive canals (Israel, *Development Options*, 1994, 1996, 1997). Shimon Peres, the former prime minister, published a book titled *The New Middle East*, which includes an ardent chapter on regional peace and water transfer through Syria to Israel (Peres, 1993). Many studies have been published on the states and rivers of the region and how, with a rational approach, the water problems of the area may be solved (Kally, 1990; Watchtal, 1993; Libiszewski, 1995; Wolf and Lonergan, 1995).

Biswas (1994) and others (Lowi, 1993; Rogers and Lydon, 1994; Wolf, 1994: 95; Hamdy et al., 1995; Allan, 1996b) offer solutions for the Nile, the Euphrates and Tigris, and the Jordan in a series of proposals for treaties, cooperation in water transfers, information exchanges, and rational distribution of resources.

Israeli economists have suggested trade in water as a purely commercial good, and similarly, transfer of water to one state at the expense of another through an exclusively economic calculation (Eckstein et al., 1994). The Turks have considered building huge dams on the Euphrates and the Tigris to facilitate the use of the rivers' waters by Syria and Iraq (Bilen, 1994: 99). Three professors at Tel Aviv University have written about regional cooperation, and the transfer of Nile water to Israel and the Palestinians, and Turkish water to Israel via Syria (Ben Shachar et al., 1989). As stated, all these proposals are rational and practicable.

Are we indeed in a new era in a New Middle East? Do the region's leaders really perceive that reality has changed and that a transition to a New Middle East is in order? May we truly allow ourselves to be misled with illusions of optimism that sweep all before them? Or should we call out "Wait! Nothing has changed." We do not yet possess, nor does the world yet possess, the enormous sums of money needed to solve the problems of water regimes in the region. Might development come about very slowly and gradually, and without cooperation among states? Might there even be regression and war, because in fact there is no New Middle East and there are no new leaders, and the old myths have not yet been discarded?

A sober view, based on acquaintance with the region and its leaders, pointing to gathering catastrophe, may actually open the eyes of the region's leaders more quickly and more seriously than concepts of a rosy future for the region based on disregard for reality and the past.

It should perhaps be borne in mind that the region's leaders, or some of them, may not act at all to prevent disaster, and one should indeed be prepared for the worst possible scenarios.

Out of all the advice given to the peoples of the region, perhaps only the solutions applicable "at home" should be emphasized; local approaches do not involve the overlay of foreign patterns of behavior and cultural expectations.

This book attempts to provide as thoughtful an answer as possible to these questions, and indirectly, a response to the pervasive atmosphere of optimism. In this sense, the book will be an exception on the bookshelves. It describes the sources of the water conflict in each of the international river basins and presents the principles for a just division of water among the nations of the region.

The rivers under consideration are the Nile, the Tigris, the Euphrates, the Jordan, and the Orontes. In addition, Chapter 7 is dedicated to international groundwater and Chapter 6 to the Litani River, which, although not an international river, is an underlying source of international political conflict. Chapter 8 concerns unconventional solutions to water shortage, such as desalination, importing water, and the Turkish "peace pipeline." This chapter stresses that, in the final analysis, at the end of the twentieth century there are diverse solutions for the water shortage, but to benefit from them plans must be made in good time. Chapter 8 also asks if it is possible to solve the water problem by going to war. Despite the absolute illogicality of going to war over water, this difficult issue must also be addressed.

# Chapter 1

# International Rivers

An international river is one that flows along the borders or through the territories of two or more states, or whose drainage basin is situated on the borders of or within two or more nations (Briggs, 1952: 274; UN, 1977: 53).

According to the United Nations (UN) committee for international natural resources and rivers, there are about 214 international rivers in the world, including about 110 rivers whose drainage basins are very large: 69 international rivers in the Americas, 48 in Europe, 57 in Africa, and 40 in Asia (United Nations 1970; 1978). The map of international rivers shows that in fact most of the world's rivers are international, except for those of Australia, central China, the Sahara, and the former Soviet Union. Now most of the rivers of the last-named area are also international including the Dnepr, the Dnestr, the Syr Darya and the Amu Darya, the Ural, the Volga, the Ob, and the Irtysh in Siberia.

## Planning Usage of International Rivers

The international river and its drainage basin form one hydrological unit, which is divided among several nations. This factor causes many difficulties in exploiting the river's water and requires coordination and cooperation among its riparians.

The main difficulty arising from use of international river water occurs when riparians use its waters in a consumptive manner. This means that water is consumed from the average annual quantity of flow of the river or its drainage basin (as measured in seconds or in years), for example, by irrigation. Consumptive use can also occur in which the quality of the water is "consumed," for example, industrial use that pollutes the water. A distinction should be made between upstream states, through which runs the upper section of the river, and downstream

7

states, in which runs the lower section of the river. Naturally, consumptive use by upstream states affects the ability of downstream states to use the river's water. If an upstream state pollutes water through industrial use, the primary injured party is the downstream state. Cooperation among all the riparians of a river and mutual consideration of others' needs are essential.

Cooperation is difficult, because often there are conflicts of interest among the riparian countries about everything related to exploitation of water, especially as each state has the absolute sovereign right to do whatever it wishes in its own territory and with its own resources. No country readily accepts any action that might compromise its sovereignty and demand sacrificing even the most minor plans for water exploitation out of consideration for fellow riparians. Sometimes riparian states are enemies for reasons unconnected with water, and hostile relations prevent them from cooperating in any arena, especially water.

Relations between river or river basin riparian countries are therefore varied, ranging from total noncooperation to close cooperation. India and Pakistan, for example, within whose borders flows the Indus River, do not cooperate at all, and the UN was obliged to intervene to solve the problem of the shared use of water. The organization funded the creation of a complex project to isolate part of the river's drainage system so that Pakistan, the downstream state, would not be subject to the caprices of India, the upstream state. Another example is the former Soviet Union, which did not cooperate with Iran in its use of the Volga and its tributaries. The Soviet Union, the upstream state, used the Volga without considering Iran's needs and caused enormous damage to the latter. As a consequence, the level of the Caspian Sea dropped by about 30 meters and the river itself and the sea became polluted to the extent that their entire ecological system changed (Berenyi, 1994).

Some countries limit cooperation only to informal contact for consultation and information exchange, for example, the countries of the Middle East, as we shall see. By contrast, other states have formed joint authorities for the management of the water and its basin, such as the seven Western European countries along whose borders the Rhine flows, or Canada and the United States, in whose area runs the Saint Lawrence and whose mutual border traverses the Great Lakes. Still, even cooperating states run the risk of discord arising between them. Such is the case of the states of Arizona and California over the waters of the Colorado, whose dispute reached the Supreme Court. Another example is the case of the Tennessee basin's states, which clash over the use of the Tennessee River that flows through their territories. Each state makes fresh plans for exploiting the water of the shared river, thereby arousing suspicions of the other riparians; if there is misunderstanding among the states, conflict can rapidly develop.

Most of the disputes occur between upstream and downstream states. Naturally, the upstream states contribute most of the river's water, but usually the downstream states, which do not contribute to the flow, are the principal users of the river water. The downstream states are also the historical users of the water, which gives them historical rights (the world's four oldest civilizations, in China, India, Mesopotamia, and Egypt, developed on the lower sections of rivers). But upstream states feel deprived. On the other hand, upstream states' consumption of water makes downstream states feel more vulnerable.

Confrontation may also occur owing to the envy felt by a poor state toward its rich neighbor, or by a rich, strong state coveting its backward and weak neighbor's resources. Another factor for conflict is the worsening shortage of water resulting from population growth and the feverish attempt to match this with continuous economic growth. Obviously, as the number of riparians on a river or in a river basin grows, so does the chances of eruption of more involved conflicts (such as those among the Danube River countries).

We have dealt with the rivers and not with groundwater, which simply adds fuel to the flames, so to speak, because occasionally groundwater is part of an international drainage basin, but occasionally it constitutes an independent system involving many states. The problem regarding groundwater is that it is invisible, and science does not always reveal whether groundwater is being replenished or is fossilized, or whether it is international. In any event, disputes over groundwater are growing more frequent, and they too become subject to the deliberations, albeit after years of delay, of jurists in search of ways for equitable distribution among neighboring states (Hayton and Utton, 1989; Barberis, 1991).

This book presents several illustrations of this old-new issue: in fact, we have before us not only "rivers of fire" but "groundwaters of fire."

## Principles for Settling International Conflicts

As mentioned, the root of the problem with shared use of international rivers is the necessity for compromise over territorial sovereignty. This issue guides the four principles that the international community applies to solve or to prevent international conflicts, as follows.

*First principle.* Each state has complete sovereignty over the drainage basin located within its territory (the Harmon doctrine). Upstream states insist on this principle (Chapman, 1963: 22; Teclaff, 1967; Frey and

Naff, 1985: 78; Rogers and Lydon 1994: 52–53). These states control the river's sources and thus are not dependent on the other riparians, and the other riparians' use of the river does not affect them. Therefore, it is easy for them to insist on their rights to exploit the river without considering other states.

*Second principle.* There is absolute territorial integration among the basin states. This principle is used in the highly explosive situation where the downstream state has historical rights over the water but does not contribute to the flow, while the upstream state, which contributes much of the flow, has never used the water in the past and therefore lacks historical rights to it. According to this principle, the entire basin is deemed a single unit, and hence even the downstream state is considered to contribute to the river's water and is therefore allowed unlimited use of it, without taking the upstream state into account (Doherty, 1965: 38). In other words, all the states within which the river runs have equal rights to its use, regardless of whether they contribute water to the river's flow or not.

Downstream states insist on this principle, which has many implications. It elicits questions regarding the historical rights of downstream states in the basin, as well as fair distribution between those states that contribute most of the river's water and those that contribute nothing but possess historical rights. In states formerly under colonial rule this principle concerns the extent to which a downstream state's historical rights should be considered when the colonial power imposed its rule on the upstream states (Hirsh, 1956; Chapman, 1963: 23; Kliot, 1994).

*Third principle.* All states of the basin are allowed to share in exploiting the basin's water. This principle emphasizes development of the basin for the benefit of all its riparians, and it recognizes the rights of all the basin states to enjoy all parts of the basin. Hence, any state that plans to develop a water project in its territory must request permission from its fellow riparians (Naff, 1994: 203–204).

*Fourth principle.* This is termed equitable utilization, meaning that a state's sovereignty is restricted to just and equitable use of the river's water. Accordingly, a state may use water as long as this causes no harm to its fellow riparians. All riparians must refrain from using the river water in a way injurious to other states or obstructing their ability to exploit the river effectively. States may use the river basin water only through mutual agreement and equitable and just distribution of the water resources. This is the most widely accepted principle in international law regarding exploitation of international rivers, and all conventions regulating the use of international river water are based on it. The European conventions, for example, include a clause that no state may construct a water project in its territory that may harm the other riparians in the drainage basin. It also prohibits any state from altering the direction of a river's flow, its water level, or water quality, without the agreement of the other riparians in the basin. Some conventions determine the special rights of the downstream states (Chapman, 1963; Utton, 1973; Le Marquand, 1977: 154; 1981: 149; Kliot, 1994).

The first principle fixes the absolute sovereign right of each state to use its water, while the other principles limit this right. Because of the opposition between the first principle and the others, and because most of the principles limit sovereign rights, the principles cannot settle disputes where a state is unwilling to forego its sovereignty.

Aside from these general principles there are three others, which have developed over time to settle or prevent clashes:

*The mutual use principle.* A state may oppose an agreement on exploiting international river water if it seems that it will not receive suitable compensation. This principle especially affects upstream states, which demand compensation, whether economic or political, for permitting downstream states to exploit the river water widely, or for being obliged to take steps to limit damage to the downstream section of the river. For example, France, which is located upstream on the river Rhine, dumped salts into the river and refused to diminish this pollution even after repeated requests by Germany and Holland, the downstream states. To reach an agreement, Germany and Holland had to compensate France financially so that it could construct plants to halve the river pollution (Kliot, 1994).

*The linkage principle.* In return for a state's agreement to share international river water, the state may request benefits in other areas from its riparians, for example, preferential trade relations (Kliot, 1994).

*The image principle.* A state may be willing to curtail its sovereignty and act cooperatively with the other riparians if it seeks to create the positive image of a "good neighbor" (Kliot, 1994).

States will cooperate with one another when they take a different approach to the problems in the shared drainage basin and set themselves similar goals for its development, such as preserving the basin's environment and landscape for recreation and tourism. Even states with equal levels of technology whose governments refuse to establish contact may incline toward agreement on water issues (Le Marquand, 1977: 153).

## International Law on International Rivers

The documents containing the currently accepted regulations on the use of international rivers are the 1966 Helsinki Accords on Water Issues, and the International Law Commission (ILC) (1991) (Henkin et al., 1987; UN 1991; Biswas, 1994; Kliot, 1994). In the first section of the Helsinki Accords, international drainage basins are defined and the importance of applying international law in exploiting international rivers is stressed. The second section of the document is the most important. It presents the fair and equitable way of distributing basin water among riparians sharing a river. This, according to the rule, is accomplished by weighing each one of the following eleven factors (see also Table 1.1):

1. The geography of the basin. Principally, the area of the basin located within the borders of each of the riparians is to be considered.
2. The hydrology of the basin, namely, the relative amount of water each riparian contributes to the river's flow.
3. The climate of the basin in each of the riparian states.
4. The extent of use of the river water by each riparian in the past (historical rights) and in the present.
5. The economic and social needs of each of the basin riparians.
6. The dependency of each riparian on the river water.
7. The cost of alternative projects for obtaining water by each of the riparians.
8. The availability of resources other than water to each of the riparians.
9. The level of waste of river water exhibited by each of the riparians.
10. The possibility of compensating one or more of the riparians for ceding some of the basin water.
11. The possibility of fulfilling the needs of one of the riparians without causing serious injury to another riparian.

The second section also states that no riparian will be granted preferential use of the basin water, and that it is possible to maintain the existing pattern of the use of the drainage basin water as long as this does not adversely affect the riparians.

The difficulty in implementing this regulation is that the factors listed above are not fixed and clear-cut. Each of them may change over time. For example, the size of a basin alters with the years owing to the erosion of the river and the variation in its course; the river's supply changes from season to season, year to year, and decade to decade, to the point where it is hard to determine the total supply precisely, or the contribution of each riparian to its water. The climate also changes by decade and by year, as occurred often during the 1980s. Other facts may be interpreted in various ways. For example, the "historical rights" fac-

Table 1.1: International River Basin — Factors for Consideration in Water Allocation Based on Helsinki Convention

| Economy | Society | Political and Legal Systems | Geography and Hydrology |
|---|---|---|---|
| Availability of resources other than water (oil, minerals, industry, tourism) | Population size | Number of riparians | Area of drainage basin |
| | Natural growth rate | Internal conflicts | River discharge |
| | Standard of living | International conflicts | River length |
| | Other sociocultural data | Legal system: international and local | Climate consideration: humid or arid, or semi-arid areas |
| Water utilization at present, ways of use | | | |
| Land availability | | | |
| Food import, types of crops | | | |

tor: what is the period of time that imparts historical rights to a state—thousands of years or 30 years? What is wasteful use? Who is authorized to determine the economic and social needs of a state? Therefore, determining the just and equitable division of river water has been subject to much disagreement, and the Helsinki Accords cannot prevent argument and clashes even when the riparian states demonstrate good will and seek agreement.

The third, fourth, and fifth sections of the Helsinki Accords deal with sailing in international basins, river pollution, and floating logs through river systems. Several major clauses also state that exploitation of river water is permitted as long as this does not cause damage or compromise the other riparians' ability to use the water (United Nations, 1991).

The sixth section of the Accords details ways to solve international river basin conflicts peacefully and according to the UN charter. This section determines among other things that each state must provide its fellow riparians with information about the basin located within its territory and about all planned water projects that might affect them. It recommends that the riparian states form a joint body to settle disputed issues, and if the parties fail to do so alone, they are advised to appeal to the International Court of Justice.

In the long run, international law does not have the power to solve international river conflicts, and the Helsinki Accords, like other previous conventions, can only offer recommendations.

Conventions have been concluded on flooding and marine pollution (New York 1972), international water management and conservation of water in time of war (Madrid 1976), the connection between water and other resources preserving the flow regime of water in a river (Belgrade 1990), ocean pollution (Montreal 1982), and groundwater issues (Seoul 1986) (Cano, 1989; Solanes, 1992).

Groundwater is a problem for most legal experts, because it is difficult to include surface water and groundwater in the same category. In the Helsinki Accords groundwater is taken to be a part of the international drainage basin. Experts attempted to sharpen the distinction, and in 1978 groundwater and surface water began to be spoken of as belonging to the same "hydrological cycle." Subsequently, the term "basin" was removed from use by the ILC and the term "system" was adopted.

In 1991, at the 43rd session of the ILC, an updated version of the Helsinki Accords was published: "Factors Relevant to Equitable and Reasonable Utilisation, Article 6(6)." (United Nations, 1991).

The main changes in the document are the inclusion of ecological, as well as geographical, hydrographic, hydrological, and climatic considerations (paragraph a); the consideration of the effect of one country's use of the riverbed on another country's riverbed (paragraph c); and the consideration of usage (current and potential) of the river (paragraph d). This last is an important change because the historical rights that appeared in the Helsinki Accords were removed from this document.

Section 2 concludes with wording different from several of the Helsinki Accords sections, as it includes the terms "conservation" and "river protection." As in the Helsinki Accords, a number of sections were added to provide for the transfer of information on future planning among the riparians, information exchange, commitment not to cause damage to neighbors, and commitment to cooperate and furnish detailed means of communication among the riparians (United Nations, 1991).

## International Rivers in the Middle East

In this book the term Middle East covers all the countries bordering the state of Israel, and also the other states sharing the river basins of these countries. That is, the region includes Egypt, Jordan, Syria and Lebanon, the Nile riparians (Sudan, Ethiopia, and the equatorial states), and the Euphrates and Tigris riparians (Turkey and Iraq). Saudi Arabia, Iran, and Libya are also discussed briefly.

In the early part of this century, most of the accords and agreements concerning international rivers in the Middle East were signed by a Middle Eastern state and its European patron, or by two European states that controlled the area of states in the region. For example, the agreements on the use of the Tigris and Euphrates, as well as the Jordan and the Yarmuk, were signed by France and Britain. The two states formed a joint committee to study all French investment plans in Syria whose implementation might reduce the water of the Tigris and the Euphrates in the British Mandate in Mesopotamia. Another committee was appointed to deal with the Jordan and the Yarmuk rivers, and a 1922 agreement determined the rights of Syrian residents to use the Jordan River. The agreement between Egypt and Britain from 1929 determined the division of water between Egypt and the British Protectorate in Sudan.

Some agreements were signed by states in the region after the end of colonial rule. In 1959 Egypt and Sudan were signatories to an agreement on a fresh division of the Nile. In this document, as in the 1929 agreement, the river was considered one unit, requiring joint management based on mutual agreement. Finally, the treaty of friendship and neighborly relations signed by Turkey and Iraq in 1946 should be mentioned. In it the importance of working to preserve the water quality and regular flow in the Tigris-Euphrates basin is recognized. This document also prescribed the pattern of cooperation between the two states concerning the construction and maintenance of water projects (Hirsch, 1956: 218; Teclaff, 1967: 193; United Nations, 1972: 36, 37; Utton and Teclaff, 1987).

Despite these agreements, the Middle East has witnessed numerous conflicts concerning the use of international river water. The most complicated conflict concerns the Jordan River and its tributaries because of the great demand in this area and the small amount of water in the river; a solution is dependent on a settlement of the Arab-Israel conflict. The Tigris-Euphrates system also has led to serious disputes between Turkey and the other riparians. These are highly complex, because the various basins are connected to and affect each other. For example, the condition of the Euphrates affects the condition of the Tigris and vice versa. The Orontes influences the Euphrates and the Jordan, and the Euphrates influences what takes place in the Yarmuk (Rogers and Lydon, 1994).

Because of the great dependence of the Middle Eastern states on water, the conflicts associated with it often take center stage, and sometimes assume an aggressive character. They can determine relations among states. For example, Syria's water policy concerning the Orontes and the Tigris underlies its relationship with Turkey. The potential for conflict in the Middle East is also high because some of the riparian states are quite evenly matched in military power (Syria and Iraq, for example, which share the Tigris River), and they cannot enforce agreement on water issues on one another.

The chapters of this book discuss the geopolitical complexity of the Middle Eastern rivers as well as suitability of the Helsinki Accords for solving international water conflicts in Middle Eastern river basins. I present a possible weighing of the eleven factors mentioned earlier and attempt to answer the question of whether a fair and equitable division of the international river water in the Middle East is possible.

*Chapter 2*

# The Nile Basin

## The Sources and Course of the Nile

The Nile basin includes the water of two large rivers, the White Nile and the Blue Nile, and also several smaller rivers (see Figure 2.1).

The White Nile springs from the Kagera River, on the equator, which empties into Lake Victoria from the mountains to the west. (The lake's water belongs to Kenya situated on the east bank, Tanzania on the south bank, and Uganda on the north bank.) The lake covers about 26,254 square miles and lies 3,772 feet above sea level. From this height the White Nile descends gradually to the Sudan heights, which are 1,312 feet high, and passes through Lake Kyoga and Lake Albert (the latter lies 2,030 feet above sea level and its water belongs to Uganda to the east, and to Zaire to the west). Into Lake Albert flows the Semliki tributary, which runs mostly through Zaire, and which marks the boundary between Uganda and Zaire before it empties into Lake Albert. The headwaters of the Semliki are in Lake Edward (3,000 feet above sea level).

One hundred twenty-five miles north of Lake Albert, the White Nile enters Sudan, and flows gently into the Sudd region (in this area the Nile is called the Bahr el Jebel). The Sudd is a vast plain of open land, rivers, and swamps. It is about 281 miles long and 188 miles wide, covering an area of 52,120 square miles. From the west, the river Bahr el-Ghazal flows into this plain, collecting water from the Bahr el-Arab River and from an additional system of rivers before it empties into the Sudd plains. Into the Sudd also flows the Sobat River, which with its tributaries (the Akobo, the Baro, and the Pibor) forms the border between Ethiopia and Sudan for about 188 miles.

The Sudd swamp area varies both seasonally and annually. Until the 1980s its territory was estimated at about 6,560 square miles. After the floods in the early 1960s the swamps spread over an area of about

17

18

*Figure 2.1:* Water Projects in the Nile Basin

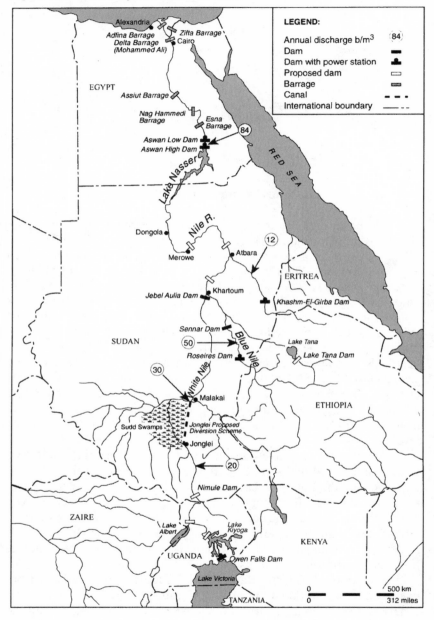

11,600 square miles (Sutcliff and Parks, 1987). The swamp region is difficult to cross because of the tangled plant growth covering it, and there is a high rate of evaporation there (20–22 billion m³ annually). The White Nile flows from the Sudd region north to Khartoum, where it joins the Blue Nile.

The Blue Nile begins at Lake Tana in Ethiopia, lying 5,576 feet above sea level. The Ethiopian highlands are basalt and impenetrable to water, so all the rainfall there drains into the many tributaries of the Blue Nile, which flows 2,000 feet below the Ethiopian highlands. In this mountainous region the course of the river and of its tributaries is canyon-like. The broken landscape impedes movement in the region and exploitation of its river water. With the exit of the river to the Sudan Plateau (on the border between Sudan and Ethiopia) its flow becomes more calm and a considerable amount of its silt also sinks here (Hurst, 1965; Said, 1993).

From the meeting point of the White Nile and the Blue Nile near Khartoum the united river flows north, and near the town of Atbara it is joined by its last tributary, the Atbara River, which also rises in the Ethiopian highlands. From here to the Mediterranean Sea, about 1,560 miles, the river receives no additional water source. From Khartoum the Nile flows through sandstone and igneous rocks, thereby creating six cataracts: the first and most southern at Sabluka, the second at Atbara, the third at Marawi, the fourth at Dalgu, the fifth at Wadi Halfa, and the most northern at Aswan.

After Aswan the igneous rocks and sandstone are replaced by limestone, and the canyon-like valley becomes the wide, fertile Egyptian Nile valley, which continues to Cairo, where the delta begins. The Nile delta today has two branches, but there is some evidence that additional branches have disappeared, and it is possible that the existing canals in the delta were carved by these vanished rivers (e.g., the Madaba Map). In 1969 evidence was found for a branch of the Nile running to the northeast. It is possible that the earlier branch followed the present path of the freshwater canal that leads to the Suez Canal in Wadi Tumilat, and from there on to Baluza (Felusium).

The entire length of the Nile is 4,266 miles, making it the longest river in the world. There are several estimates of the area of its basin, ranging from 1.08 million square miles to 1.5 million square miles (Table 2.1) (Waterbury, 1979; Sutcliff and Lazenby, 1990: 120; Hulme, 1994).

### The Flow Regime of the Nile

The drainage system and flow regime of the Nile are complicated because its sources are located in various climatic regions (equatorial,

Table 2.1: Nile Sources, Area of Drainage Basin, Mean Discharge, and Riparian Share

| River | Area of Drainage Basin (square mile) | Share per Country in Drainage Basin Area (%) | Mean Discharge (billion m$^3$) | Remarks |
|---|---|---|---|---|
| Blue Nile (Khartoum) | 12,530 | Ethiopia (90) Sudan (10) | 53.5 | Ethiopia contributes almost all the water |
| Atbara | 38,764 | Ethiopia (50) Sudan (50) | 11.8 | Ethiopia contributes all the water |
| Sobat | 86,872 | Ethiopia (50) Sudan (50) | 12.4 | Ethiopia contributes most of the water |
| White Nile | 514,312 | Kenya (30) Tanzania (18) Uganda (12) Burundi (15) Rwanda (15) Zaire (10) | 24.0 | Kenya, Tanzania, Rwanda, and Burundi contribute most of the water |

Table 2.1 (continued): Nile Sources, Area of Drainage Basin, Mean Discharge, and Riparian Share

| River | Area of Drainage Basin (square miles) | Share per Country in Drainage Basin Area (%) | Mean Discharge (billion m³) | Remarks |
|---|---|---|---|---|
| Bahr al Razal | 20,077 | Sudan (100) | 16.0 | Sudan contributes all the water |
| White Nile (Khartoum) | 38,610 | Sudan (100) | 30.0 | Sudan contributes all the water |
| Main Nile (Khartoum-Mediterranean) | 104,247 | Sudan (35) Egypt (65) | 94.0 (At Atbara) 84.0 (At Aswan) | |
| Total Basin | about 1,158,301 | Ethiopia (10) Sudan (63) Egypt (12) Equatorial States (15) | 84.0 (Aswan, 1912–1965) | |

monsoon, savannah, and desert), and because it loses large quantities of water by evaporation and seepage from the Sudd swamps and beyond, across the thousands of kilometers of desert through which the river flows en route to the Mediterranean (Table 2.1).

The source of the Blue Nile, as mentioned, is in the Ethiopian highlands, and the river is influenced by the summer and fall monsoon winds, which are accompanied by strong rains. The rainy season begins in June and lasts about five months, until the end of October. In this period the monthly precipitation reaches about 20 inches. In winter there is almost no rain.

The basalt structure of the Ethiopian highlands prevents the rainwater almost entirely from seeping into the ground, and most of it runs off into the Blue Nile. In the summer and fall months about 10 billion $m^3$ of water flow to Khartoum. By comparison, the yearly flow of the Jordan River, including the Yarmuk water, at the entrance to the Dead Sea, before the construction of the water projects, was 1 billion $m^3$. The Atbara, which also originates in the Ethiopian highlands, contributes about 2.2 billion $m^3$ to the Nile during each of the five rainy months (Table 2.2).

The White Nile originates in an equatorial climate, in which large amounts of rain fall in all months of the year (about 62 inches annually). Because it rises in Lake Victoria, the quantity of monthly water which flows to the Sudd is far more regular, amounting to about 2–3 billion $m^3$ in summer and winter (Table 2.2).

The Bahr el-Ghazal River, which flows with all its tributaries to the Sudd region, is located in a region with a savannah climate, with summer rains. During the summer the river contributes about 1.5 billion $m^3$ monthly to the Sudd. The Sobat River, which flows north of the Sudd, originates in the monsoon climate of the Ethiopian highlands. It contributes about 2.5 billion $m^3$ to the river from the east during each of the five rainy months of the summer and fall (Table 2.1).

Ultimately, this quantity of water does not influence the White Nile's discharge because of the high evaporation occurring in the Sudd and the northern swamps. Annually about 16 billion $m^3$ of water enter the Sudd swamps from the Bahr el-Ghazal, 12 billion $m^3$ from the Sobat, and 24 billion $m^3$ from the White Nile (Table 2.1), a total of 52 billion $m^3$. The amount of White Nile water leaving the swamp is only about 30 billion $m^3$. This indicates that in the Sudd swamp region about 20–22 billion $m^3$ of water are lost, equal to about a quarter of the Nile's discharge at Aswan (Shahin, 1985; Sutcliff and Lazenby, 1990: 117). According to Abdel-Mageed, losses in the Sudd region alone reach 41 billion $m^3$ (Abdel-Mageed, 1994: 111). Anyone wishing to utilize the White Nile's

Table 2.2: The Average Flow of the Nile (1912–1965) (billion m³)

| Sources | Summer Monthly Flow | Number of Months | Total in Summer | Winter Monthly Flow | Number of Months | Total in Winter | Total |
|---|---|---|---|---|---|---|---|
| Blue Nile | 10.0 | 5 | 50.0 | 0.5 | 7 | 3.5 | 53.5 |
| Atbara | 2.2 | 5 | 11.0 | | | | 11.0 |
| White Nile | 3.0 | 5 | 15.0 | 2.2 | 7 | 15.4 | 30.4 |
| Evaporation | | | | | | | -10.0 |
| Total | 15.2 | 5 | 76.0 | 2.7 | 7 | 18.9 | 84.9 |

Table 2.3: Nile Water Utilization Prior to the Construction of the Aswan High Dam (billion m³)

| Storage Capacity in Dams | 9.0 |
|---|---|
| Utilization of Nile during the low tide (7 months) | 15–16 |
| Total use during low tide months | 24–25 |
| Utilization of Nile water during flood period | 23–24 |
| Total yearly utilization | 48.0 |

water effectively must take into consideration the great evaporation of
the Sudd swamp waters and find a means of halting this process.

Until the Jebel Awliya dam was built, the large quantities of water
flowing in the Blue Nile in the Khartoum region blocked the flow of the
White Nile for several of the summer months, and sometimes the Blue
Nile even flowed up the course of the White Nile. For this and other
reasons the growth rate of the Sudd swamps increased, since during this
period they received water from the Sobat in the east, Bahr el-Ghazal in
the west, and the White Nile in the south. Only at the conclusion of the
summer and fall rainy seasons on the Ethiopian highlands and the ending of the powerful current of the Blue Nile does the White Nile begin
to flow northward toward Khartoum (Tables 2.1, 2.2). At first, the water
is green owing to the many swamp plants carried by the water; later the
White Nile becomes clearer.

The seven or eight winter and spring months (December to July) are
the low season of the Nile, during which time the Blue Nile carries only
about 0.5 billion m$^3$ of water monthly, and the White Nile, leaving the
Sudd, about 2 billion m$^3$. The tributaries' discharge into the Sudd decreases. The low season in the united Nile reaches its peak in July, after
the dry winter months and before the rainwater from the Ethiopian
highlands, which begins to fall in June, reaches the river. (Table 2.2
shows the discharges of the Nile sources in the summer and fall season
[July to November] and in the winter and spring season.) The annual
average discharge at Aswan reaches about 85 billion m$^3$ (76 billion m$^3$
in summer and 18.9 billion m$^3$ in the winter), but about 10 billion m$^3$
are lost due to evaporation in Lake Nasser. Eighty percent of the water
is discharged in five months only, while the remaining 20 percent is discharged during the seven months (Table 2.2). The data in Table 2.2 are
averages, and they do not reflect the monthly discharge and the annual
discharge over time. Sometimes there are significant variations from
year to year in the monthly discharge as can be seen in Figure 2.2. The
annual discharge of the Nile at Aswan in an average year (e.g., 1943)
was 81.1 billion m$^3$, a figure close to the average in Table 2.2. The years
1964 and 1913 are each extreme, a maximum and a minimum. In the
three years shown in Figure 2.2 there were only three months of significantly high discharge—August, September, and October. The discharge in the winter and spring months was 2–4 billion m$^3$, this being a
very small variation compared with the summer months. Just as the
monthly discharge of the Nile varies from year to year, so does the river's total annual discharge. In 1879, for example, the annual figure was
137 billion m$^3$ and in 1885 it was 126 billion m$^3$, while in 1913 the total
discharge was 45.5 billion m$^3$ and in 1987 it was 37.5 billion m$^3$ (Figure

*Figure 2.2:* Monthly Discharge of the Nile at Aswan (1913, 1942, 1964)

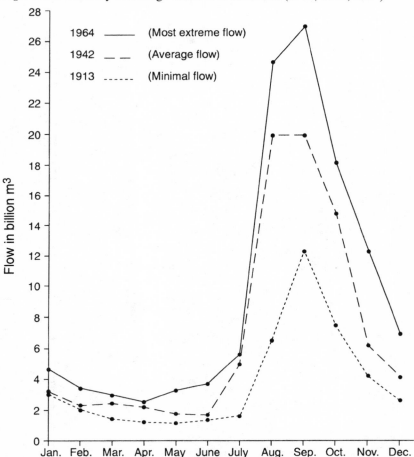

2.3). The large variations exert a powerful influence on the Egyptian population, who are greatly dependent on the river for their existence.

The above data are based on about 100 years of measurements. In the 1980s a new phenomenon began, one causing great concern. We seem to be witnessing a process of climate warming in the Nile basin, which has led to an increased rate of evaporation of its water (Figure 2.3 and 2.4). In that decade likewise there were years of severe drought in both north Ethiopia and central Sudan. The amount of precipitation in the northern regions of the basin (e.g., the Ethiopian highlands) fell sharply (Hulme, 1994; Alvi and Elagib, 1996).

26

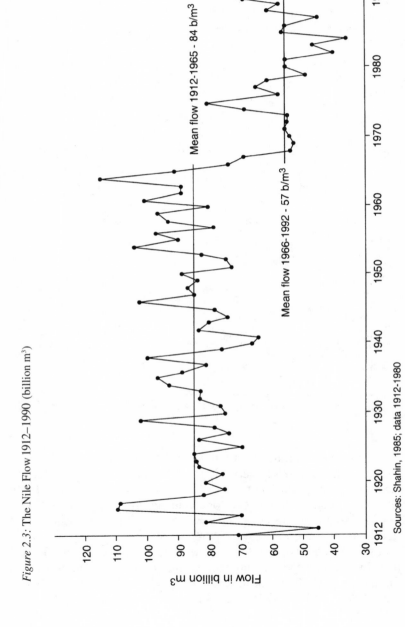

*Figure 2.3*: The Nile Flow 1912–1990 (billion m³)

Sources: Shahin, 1985; data 1912-1980

*Figure 2.4:* Desertification Region in Northeast Africa

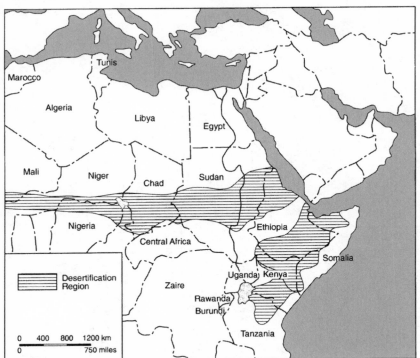

The drought years did not alter the flow of the White Nile; however, while much more water flowed into the Sudd swamps, more water was lost there through evaporation. The warming of the Nile basin and the years of continual drought have significantly reduced the amount of water that reaches Egypt. This country was saved from disaster in 1988 thanks to the Aswan dam and the stored water in Lake Nasser, but if the warming and the years of drought continue it will no longer be possible to save Egypt (Figure 2.5). The country will be obliged to transform its water management; otherwise it may expect the catastrophe of drought years that struck Sudan and Ethiopia, when millions died of starvation and thirst.

The spatial configuration of the Nile basin and its flow regime serve as connecting links between hydrology and geopolitics. As mentioned in Chapter 1, one of the factors that determines fair distribution of international river water among riparians is the area of the drainage basin of the river located within each state (Table 1.1). Another factor is the

28

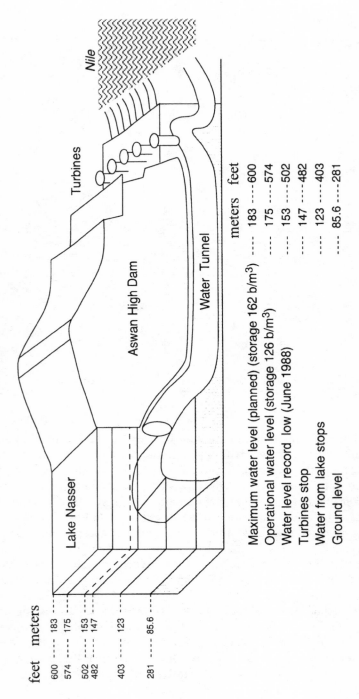

*Figure* 2.5: Critical Water Levels of the Aswan High Dam

feet   meters

600 ---- 183 ---
574 ---- 175 ---

502 ---- 153 ---
482 ---- 147 ---

403 ---- 123 ---

281 ---- 85.6 ---

Maximum water level (planned) (storage 162 b/m³)  ---- 183 ----600
                                                   ---- 175 ----574
Operational water level (storage 126 b/m³)
Water level record  low (June 1988)                ---- 153 ----502
Turbines stop                                      ---- 147 ----482
Water from lake stops                              ---- 123 ----403
Ground level                                       ---- 85.6 ----281

meters  feet

quantity of water the state contributes to the river. In the case of the Nile, Ethiopia contributes about 80 percent of the discharge of the entire river, and the equatorial states (Tanzania, Kenya, Uganda, Sudan, Zaire, Burundi, and Rwanda) contribute the remaining 20 percent. Sudan's contribution is very small. From Sudanese territory large amounts of water reach the Bahr el-Ghazal and other tributaries that empty into the Sudd swamps from the west, but most of this water evaporates or is absorbed into the swamp and little is added to the White Nile as it flows to Khartoum. Egypt contributes nothing (Table 2.1): yet paradoxically, Sudan and Egypt are the principal consumers of the water and therefore have historical rights to its use (Whittington et al., 1995).

Following the climatic changes described above, the share of the White Nile in the water of the Nile basin has increased (as have the shares of the equatorial states), and the share of the Blue Nile (namely, Ethiopia's share) has lessened. According to several experts, in the last decade the White Nile's contribution to the river has been about 44 percent, and that of the Blue Nile 56 percent (Allan, 1990). This could have implications in a just division of the water, and in any discussions on allocation arrangements the basin's riparians will undoubtedly raise this issue. In any event, the fact remains that the contributions of Egypt and Sudan to the Nile's water is very small, but they are its principal users.

## Use of the Nile Water Prior to the Construction of the Aswan High Dam

Attempts to use the Nile water for human benefit began under the rulership of Manes, 5,400 years ago. Manes dug canals to prevent floods and to enlarge agricultural areas. Among other things, a canal was dug to carry water to the Fayum depression (Wilcocks, 1904: 62; Teclaff, 1967). The irrigation systems implemented by the ancients—the lake system and the Kilon pumping system—were common in Egypt until the time of Muhammad Ali (1805–1849) and even later. Muhammad Ali wished to extend the irrigated land in the delta to grow cotton by raising the water level of the Nile, and in 1847 he attempted to construct barrages (diversion dams) from north of Cairo to the branches of the delta, the Damietta and the Rosetta (Figure 2.1). But the attempt did not work and the first and only barrage that was constructed collapsed. In 1890 British engineers succeeded in restoring the barrage (Figure 2.1). It raised the Nile level in the flood season, at the beginning of the summer, and allowed extensive irrigation of the delta (Howell and Allan, 1994).

Additional barrages were built along the river, north of Aswan. The

Assyut barrage was built in 1902 and was improved in 1933 and 1938; the Zifta barrage was built in 1902 and improved in 1953; the Isna and Naj Hammadi barrages were built in 1909, and the latter was improved in 1930. The Isna barrages raised the water level by 2.5 meters, and the Naj Hammadi barrage raised it by 4.5 meters. In 1951 the Adfina barrage was constructed. In addition, improvements were made on the barrages at the mouth of the delta in 1939.

In 1902 the first storage dam was built in Egypt, the old Aswan dam. It was elevated for the first time in 1912, and again in 1933. The storage capacity of the dam rose from 1 billion m$^3$ in 1902 to 5.7 billion m$^3$ in 1933; after the construction of the Aswan High Dam the capacity increased to 6.3 billion m$^3$. In addition, two other dams were built outside of Egyptian territory, the Senar dam and the Jebel Awliya dam. These were intended to prevent the outflow of the river water into the Mediterranean in the high summer season. The Senar dam was built in 1925 in Sudan on the Blue Nile. It has a carrying capacity of 1 billion m$^3$ and it serves the needs of Egypt (in the low months of early summer) and of Sudan (during the rest of the year) for irrigating the Jezira (Collins, 1990a: 248–249). The Jebel Awliya dam (1937) was also built in Sudan, on the White Nile. It has a carrying capacity of 2.5 billion m$^3$ and is meant to serve Egyptian needs (Figure 2.1). Thus, the total water carrying capacity of Egypt prior to the construction of the Aswan High Dam amounted to about 9 billion m$^3$ and Egypt used about 48 billion m$^3$ (Table 2.3).

All these projects proved unable to satisfy Egypt's needs, which grew owing to rapid growth of its population. The quantity of water required by this population reached about 52 billion m$^3$ in the 1950s and even larger amounts were envisioned. At the beginning of the twentieth century Egypt embarked on a demographic revolution, brought about by a rise in the level of health services and a decline in the mortality rate without a change in the birth rate. Table 2.4 shows the widening gap between added irrigated land in Egypt (namely the additional water used) and population growth. Egypt seems to be caught in a demographic upheaval, which endangers all its achievements in water exploitation.

**The Century Storage Plan**

At the beginning of this century the British realized that it was possible to use the Nile's water more efficiently in view of the large quantities of water that were wasted and the fluctuating annual discharge created by its complex flow regime. They therefore prepared a plan to solve the problems of evaporation in the Sudd swamps area and of the

**Table 2.4: Egypt: Additional Irrigated Area Versus Population Growth (1902–2000)**

| Period | Additional Irrigated Area (million acres) | | Population Growth (million) |
|---|---|---|---|
| | A | B | |
| 1902–1933 | 1.0 | 0.7 | 5.0 |
| 1933–1952 | 0.6 | 0.8 | 3.0 |
| 1952–1960 | 0.1 | 0.8 | 4.0 |
| 1960–1976 | 0.8 | 0.5 | 15.0 |
| 1977–1987 | 0.3[c] | 0.7[c] | 14.0 |
| 1988–1992 | 0.8[d] | — | 7.0 |
| 1992–2000 | 4[d] | | 10.0 |

*Sources:* Population Reference Bureau (1996)
[a]According to Little, 1965: 17; Voll. 1980; *Middle East and North Africa Yearbook,* 1994.
[b]According to Chesworth, 1990: 45; Waterbury, 1979.
[c]Specialists do not accept these data for economic, hydrological, and social reasons.
[d]1988–2000 plans according to President Mubarak, Oct. 3, 1993 (interview, Cairo).

great fluctuation in the river's discharge from season to season. As a spin-off they hoped also to solve the problems of wasted land in the Sudd region and shipping on the Nile. Their intentions were primarily to use the water for agricultural development, first for cotton to export to Britain, and secondly for industrial development and the domestic needs of Egypt and Sudan. In the long term they planned to use the Nile water also to satisfy the needs of Uganda, Kenya, Tanganyika, and Ethiopia (Collins 1990a; 1990b; 1994: 109–136).

Due to the complicated system of the Nile the British abandoned their plans for developing only one part of the basin in favor of collective use of the basin. For example, the problem of the Sudd swamps cannot be solved by diverting the White Nile to skirt the swamps and flow directly to Khartoum without restricting the flow of the Blue Nile. Britain's rule at the time over most of the states of the Nile basin—Egypt, Sudan, Uganda, Kenya, and later Tanganyika—made the collective planning of water use easier.

At the beginning of the century W. Garstin, the adviser to the Egyptian government on public works, introduced general ideas for collective use of the river water, especially above the White Nile (Garstin, 1904). Macdonald, who came afterwards, presented similar ideas. In 1919 Hurst was appointed to this position, and he formed a plan for use of the Nile water called the Century Storage plan. The name originated from Hurst's view that it would take a hundred years to fully implement the project (Evans, 1990: 18; Hurst et al., 1966). The goal of the plan, which was presented in a voluminous agreement in the 1960s, was to use 84 billion $m^3$ of water from the Nile to regulate the discharge and to control the floods of high season, to produce large amounts of electricity, and to make the river suitable for shipping.

Hurst proposed constructing one dam at the mouth of the Blue Nile, on Lake Tana in Ethiopia, and two dams further downstream, at Roseires and at Senar in Sudan. He suggested building a large dam on the White Nile at its exit from Lake Victoria to regulate its flow and produce electricity, and dams on the equatorial lakes through which the Nile flowed (Lake Kyoga and Lake Albert). The most elaborate project was to cut a canal, the Jonglei canal, which would divert the White Nile from the Sudd swamps directly north to Khartoum (Figure 2.1). The great loss of water in the Sudd swamps would thus be prevented. Reducing the amount of water entering the Sudd would solve the problem of shipping in the region and would allow large areas of land in the swamps to be reclaimed and cultivated. Hurst proposed building dams at four of the united river's cataracts (Hurst et al., 1966).

Some of Hurst's proposals were implemented in the region over the years, some even during the period of British rule, but not in an overall framework. The following are the parts of the plan accomplished outside Egypt (Figure 2.1): the Senar dam (1925), and the Jebel Awliya Dam (1937); the Owen Dam, constructed by the British in 1952 at the mouth of Lake Victoria; the Roseires Dam, constructed by Sudan in 1966 on the Blue Nile, whose carrying capacity is 2.3 billion $m^3$, and which is intended to supply the electricity and water needs of the Sudanese population; and the Khasm el-Girba Dam, constructed by Sudan in 1964 on the Atbara, whose carrying capacity is 1.3 billion $m^3$, and which is intended to supply the needs of the Nubian population that was transferred from the Wadi Halfa region with the onset of the flooding of Lake Nasser.

With all these storage dams there are serious problems of evaporation and seepage. The water lost in all of them and in the old and new Aswan dams amounts to 16–17 billion $m^3$ annually (Waterbury, 1979; Haynes and Whittington, 1981; Shahin, 1985; Chesworth, 1990).

The Jonglei Canal was begun in 1978 (Figure 2.1). The decision to cut it and to commence work on it was preceded by a series of discussions and disputes between the Egyptian and Sudanese governments. In the 1920s the Egyptian government supported the plan. The Sudanese government fiercely opposed it, however, because it centered primarily on Egypt and its developmental needs and disregarded the hundreds of thousands of Nilotics who lived in the Sudd swamp area. In 1954 a compromise was proposed, whereby the canal would be diverted eastward to lessen the damage to the residents of the area who lived off fishing and grazing cattle in the swamp waters. In 1974 the revised plan was approved. It was decided that the additional discharge from the canal would be divided between Sudan and Egypt equally (according to the Sudan–Egypt agreement signed in 1959).

The goals of the complex project, as detailed in the agreement, were to reduce flood damage in the Sudd swamps, increasing the White Nile's discharge by 4.7–5 billion m³ annually; to improve shipping in the region along a 188-mile stretch; and to irrigate land along the canal.

The canal was planned to be 225 miles long, 122 feet wide, and 16–26 feet deep. In 1984 about 150 miles had been cut, but that year the work was halted because of the Sudanese civil war, and everything accomplished until then was in fact lost (Waterbury 1994: 54). It is doubtful that it will be possible to restore the canal; the indigenous inhabitants of the Sudd would object because the canal would be disadvantageous to them, while serving the northern Sudanese. In fact, the question of the canal, like the development of the entire southern region, is one of the issues over which the civil war broke out again in 1983 (Collins, 1990).

Hurst made similar plans to drain part of the Sobat, the Baro, and the Mashar swamps, lying east of the Sudd swamps (Figure 2.1, Hurst, 1965); these plans have not yet been executed even though they could increase the Nile's discharge by about 4 billion m³. Similar plans have been made for the Bahr el-Ghazal region, and there too the diversion canals would prevent water evaporation and a resulting increase in the Nile's discharge by about 5 billion m³. If all the diversion plans and the development in south Sudan in the Sudd swamps were realized along the lines of Century Storage plan, an extra 13 billion m³ of water would be added to the Nile; but owing to the current geopolitical situation in the Sudan implementation is doubtful in the near future.

Even though some of Hurst's suggestions were implemented, most of the plan was not, mainly because most of the projects were planned for the south at the sources of the White Nile and of the Blue Nile. This was not particularly problematic when Britain ruled the whole area. But when separate states were formed in the region, the issue of Egypt's dependence on water projects not within its borders arose, incurring a conflict of interests between Sudan and Egypt. With the geopolitical changes in the Nile valley after the Second World War, and especially after Sudan gained independence, the Sudanese interest in this plan lessened because of fears that Egypt would take control of the entire basin. After the Egyptian army officers' coup in 1952 the plan seemed to be doomed forever. Egypt's President Nasser rejected it, preferring to construct a dam within Egypt's borders that would satisfy Egypt's needs quite independently of the river's other riparians. Nasser also wanted to solve Egypt's problems in a shorter period than that needed for the Century Storage plan. Thus, the idea of the Aswan High Dam was born.

Hurst's plan, however, continued to exist in the background. The new Aswan dam's carrying capacity was determined largely according to Hurst's calculations, assessing the Nile's discharge at an annual average of 84 billion m$^3$. Moreover, it seems that this plan's general outline may again appear on the agenda of the Nile basin as it becomes increasingly clear at the end of the twentieth century that the Aswan High Dam has not solved, and perhaps could never have solved, Egypt's problems.

## The Aswan High Dam

As mentioned, despite all the development projects Egypt still faced a water shortage in the 1940s and 1950s due to its population growth. The critical period came in July each year. Before Ethiopia's June monsoon rains could reach Egypt the depleted reservoirs contained only 20 percent of Egypt's carrying capacity. The possibility of using this water depended on whether the monsoon rains came on time or not. At the beginning of each July, between the first and twentieth of the month, Egyptian hydrologists traveled to the Ethiopian-Sudanese border, and according to the amount of rain in the region decided whether it was feasible to use the water. This situation could not long continue. Sudan's water needs grew and Sudan demanded the exclusive right to use the Senar dam, which until then had supplied Egypt's needs in the summer and Sudan's needs during the rest of the year; now Sudan wanted use of the water all year-round. Egypt was therefore in critical need of a water project that would relieve its worsening shortage.

## The Objectives of the Dam

The decision to construct the Aswan High Dam was made after Nasser came to power in 1952. Some in Egypt objected to the plan, but Nasser prevailed (Little, 1965).

The Aswan High Dam was intended to ensure a regular supply of drinking and irrigation water all year-round, during flood season and low water season, and every year, whether wet or dry (Waterbury, 1978; White, 1988; Said, 1993; Howell and Allan, 1994).

A regular supply would promote more effective use of arable land by increasing the number of crops from two to three per year. The plan was also to use 300,000 hectares (750,000 acres) of farmland more efficiently in the sector from Aswan to Isna through irrigating during the Nile high water season. The abundance of water would allow cultivation of rice on the irrigated land.

The expected increase in the amount of water to be used after the construction of the dam was 7.5 billion m³, from 48 billion m³ to 55.5 billion m³. This increase would permit reclamation of the desert on both sides of the delta and its transformation into agricultural land. It was hoped that this would solve the problem of land shortage for several million fellahin (farmers). The calculation was that 7,400 m³ of water annually were needed to reclaim one feddan (about 1 acre), so the additional 7.5 billion m³ that would become available would allow reclamation of about 400,000 hectares on which 2 million fellahin could settle. The plan was to reclaim: 12,000 hectares in the Abiss project, southeast of Alexandria; 240,000 hectares in the El-Tahrir project, at the western end of the delta; 10,000 hectares in the Ras el-Hakma project, west of Alexandria; and 60,000 hectares in the Mariot project, northwest of the Cairo-Alexandria road. Smaller projects were planned for the Sinai peninsula, Lake Idko, and Wadi Natrun. The largest and most ambitious project was the "New Valley" plan—irrigation of the depressions in the Western Desert with Nile water and groundwater and reclamation of 1.4 million hectares (3.5 million acres). The completion date was set for the end of the twentieth century.

The dam was intended to prevent the destructive floods that cause the Nile to overflow. Prevention of flooding would make possible an improvement of the poor drainage system throughout Egypt, which would enlarge the crops by 20 percent. It would also improve the transportation system on land and on the river. The dam was intended to produce electricity by construction of a large power station there. This would foster the industrialization of Egypt and the electrification of the villages. The Aswan High Dam would also permit the construction of power stations on the old Aswan dam and on the Isna and Naj Hammadi barrages that until that time were not used for producing electricity. In addition, the large lake that would be created behind the dam (Lake Nasser) would be used for fishing as well as a recreational area. The final and most important objective was to release Egypt from its dependence on the other Nile riparians. In vindicating the decision to construct the Aswan High Dam, Nasser said, "Once the Aswan High Dam is built, Egypt will no longer be a historical hostage of the upstream riparians of the Nile basin" (Pomp, quoted in Sayed, 1960: 213; Collins, 1990: 163; Little, 1965). The quest for freedom from dependency on the other basin riparians merged with the new regime's desire to accomplish an enterprise of monumental proportions.

**The Events Preceding the Construction of the Dam**

In 1952 two German companies arrived in Egypt to plan the dam. That year a reparations agreement was signed between Germany and Israel, and the German government, seeking a balance between aid to Israel and aid to Arab countries, gave the Egyptian government a grant to finance the work of these two companies.

The United States, Britain, and Germany offered to finance jointly the implementation of stage 1 of the dam. But Nasser, wary of political dependence, asked that they finance both stages. In 1955–56, following the Czech-Egyptian arms deal, the nationalization of the Suez Canal, and the Suez War, negotiations with the three Western countries, which now refused to finance even stage 1 of the dam, ceased and Egypt turned to the Eastern bloc (Soffer, 1992).

In 1956 the Soviet Union agreed to finance the two stages of the dam. The Russians accepted the general lines of the German companies' plan, but required certain structural modifications. In October 1958, after all the alterations were inserted, Egypt and the Soviet Union signed the final agreement.

In 1958–1959, tension arose between Sudan and Egypt. Sudan wanted to amend the 1929 water agreement, according to which Sudan received 4 billion m³ of the river water and Egypt received 48 billion m³. Sudan claimed that according to its population growth in comparison to Egypt's, it was entitled to about one-third of the total water. Similarly, Sudan objected to Lake Nasser spreading into its territory, which would oblige the Nilotic Nubian population to leave their homeland.

On October 8, 1959, Egypt and Sudan signed a new water agreement, whereby Egypt would receive 55.5 billion m³ and Sudan would receive 18.5 billion m³. Egypt therefore received an additional 7.5 billion m³ and Sudan an additional 14.5 billion m³ (Table 2.5). It was also agreed that Sudan would be compensated for the population resettlement necessitated by the creation of Lake Nasser. It was likewise resolved that

**Table 2.5: Nile Water Allocation between Sudan and Egypt (billion m³)**

|                              | 1929 Agreement | 1959 Agreement | Additional Water (1929–1959) |
|------------------------------|----------------|----------------|------------------------------|
| Egypt                        | 48.0           | 55.5           | 7.5                          |
| Sudan                        | 4.0            | 18.5           | 14.5                         |
| Not utilized                 | 32.0           |                |                              |
| Water loss in the new lake   |                | 10.0           |                              |
| Total                        | 84.0           | 84.0           |                              |

a dam would be built on the Atbara, which would assist the resettlement of the Nubians, and another at Roseires on the Blue Nile. This agreement was without doubt a political gain for Sudan and greatly improved its status on the Nile (Waterbury, 1979; 1994).

## Construction of the Dam and Basic Data

The site of the dam at Aswan, six miles south of the existing dam, was selected because the igneous rocks there could bear the weight of the dam except in the event of earthquakes and tremors. The issue was of supreme importance, as an entire nation could be harmed by a flood if the dam were destroyed, sank, or fractured. In this respect, the planners and decision makers assumed unique historical responsibility.

On January 9, 1960, eight years after the start of discussions on the project, stage 1 of the Aswan High Dam began. It was completed in 1964, and construction of stage 2 commenced, being accomplished in 1970. Eighteen years had passed since the discussions began and ten years since the construction got under way.

In the first stage the river water was diverted from the dam site. This necessitated the erection of two small dams and a diversion canal for the Nile water. The second stage was the building of the Aswan High Dam itself, and its connection to the two smaller dams. At the same time twelve electricity generators were set up on the dam, each with a production capacity of 175,000 kilowatts.

The Aswan High Dam rises to a height of 360 feet, runs 2.38 miles in length, and is 3,200 feet across at the base on the river (Figure 2.5). Its lake is 280 miles long (including 94 miles in Sudan) and its average width is about 6 miles. The reservoir can retain about 160 billion m$^3$ of water, and when full it rises to 597 feet above sea level. Usually the lake is not completely filled, for several reasons. First, room must be left for water during unexpected floods. Second, at a height of 597 feet above sea level the lake attains maximum level, and evaporation and seepage also reach their maximum. The evaporation level was planned to reach 10 billion m$^3$ of water annually, but at 597 feet above sea level it increases to reach 15–16 billion m$^3$ annually (Tables 2.6, 2.7). And third, at 597 feet the pressure on the dam and its foundations is enormous, to the point of endangering its stability.

The water tunnels from the lake are 122 feet above the dam's foundations (or 403.5 feet above sea level), so that the silt that accumulates on the lake bottom will not block the openings (Figure 2.5). It is calculated that the gathering silt will attain this height in 500 years. The volume of water below this level (403 feet) is about 6.8 billion m$^3$. It is unused.

The critical height of the reservoir is 482 feet above sea level, the height of the uppermost openings of the tunnels. When the water drops below this level electricity production stops (Figure 2.5 and Tables 2.6, 2.7).

Since completion of the dam the water level has never exceeded 567.5 feet, that is, the lake has not held more than 110–111 billion m³ annually. This is the volume needed to obtain 55–60 billion m³ of usable water. The calculation of water available for use is the following: 110–120 billion m³ minus 30 billion m³ (the volume of water at the 482 feet level, required to produce electricity, which cannot be lowered) leaves 80–90 billion m³; 80–90 billion m³ minus 10 billion m³ (evaporation rate) leaves 70–80 billion m³; 70–80 billion m³ minus 18.5 billion m³, intended for Sudan according to the accord, leaves Egypt with 51.5–61.5 billion m³. However, because Sudan is engaged in civil war it is unable to use all the water allocated to it and uses only about 12–13 billion m³; Egypt takes the remainder, about 5 billion m³, and therefore uses a total of about 55–65 billion m³ (Waterbury, 1994; Whittington et al., 1995).

**The Dam Saves Egypt**

In 1978 the volume of water in the basin was 110 billion m³, the volume required to satisfy Egyptian water needs, but subsequently the amount of water in the lake fell owing to a continual decrease in the Nile's discharge (Table 2.7). In 1984 the discharge reached an unprecedented low, 35 billion m³. The years 1985–1987 were likewise poor, the result being a constant drop in the volume of Lake Nasser water, declining by 1987 to another low, 42 billion m³ (Figure 2.5 and Table 2.7) (Howell and Allan, 1994). As Table 2.8 shows, the Egyptian authorities ignored this: the lake's volume fell from 110 billion m³ to 80 billion m³ in 1982, but the outflow of water from the lake to the Nile valley remained constant at about 55–60 billion m³ annually—as if nothing had happened and better years were hoped for. After all, this was the *raison d'etre* of the dam, to provide Egypt with water every year, even dry ones. The drop in the river's discharge in the 1980s resulted from the dry years that visited Ethiopia and Sudan. In those years millions of people died of thirst in those two countries, while in Egypt life was sustained as usual. Thanks to the Aswan High Dam the dearth of water was not felt in Egypt, and the country was saved from disaster.

However, the dry years did not end, and the reserves in the lake became even more depleted. In July 1988, at the end of the dry season and before the June monsoon rainwater from Ethiopia arrived, the water level of the lake fell to 502 feet above sea level, and by the end of July the level was expected to drop to 492 feet, a mere 9.8 feet above the

Table 2.6: Lake Nasser: Critical Levels

| Water Level (meters above sea level) | Lake Area (miles square) | Volume of Water (billion m³) | Evaporation (billion m³) | Electricity Production (megawatts) |
|---|---|---|---|---|
| 185 | 2,770 | 182.7 | 15.3–16 | 1,750 |
| 175 | 1,972 | 126.5 | 14.0 | 1,750 |
| 164 | 1,333 | 74.3 | 9.4 | 1,200–1,500 |
| 150.0 | 757 | 37.2 | 5–7 | 850 |
| 147.0 | 671 | 31.6 | 3–5 | 0 |
| 123.0 | 208 | 6.8 | 1 | 0 |

*Sources*: Gischler, 1979; Waterbury, 1979; Shahin, 1985.

Table 2.7: Operation of Lake Nasser — Various Years (billion m³)

| Year | Flow to Lake | Water Level (feet above sea level) | Volume of Water | Release of Water from Lake to Valley | Evaporation and Seepage |
|---|---|---|---|---|---|
| 1970 | 77.2 | 508 | 45.0 | 54.7 | 9.3 |
| 1974 | 69.0 | 511 | 67.0 | 56.1 | 10.8 |
| 1978 | 62.1 | 567 | 111.0 (approx) | 61.9 | 13.9 |
| 1982 | 40.7 | 544 | 99.0 | 59.1 | 12.5 |
| 1984 | 35.0 | 515 | 72.9 (approx) | 57.3 | 9.7 |
| 1988 | 45.0 | 502 | 42.0 | 55.0 | 9.0 (approx) |
| 1989 | 80.0 | 521 | 75.3 | | 9.8–10 (approx) |
| 1991 | | 535 (approx) | 88.0 | 54.5 | 10.0 (approx) |

*Sources*: Shahin, 1985; Howard and Allan, 1990; *October* (Egypt) May 3,1991; Kliot 1994

Table 2.8: Water Supply and Demand in Egypt (billion m³)

| | Mid-1970s W | Mid-1970s E | 1980 W | 1980 E | 1990 W | 1990 C | 2000 Sr | 2000 Sd | 2000 E | 2000 A[b] |
|---|---|---|---|---|---|---|---|---|---|---|
| **Demand** | | | | | | | | | | |
| Irrigation | 33.0 | 29.4 | 37.2 | 37.9 | 44.2 | 33.6 | 50.7 | 45.2 | 40.9 | 58 |
| Domestic | 5.0[a] | 1.8 | 3.0 | 2.2 | 4.0 | 2.4[a] | 4.8[a] | 4.8[a] | 3.5 | 6 |
| Industrial | - | 4.1 | 3.5 | 2.4 | 3.6 | - | | | 3.0 | 5 |
| Drainage | 12.0 | 16.0 | 15.0 | 14.2 | 14.2 | 17.5 | 11.7 | 11.7 | 23.4 | 4 |
| Evaporation | 1.4 | 2.7 | 6.7 | 2.2 | 7.4 | 2.0 | 2.0 | 2.0 | 2.3 | 2 |
| Total demand | 51.4 | 54.0 | 65.4 | 58.9 | 73.4 | 55.5 | 69.2 | 63.7 | 73.1 | 75 |
| **Supply** | | | | | | | | | | |
| Aswan release | 55.5 | 57.5 | 60.0 | 61.7 | 58.9 | 55.5 | 55.5 | 50.0 | 57.5 | 58 |
| Water reuse | - | - | 2.5 | 5.4 | 6.0 | - | 6.0 | 6.5 | 4.5 | 6 |
| Drainage reuse | - | - | 4.0 | - | 4.0 | - | 3.0 | 3.5 | 6.0 | 3 |
| Groundwater | | | | | | | | | 4.9 | 5[c] |
| Total supply | 55.5 | 57.5 | 66.5 | 67.1 | 68.9 | 55.5 | 64.5 | 60.0 | 73.9 | 72 |
| Balance | +4.1 | +3.5 | +1.1 | +8.2 | -4.5 | - | -4.7 | -3.7 | - | -3 |

Sources: E - Egyptian Water Master Plan; W - Waterbury, 1979, 1988, 1991: C - Chesworth, 1990; S - Stoner, 1990 (r-rainy year; d-drought) ; A- Author

[a] Domestic and industrial use together

[b] Soffer's assumptions, based on E and the great efforts to reclaim more Western Desert

[c] Groundwater use can slightly change the balance positively

critical level for electricity production (Table 2.6, Figure 2.5). The Egyptians began to slow the electricity production in the dam, and several regions in Egypt, mainly Alexandria, were blacked out. Even the pumping of water for agriculture was curtailed, and for the first time Egyptians were asked to save water in their domestic use. A large island appeared in the middle of Lake Nasser, dividing it into two. Villages in Sudan on the lake's shores now found themselves about 19 miles distant from it. Lake Nasser reached the lower limit of its capacity to serve for irrigation and for the production of electricity (Hulme, 1994).

Salvation came in August. On the night of August 3–4, 1988, torrential rains fell in Sudan, and the Khartoum area suffered serious flooding, the worst since 1946 (Hulme and Trilbach, 1989). In consequence, the annual discharge of the Nile rose to about 80 billion $m^3$ and the volume of water in Lake Nasser rose to about 60 billion $m^3$, its level attaining 512 feet. Had the drought continued, in six weeks the level would have dropped to 482 feet and electricity production would have ceased. The volume of water would have fallen from 37 billion $m^3$ to 31.6 billion $m^3$ (Table 2.6). If we subtract the volume of "standing" water (Figure 2.5), Egypt would have been left with only 24.8 billion $m^3$ (half its annual demand). This amount could provide Egypt with only six months' supply. What would have happened then?

The case of July 1988 taught Egypt several important lessons. The first was not to rely on the dam alone for electricity production. In 1988 Egypt purchased several thermal power stations, intended to replace some of the generators in the Aswan High Dam. The second lesson was to match the amount of discharge from the lake with the amount of discharge into the lake. Egypt reduced the water supply for agriculture and postponed several projects for desert reclamation.

However, none of this solved the fundamental problem: the long years of drought produced a growing deficit in the lake's water. Since 1978 the volume has fallen from the necessary 110–120 billion $m^3$ and even with the 1988 flood the water did not return to this level. Since Egypt added 55–60 billion $m^3$ to its needs, a deficit was created that has grown larger with the years. According to one observer, in 1987 this deficit had already reached 129 billion $m^3$ (Allan, 1988–1989: 48).

It thus seems that in the future the dam will not be able to save Egypt in dry years as it did in the years of drought in the 1980s, since the volume now does not exceed 70–90 billion $m^3$. If the water in the lake attains a volume of 60 billion $m^3$ and in the rainy season 84 billion $m^3$ reaches the lake (average annual discharge of the Nile), then in July of the following year the lake's volume will return to 60–65 billion $m^3$ (the existing volume), and an additional 84 billion $m^3$ (average annual discharge) minus 10–15 billion $m^3$ (rate of evaporation) equals 130–135 billion m³. From this about 70 billion m³ are pumped for use, and only 60–65 billion m³ remain. If the region suffers another drought there will not be sufficient reserves in Lake Nasser for both countries' use. Egypt has therefore returned to the situation of the 1940s and 1950s, when it was completely dependent on rainfall in the south.

Another problem is that due to population growth, even in normal years, which are not dry, the amount of water supplied by the dam will not satisfy Egypt's growing demand for water.

### Have the Dam's Goals Been Realized?

The Aswan High Dam cost Egypt more than $1.5 billion ($820 million for building the dam and about $1 billion for land reclamation). In Nasser's time the dam was an important political symbol and was considered, like the Egyptian pyramids, to be one of the wonders of the world. However, since its construction it has been subject to dispute, which became sharper when it became clear that the unexpected side effects of its construction would generally become more severe with time. In contrast to these effects, one should consider the achievements of the dam. Has it achieved the goals that were set? The dam supplies water to Egypt all year, every year, including dry years. The threat of water shortage in July has been alleviated, as has the danger of dry years generally. The dam saved Egypt from drought in 1972–1973 and in the 1980s, when the Ethiopian highlands suffered constant lack of rainfall and the Nile's discharge fell to a level not witnessed during the previous century. It can be said with certainty that without the reservoir at Aswan the Egyptian population would have endured thirst and a drastic cutback in its agricultural lands throughout the 1980s, and in 1985–1988 a national disaster would have occurred. As noted, however, because of the large deficit that accumulated in the lake during these years, it seems that the dam will not be able to fulfill its purpose if the area is again struck by drought.

Because of the reliable supply of water, 300,000 hectares of agricultural land between Aswan and Isna were made more useful by increasing the number of crops. In a few short years from the construction of the dam the food crops were almost doubled in Egypt (1.6 crops per unit area). Yet this achievement may be short-lived because the dam's construction harmed the drainage system and raised the salinity of the agricultural land in this area, which is likely to damage crops. In recent years efforts have been made to improve drainage, but they are not sufficient; the problem has still not been solved.

In consequence of the increase in quantities of water the irrigated areas for growing rice expanded somewhat and exports of Egyptian rice grew as well (White, 1988: 34).

Egypt reclaimed 912,000 feddans (about 1 million acres) of desert land for agriculture, thereby solving the problems of four million fellahin. However, the general issue of landless fellahin has not been resolved because by the time the dam was completed the Egyptian population had grown by 12 million people, including at least six million fellahin. Moreover, the total territory reclaimed included 55,000 hectares (139,000 acres) for public, not agricultural use. Forty percent of the remaining land gave a medium yield and the remaining 60 percent gave a low yield, or was abandoned or not developed for other reasons. Moreover, while millions of acres of new agricultural land were reclaimed, existing agricultural land was lost (owing to spreading urbanization and sale of land for brick manufacture and for building). In 1973 the Egyptian minister of agriculture stated: "Egypt's agricultural land is limited, and this is not only because it is not growing larger but because it is shrinking, despite the fact that 912,000 feddans (1 million acres) of new land have been created. Between 1963 and 1973 we lost 200,000 feddans (200,000 acres), while the population grew in this period by eight million" (*Middle East and North Africa Yearbook*, 1994).

The conclusion is that there is no justification to continue development, and other ways should be found to solve the agricultural land shortage in Egypt, for example, by changing the nature of the fellah and his work methods. However, it seems that the development will continue because of ideological commitments (Voll, 1980). But, at the end of the 1980s the attempt at land amelioration appeared to be diminishing (Table 2.4). The "New Valley" plan was postponed because of the water deficit of the dry years. Waterbury comments: "The irony is that before the construction of the dam there was a greater effort to develop new land than afterwards" (Waterbury, 1979).

Following the construction of the dam the floods during high water in the Nile ceased. The transportation routes on and alongside the river improved. However, this improvement did not solve the principal transportation problems of Egypt, which are concentrated mainly in the large cities and stem from a lack of infrastructure—highways and railways. The goal of connecting Sudan to Egypt via Lake Nasser was not realized.

The dam's power station provides Egypt with electricity. For technical reasons (the fear of the dam's instability) and because of the drop in the water level in the lake, not all twelve generators work, and Egypt therefore needs additional power stations. Electricity is also generated at the power stations built after the construction of the Aswan High Dam at the old Aswan dam and at the Isna and the Naj Hammadi barrages. During the 1990s more power stations have been installed at the barrages. Many Egyptian villages have been connected to the electricity grid. Electricity has also boosted Egyptian industry, which provided employment for millions of fellahin who flocked from the villages to the cities; but this goal has only partly been fulfilled because the rates of industrial growth are lower than the rate of population growth.

In the long term, the dam power station seems to be a factor whose importance is gradually diminishing: in Egypt new thermal power stations are being constructed continually. In 1982 the share of the dam in electricity production in Egypt was about 54 percent of the whole. In 1992 it was 13.3 percent and the outlook for the year 2000 is that it will drop to about 11 percent only (*Middle East and North Africa Yearbook*, 1994).

Lake Nasser has a rich supply of fish, and its annual fish crop is about 22 thousand tons. However, because of the great distance of the lake from the population centers close to Cairo the crop must be stored in cooling tanks, with the result that it is more expensive than fish from the Mediterranean and the delta lakes; moreover, because of the shortage of cooling tanks, it is not possible to fully exploit the fishing potential, which is 100,000 tons a year.

Lake Nasser has not become a recreation site. Tourism is only beginning and hotels and leisure centers have not yet been built along the lake's shores. While hundreds of thousands of tourists come every year to the lake region to see the city of Aswan, whose beauty has always drawn travelers, and to travel to the Abu Simbal temple, the lake itself has no tourist value, and it is not used as a vacation site in itself. The tourists reach the area by plane and do not remain at the site.

**Side Effects of the Dam's Construction**

As with other major world projects that altered the natural environment, construction of the new Aswan dam and changing the Nile's flow regime caused great disturbance to the ecological balance. The enterprise has incurred serious side effects, some short-term and some that will only be felt several years into the future, and maybe even far later. Meantime, much research has been conducted to determine the nature and extent of the damage to find ways to counter it. The following are the primary side effects of the construction of the Aswan High Dam (Waterbury, 1978; White, 1988).

*Soil Loss*

Before the erection of the High Dam the Nile water carried 100 million tons of soil annually. Eighty-eight percent of it flowed into the

Mediterranean, and the remaining 13 million tons fertilized Egyptian fields annually in the flood season. (The principal source of the fertilizer is silt, which comprises 40 percent of the soil. The fine sand, which comprises 30 percent, improves the physical makeup of the soil and helps to preserve soil moisture and plant root penetration into the soil.) Since the dam was built, most of the soil has collected south of it in Lake Nasser. Instead of this natural fertilizer Egypt must now supply millions of fellahin with artificial fertilizer. Some of this is imported and some is produced in plants near the dam itself, making use of the cheap electricity. Besides the economic cost involved, the fertilizers salinate the soil and some of them reach the river and pollute it. Erosion of land into the river flow causes Egypt to lose thousands of acres of good agricultural land.

The production of red brick, the principal building material in Egypt, has suffered serious damage from the loss of silt, which before renewed the topsoil used for manufacturing bricks. Demand for the bricks has risen accordingly. Only the soil of agricultural land was never used for producing bricks, but now fellahin are being offered large sums of money for the topsoil or for the land itself. The loss of topsoil has severely harmed agriculture, and sale of agricultural land for brick manufacture reduces its total area in Egypt. According to one source, during 1984 alone about 100,000 hectares (250,000 acres) were lost in this way (White, 1988: 11). A new law was passed at the end of the 1980s that forbids the use of agricultural land for construction purposes and recommends using desert sand as building material. Until 1992 this law was ignored.

Due to the loss of soil the Nile now flows from Aswan smoothly and quickly, which increases erosion of the riverbed and banks. This process is especially dangerous near the foundations of dams, bridges, and dikes from north of Aswan to Cairo.

The soil loss has also disturbed the balance between the advance of the delta and the destruction of the coast by sea waves, and a serious problem of coastal erosion has developed. According to some, the process occurs in the mouth of the Rosetta and the Damietta, mostly in the latter. On the coast of Alexandria recessions of the shoreline of 16–32.8 feet annually have been registered (al Ahram, April 7, 1989), and in the Rashid area there has been a recession of about 3.1 miles (al Akhbar, May 7, 1989).

The subsidence of the delta in the northeast is also noted. The process was already observed many years ago owing to the weight of the material that forms it, but it has accelerated in recent years (Stanley, 1988). In these places wave action has caused great damage. Coastal erosion is liable to damage the offshore bars that separate the Mediterranean from the five delta lakes, whose water is relatively fresh, and even burst them. If the salinity of these lakes rises they will salinate the groundwater, which could imperil agriculture in the northern delta region. The dam's planners predicted this process, and proposed a stone wall about 125 miles long on the shoreline from Port Said to Alexandria. Fresh evidence of coastal erosion has stimulated great efforts on the part of the Egyptian government to counteract its full consequences.

The silt provided food for the sardines in the Nile, the delta lakes, and the Mediterranean. Due to the loss of the silt, a significant decrease of fish has been noted in the southeastern basin of the Mediterranean, the Nile, and the delta lakes.

### Loss of Water Due to Evaporation and Seepage

Lake Nasser is located in a hot arid climate and the dam's planners expected great water loss through evaporation. Another factor that increases the evaporation in Lake Nasser is the unchecked spread of water lilies in the lake, covering a wide area of its surface. The plant also obstructs shipping.

From calculations made under laboratory conditions, it emerged that if the average daily evaporation reaches about 0.29 inches, and the average area of the lake is 1,776 square miles, water loss due to evaporation will be 12.6 billion $m^3$ annually. In times of strong desert winds in the region the evaporation rate will reach 17.6 billion $m^3$ annually (0.59 inches daily). The calculation is this: Assuming evaporation of 0.29 inches daily, $365 \times 0.0075 \times 10 \times 4600 = 12.592$ billion $m^3$. Assuming evaporation of 0.59 inch daily, $365 \times 0.0105 \times 10 \times 4600 = 17.629$ billion $m^3$. Evaporation is thus calculated to fluctuate between 12 billion $m^3$ and 17 billion $m^3$ annually. The actual evaporation rate is in fact close to these figures. According to Egyptian hydrologist M. Shahin, 11.1 billion $m^3$ and 12.5 billion $m^3$ evaporated in 1975 and 1976, respectively (Shahin, 1985).

Water loss on account of seepage was also foreseen, although opinions were divided on this issue. Government researchers calculated that when the lake's level was 492 feet above sea level the water loss through seepage would reach 0.6 billion $m^3$ annually. If the lake's level reached 590 feet above sea level, the loss would reach 2 billion $m^3$ annually. A more pessimistic evaluation, based on experiments conducted in the old Aswan dam's reservoir, calculated that water loss due to seepage could reach 9 billion $m^3$ annually. Findings from the 1980s favor the more optimistic evaluation (White, 1988).

If we summarize water loss due to seepage and evaporation in Lake Nasser, according to government estimates it amounts to about 10 billion m³ annually; and according to unofficial estimates it could, under certain circumstances, reach 18 billion m³ annually. If the loss does surpass 10 billion m³ it seems that not only will all Egypt's additional water obtained through the construction of the dam be lost, but also the country will have less water following the construction of the dam than preceding it (Allan, 1988–1989: 48; Chesworth, 1990).

According to Shahin (1985), this is in fact what occurred. In eleven years, from 1960 to 1971 (before the dam started functioning) the lake lost a total of about 12 billion m³, while in 1974 and 1976 alone it lost 14 billion m³.

### Cultural Damage

One of the principal arguments against Lake Nasser was that no project, no matter how effective, would justify the destruction of the cultural treasures of the region. The dam's construction ruined many of Egypt's landscapes and antiquities. The lake region was rich in remains of river civilizations from the Paleolithic period onward. The intensive rescue work carried out by archaeologists from UNESCO managed to save many treasures in the short time at their disposal (for example, the Abu Simbal Temple and the Kalbasha Temple), but nonetheless many remains and cultural treasures were lost or damaged, such as Kasr Ibrim on the eastern side of the river, facing Abu Simbal, which was a fortress from pharaonic times to the Mamluk period, and the Addar and Amda temples. Other temples were moved, almost in their entirety, to museums in Cairo and in Aswan and to other museums around the world, notably London, Madrid, and New York.

### Salination of Soils

Due to intensive irrigation and the drainage system, soil salinity in Egypt has risen. Salinity has also been caused by the rise in salinity of Lake Nasser water, through evaporation. Similarly, saline water penetrates the Nile delta and salinates the delta soils. According to estimates, 35 percent of the land and 90 percent of Egyptian water is subject to salination. The problem of soil salination should be eased somewhat in the year 2000, when the drainage project is completed, having been in progress in the delta since the end of the 1980s.

### Spread of Disease

One of the most damaging results of the dam's construction is the spread of waterborne epidemics, such as malaria and bilharzia. The dam's planners foresaw the spread of bilharzia. This disease has existed in Egypt for about 4,000 years, but since the construction of the dam it has expanded. The Nasser government paid much attention to the disease and constructed village water supplies, built rural health centers, and provided education and prophylactic treatment (White, 1988).

Bilharzia is caused by a parasitic worm. People are infected with it through contact with water infested with bilharzia larvae in one of their immature stages. The larvae penetrate the skin and pass to the liver where they mature; from the liver they enter the mesentery or the urinary tract. There they reproduce and lay their eggs, which return to the water in feces or urine. In the water the eggs hatch and the larvae that emerge penetrate the bodies of certain snails, which are their intermediate hosts. In the snail they multiply 100,000 times, and after a period of development in the body of the snail, they swim in the water and can again penetrate a human host. The bilharzia causes intestinal and urinary tract infections, resulting in debility and sometimes death.

Prior to the erection of the Aswan High Dam the bilharzia species in the Nile were limited, because the habitat conditions of their intermediate host, the snail, were not stable. After construction of the dam the water conditions became more stable, both in Lake Nasser and in the Nile after emerging from the lake, and the marine flora that formed the snails' habitat expanded, as did the population of snails and their parasites. The numbers of people infected with bilharzia likewise increased, both in the Nile valley and along the shores of Lake Nasser. Preventing the spread of the disease is difficult because to destroy the host snail population, the spread of the marine flora must also be curtailed, among other things. The chances of overcoming bilharzia are fairly slight, and the forecasts concerning the spread of the disease made in the 1960s, before the construction of the dam, have already been realized.

### A Safety and Security Risk

The construction of the dam exposed the Egyptian people to great safety and security risks, as any impairment to the dam caused by human or natural means (an earthquake, for example) could flood the entire Nile valley. Damage to the power station and the four transformer stations that supply electricity from Aswan to Cairo, could greatly endanger Egypt. This risk did not exist, of course, before the creation of the dam. Since then, Egypt has feared that Israel might drop an atomic bomb on the dam. Israel itself intimated this to Egypt in the War of Attrition. Egypt also fears that Libya, Sudan, Iran, or Iraq might attack the dam.

In 1981 there was a powerful earthquake in the Aswan area, which caused grave anxiety in the Egyptian government. In 1990 another strong tremor in the Cairo area severely damaged the city. Many studies were conducted to ascertain whether the dam would withstand a powerful earthquake and the findings show that it indeed will. Still, the Egyptian government is disturbed about the dimensions of the disaster that could befall the Egyptian nation if such an event should occur (White, 1988: 10).

## Supply and Demand of Water in the Nile Basin in the Year 2000

### Egypt

The principal goal of the Egyptian government in the field of water policy has been to ensure a free flow in the Nile of sufficient water to assure agricultural production for domestic use and for export, and to expand agricultural lands for the increasing population (Waterbury, 1990: 65). Until the end of the 1980s Egypt met this goal, in part because Sudan did not use all its allocated water, and Egypt exploited what was unused. Table 2.9 demonstrates that if Sudan had used all the water it was entitled to in the 1970s and the 1980s, then by 1990 Egypt would have suffered a water shortage (according to Waterbury). At the beginning of the 1990s Egypt still had adequate water because it used Sudan's excess water, and because it attempted to recycle water. But

Table 2.9: Water Supply and Demand in Sudan (estimation, billion m$^3$)

|  | 1990 | 1990 | 2000 | 2000 |
|---|---|---|---|---|
|  | Estimate A | Estimate B | Crisis Continues | End of Political Crisis |
| *Demand* |  |  |  |  |
| Irrigation | 17.0 | 12.0 | 12.0 | 30.0 |
| Domestic and industrial use | 2.0 | 1.0 | 2.0 | 2.7 |
| Total | 19.0 | 13.0 | 14.0 | 32.7 |
| *Supply* |  |  |  |  |
| Groundwater | 0.3 | 0.3 | 0.3 | 0.3 |
| Nile | 20.5 | 20.5 | 20.5 | 20.5 |
| Total | 20.8 | 20.8 | 20.8 | 20.8 |
| Balance | + 1.8 | + 7.8 | + 6.8 | − 11.9 |

*Sources:* Waterbury 1979, 1988; Whittington and Haynes, 1985; Chesworth, 1990; Knott and Hewett, 1990.

toward the year 2010, due to population growth, Egypt will be deficient in water, even with the benefit of Sudan's water, and if the water projects in the Sudd region are implemented and Egypt receives some of the additional water from them. According to the most optimistic estimates, Egypt's water deficit will be solved by the addition of water from the Sudd projects.

The Egyptian government is aware of the problem of water shortage and makes great efforts to save water by implementing modern irrigation methods, such as the installation of a subterranean pipe in the fields in the lower portion of the Nile Valley, and by reducing water intensive crops and increasing nonwater intensive crops, as well as increasing the supply of groundwater (Allan, 1990; Whittington et al., 1995; Fahmy, 1996). But all this will not be enough. An important measure that would result in considerable savings in water use for agriculture would be to put a price on water. But the Egyptian government refrains from this step for fear of resistance by farmers. Egypt will have no choice but to change its policy of subsidizing water and fix a price for the commodity, which is currently free of charge. The move would reduce the cotton, rice, and sugarcane crops, and enlarge those requiring less water.

But even water saving, great as it may become, will not solve the problem; when Egypt's population reaches about 70 million (close to the year 2000) the government will have to undertake a structural revolution and reduce agriculture, the only sector in which it is possible to cut back demand, to bridge the gap between supply and demand (Table 2.8) (Whittington et al., 1995; Fahmy, 1996).

However, the Egyptian government constantly makes announcements on the extension of irrigation by 2025 to about 2 million more hectares (5 million acres) of new desert areas, with an additional 20 billion m³ of water being used (Rogers and Lydon, 1994: 306–307); it is not clear from where the government plans to draw this water, and why it has decided to irrigate this land, considering that it has already been proven that its yield is low and unprofitable. Perhaps the Egyptian government believes that the great projects in south Sudan will still materialize (Rogers and Lydon, 1994; Fahmy, 1996).

### Sudan

Sudan is more dependent on the Nile than Egypt. While much rain falls in southern Sudan, whose economy is therefore not dependent on the Nile waters, in the north, as the climate becomes more desertlike, settlement on the banks of the Nile and its tributaries becomes sparse and dependence on the Nile increases. In Egypt 50 percent of the population are farmers while in Sudan the figure is 72 percent, and agriculture comprises about one-third of the total GNP and about 90 percent of exports.

Nonetheless, Sudan does not use all the water allocated to it (Table 2.9). Waterbury estimates (personal communication in June 1991; Waterbury, 1995) that in 1990 the water consumption in Sudan was between 12 and 14 billion m³. This is the amount that Sudan consumed in the 1970s and 1980s, but although the population rose, water consumption in Sudan actually dropped. This was due to the civil war and the drought that beset the country. If this analysis is correct, it can be understood why Sudan does not suffer a water deficit despite its large dependence on agriculture, but has excess water (about 5 billion m³), which Egypt uses.

If Sudan recovers from the shocks of the 1980s and 1990s, its irrigated land will expand significantly toward the year 2000 and beyond. Subsequently there will be a water shortage even if Sudan receives some of the additional water from the Sudd projects (Table 2.9).

### Ethiopia

Until the 1970s Ethiopia was not dependent on the Nile because of the high rainfall it enjoyed. In the 1970s and 1980s there were climate changes in Ethiopia due to the drought that struck the entire Sahal region. Until then much rain fell in the northern part of the state and very little in the south. Following the change plentiful rain falls in the southern and central areas of the country, while the northern area receives less. Consequently, and due to rapid population growth, Ethiopia's water consumption has risen. Ethiopia still contributes most of the Nile waters, but still uses only 1 percent of the river's discharge.

The land and water potential in Ethiopia are presented in a development plan prepared by the U.S. Agricultural Rehabilitation Department (Jovanovic, 1985). The plan states that Ethiopia has three sites for reservoirs with carrying capacities of 85 billion m³, and seventy-one sites for building dams on the Nile, including nineteen that are suitable also for electricity production at a rate of about 8,700 megawatts (30 billion kilowatt hours). The planners propose to construct these nineteen dams for water storage and hydroelectric production, but so far only one of them has been built, at the Pisha site. According to the plan, Ethiopia will be able to reclaim 4.3 million hectares (10.7 million acres) of land for agricultural use if the Blue Nile is diverted east to the Awash River basin and the Dankil depression, and if use is made of the water of the River Umo and of the two Sobat tributaries of the White Nile that flow through its territory, the Akobo and the Baro.

If Ethiopia exploits all these opportunities, it will take up about 40

billion m³ of Blue Nile water annually (Jovanovic, 1985). According to
a recent estimate, Ethiopia will use only about 5–6 billion m³ (Collins,
1990b: 166). Whittington et al. mention the use of 900,000 hectares in
the Blue Nile basin and 1.5 million hectares in the Sobat basin, a total
of 20–30 billion m³ (Whittington et al., 1995).

In the early 1990s Ethiopia ended a long bitter war with Eritrea,
which formally became an independent state. The central government
of Ethiopia conducted a war against the Tigre tribe in the north, and in
1991 the latter won a victory and toppled the central government; yet
even this victory does not bode well for the country, and as long as there
is no quiet Ethiopia cannot set about constructing water development
projects. Even if the peace in the country endures, development projects
in Ethiopia will be obstructed by Egyptian objections to any change in
the existing distribution of water. Egypt is the most powerful state in
the region, and it can force the other states to accept its demands. Still,
it seems that Ethiopia's as well as Eritrea's needs will continue to grow,
and the riparians of the Nile basin will have no choice but to introduce
a more equal division of the river water (Vestal, 1985; Wood, 1985;
Abebe 1995; Whittington et al., 1995; Allan 1996b).

**The Equatorial States**

Six White Nile riparians (Zaire, Rwanda, Burundi, Uganda, Kenya,
and Tanzania) enjoy an equatorial climate, and therefore do not need
the Nile water as badly as Sudan, Egypt, and Ethiopia. At present their
combined consumption is 1.7 billion m³ of Nile water (Waterbury,
1979: 80, 1994). But the countries located on Lake Victoria (Kenya,
Tanzania, and Uganda) have substantial semiarid areas. They presently
reclaim land for agriculture there at a steady pace, but because they too
are experiencing rapid population growth, they will need more river
water to prepare wider areas for settlement (principally in the south Tan-
zanian highlands, the Karyo River Valley in Kenya, and the western valley in Uganda) (Okidi, 1990: 216). At a meeting with Egyptian and Sudanese representatives at the end of the 1980s, Tanzania, Kenya and
Uganda demanded about 5 billion m³ of water for their future needs.
The three other states (Zaire, Rwanda and Burundi) also require the use
of Nile water. In 1984 the three last states decided to build a multipurpose dam on the Kagera River, which empties into Lake Victoria, for
electricity, recreation, and irrigation. For various reasons the project has
not yet been implemented (Okidi, 1990: 212).

Between Sudan and the Lake Victoria states an agreement will be
needed to regulate the White Nile's waters. Between 1961 and 1964
large quantities of rain caused flooding in the lake region, and Lake

Victoria burst its banks in Kenya and caused serious damage. At the lake countries' request, the Owen Dam was opened to allow excess water to flow from the lake. In consequence, the Sudd region was inundated and thousands of resident Nilotics were drowned. The dam was closed once more, so the devastation around the lake grew worse. Securing the banks of Lake Victoria without damaging the Sudd swamps has become a geopolitical problem requiring a solution.

## Economics and Society in the Nile Basin States

All the basin states suffer from a single socioeconomic problem: rapid population growth is not matched by food production (Table 2.10). Of all the basin states only Egypt is abundant in industry, tourism, and foreign aid. Egypt's dependence on agriculture is less than that of the other riparian states, and therefore Egypt can solve its food problem. Ethiopia, Sudan, Burundi, Kenya, and Rwanda lack these advantages, thus they cannot import food and their residents suffer from hunger.

Egypt, however, imports most of its food. Until the 1960s Egypt was a wheat exporter and satisfied all its own food requirements. However, in the 1980s its wheat crop supplied only about 20 percent of the population, even though the yield per dunam (about 0.23 acres) in Egypt is one of the highest in the world. The reason for this gap is population growth. From the 1960s until the 1990s, Egypt's population grew by about 102 percent, while its wheat production rose by only 71 percent. Egypt was therefore forced to import about 7–8 million tons of cereal annually (75–80 percent of all Egypt's cereal needs) at the cost of $4 billion, which placed Egypt in second place among the Third World grain importers (Table 2.11). In 30 years, Egypt's cereal imports grew by 612 percent (Dethier and Funk, 1987: 26).

Only by decreasing dependence on agriculture and importing food can Egypt solve its food shortage problem, because it has exhausted almost all ways of increasing the yield of agricultural crops. As mentioned, Egypt's yields are some of the largest in the world, and any enlargement in the yield of the land increases its salinity and creates serious drainage problems. Also, land reclamation contributes only slightly to food production. The yield in reclaimed regions is low and great investment is required for soil improvement. According to 1980s data, the desert lands reclaimed after the construction of the Aswan High Dam contribute less than 1 percent of the agricultural production in Egypt (Richards, 1980: 127–8; Voll, 1980: 9; White, 1988; *Middle East and North Africa Yearbook*, 1994). Moreover, while Egypt has been making a supreme effort to reclaim new lands it has lost about

Table 2.10: Economics and Society of Nile Basin Riparians — Basic data

| Country | Population (in millions) | | Annual Population Growth Rate (%) | | Annual Food Production Growth Rate (%) | | GNP per Person ($) | Dependency on Agriculture (as % of GNP) | |
|---|---|---|---|---|---|---|---|---|---|
| | 1995 | 2010 | 1980–90 | 1991–2000 | 1980–90 | 1990–94 | 1995 | 1965 | 1994 |
| Ethiopia | 56 | 90 | 3.1 | 3.4 | 0.4 | - | 100 | 58 | 57 |
| Zaire | 44 | 69 | 3.2 | 3.0 | 2.5 | - | 120 | 20 | 30[b] |
| Tanzania | 29 | 43 | 3.1 | 3.1 | 4.9 | 5.8 | 120 | 46 | 57 |
| Burundi | 6 | 10 | 2.8 | 3.1 | 3.0 | -3.1 | 160 | 71 | 53 |
| Uganda | 21 | 32 | 2.5 | 3.3 | 2.3 | 3.3 | 240 | 52 | 49 |
| Rwanda | 8 | 10 | 3.3 | 3.9 | 0.7 | -13.8 | 180 | 62 | 51 |
| Kenya | 28 | 44 | 3.8 | 3.5 | 3.3 | -1.5 | 280 | 35 | 29 |
| Sudan | 28 | 42 | 2.7 | 2.8 | - | - | 340[a] | 43 | 34[b] |
| Egypt | 62 | 81 | 2.4 | 2.3 | 1.5 | 1.8 | 790 | 29 | 20 |

*Sources:* World Bank, *World Development Report*, 1994, 1996; World Resources Institute 1997; Population Reference Bureau 1996

[a] 1991
[b] 1990

**Table 2.11: Cereal Import and Donations in Various Years (thousands of metric tons)**

| Country | Imports | | | Donations | | |
|---|---|---|---|---|---|---|
| | 1974 | 1990/91 | 1992 | 1974 | 1990 | 1992 |
| Ethiopia | 118 | 687 | 1045 | 54 | 646 | 963 |
| Zaire | 343 | 336 | | 1 | 113 | |
| Tanzania | 431 | 73 | 252 | 448 | 58 | 15 |
| Burundi | 7 | 17 | 19 | 6 | 4 | 2 |
| Uganda | 36 | 7 | 22 | 0 | 27 | 25 |
| Rwanda | 3 | 21 | 14 | 19 | 6 | 14 |
| Kenya | 15 | 188 | 669 | 2 | 97 | 162 |
| Sudan | 125 | 586 | 654 | 46 | 383 | 481 |
| Egypt | 3877 | 8580 | 7330 | 610 | 1427 | 1611 |

*Sources:* World Bank, *World Development Report*, 1994, pp. 224–225; World Resources Institute 1994–5: 298; 1996–7

300,000 hectares of fertile agricultural land to urbanization (White, 1988). But the principle problem in reclaiming new land is that it requires a large amount of water. In the mid-1980s Egypt devised a plan for the reclamation of 0.5–0.6 million hectares of desert land for agriculture. The work was supposed to be completed by 1997, but it requires an additional 8 billion m³ of water annually. In the early 1990s, the plans reached figures of 2.0 million hectares and 20 billion m³, and it is not clear where Egypt will find this additional water (Mideast Market, Feb. 8, 1988; South, June 1988).

Egypt can increase its food production by mechanizing agriculture, improving drainage, and destroying pests, but this is a slow and continuous process, and will not solve the fundamental problem (Fahim, 1981; White, 1988).

Sudan, until two decades ago considered the potential "bread basket" of the Arab world, today spends about 50 percent of its income on food imports. Sudan has about 35 million hectares suitable for agriculture (about 3 percent of all Sudan's territory), but only about 10 million hectares are cultivated, and only about 1.8 million hectares (0.6 percent of Sudan's total territory) are irrigated. Sudan's agricultural potential is therefore particularly large, and if it solves its political, economic, and social problems, its chances to be food self-sufficient are even better than Egypt's.

Ethiopia also has abundant water and large areas earmarked for agricultural development, but because of its political, economic, and social situation it cannot exploit these resources. In 1985 famine struck

eight million people in Ethiopia, and about one million died of starvation.

All the equatorial states contain large areas of land for agricultural
development and abundant water (from rain and rivers). Because of
their economic and social position, however, these states lack financial
resources and labor to utilize these resources. Some of the equatorial
states (Burundi, Uganda, Kenya, and Rwanda) suffer from serious food
shortage (Table 2.10).

In all of the states the population is growing rapidly. From an exami-
nation of predicted population growth until the year 2010 it appears that
the situation in the future will be even worse: in 1990 the population of
the Nile basin states was about 251 million people; in 2000 it will be
338 million people (Table 2.10). Because no growth in water utilization
is expected in the coming decade, it seems unlikely that these states will
increase their food production, and because they cannot import food
they will not be able to feed all their populace (Ehlers, 1979; Stork and
Pfeifer, 1987; Canaan, 1990).

The only way to prevent starvation in the Nile states is by importing
food through humanitarian aid. Until 1995 humanitarian aid came
mainly from the West and was intended principally for Ethiopia, Zaire,
Kenya, Sudan, and Egypt (Table 2.11). But the aid shipments will have
to be much larger to meet the population growth forecast, and it is
doubtful whether the Western world will have so much excess food.
Without food, at least some of the population in these countries will die
(World Resources Institute, 1997).

The 1990s did in fact manifest such an apocalyptic outcome. In
Rwanda and Burundi there was genocide as a result of tribal war; in
Ethiopia millions died of starvation and in tribal warfare; in Sudan the
civil war went on incessantly; and Egypt alone is barely surviving, with
massive western support that serves as a substitute for Nile water.

## The Geopolitical Array in the Nile Basin

Two principal elements determine the geopolitical array in the Nile
basin: international agreements for water management in the basin and
the complex relationships among the basin states. The nature of the
array is determined by Egypt's dominance concerning discharge water
exploitation, the colonial history of the basin states, and the political
instability in most of these countries.

### International Agreements on Nile Water Utilization

Most of the agreements among the Nile basin states were signed in
the colonial period at the initiative or under the influence of the colonial

states (Table 2.12). Britain, which played a dominant part in these agreements, protected first and foremost Egypt's interests, and later also Sudan's. The agreements do not deal with the development of use of Nile water, but rather with preventing the other riparians from using it. The other colonial powers that signed these agreements, such as Italy, France, and Belgium, did not protect the interests of the lands under their rule. They were more concerned with their own problems and interests in the Nile basin area than with what was being done within the borders of their colonies or with improving the conditions of the population living in these areas. Therefore, these colonies suffered under their rule, especially Ethiopia; no agreement exists protecting Ethiopia's natural rights to use Nile water.

Two postcolonial agreements are exceptional: the 1959 accord between Sudan and Egypt and the Kagera Accords. In the 1959 accord between Egypt and Sudan, Egypt recognized Sudan's rights to use the river water and abandoned its own historical rights. As mentioned, it was agreed that all additional water that accumulated as a result of the development projects would be evenly divided between the two states. But Egypt entered this agreement with obvious displeasure. It was obliged to sign the accord with Sudan because it had harmed Sudan and had forced a Sudanese Nubian population to abandon territories flooded by the Egyptian reservoir, which had overflowed into Sudan. Egypt also feared that Sudanese opposition to the dam would delay its construction, already well behind schedule, for several years more. Furthermore, behind the Sudanese demands stood the basic fact that in the 1929 agreement Sudan had been put at a disadvantage by the British and now it was necessary to set matters right.

Sudan in fact gained from the new agreement, and the major quantity of water that was added as a result of building the Aswan Dam was transferred to Sudan. However, Egypt and Sudan ignored the rights of the remaining basin states, and the upstream states, and they also agreed to cooperate in rejecting any future claims that these states might make (Howell et al., 1988: 47).

The Kagera Accords, signed in 1977 among the upstream states without Egypt's approval, concern development projects for utilizing Kagera River water; but the signatories are unable to realize these plans because of their social and economic situation, and no changes are expected in the near future.

After colonial rule, a dispute arose concerning the status of the colonial accords. Egypt claimed that they should be upheld to the letter, on the basis of international decisions and precedents. The world states in fact agreed, and at a conference held in Vienna in 1978 colonial accords and treaties made throughout the world were held to be binding in the

Table 2.12: International Agreement on Nile Water Use

| Year | Place of Agreement | Sides to the Agreement | Contents of Agreement | Benefi-ciaries | Legal Status at Present |
|------|-------------------|------------------------|----------------------|----------------|------------------------|
| 1891 | Addis Ababa | Italy and Great Britain | Italy agreed not to construct any work on the River Atbara. | Egypt | According to Ethiopia no longer effective with end of Italian and British colonial rule. |
| 1902 | Addis Ababa | Great Britain and Ethiopia | Ethiopia committed itself not to construct any work across the Blue Nile, Lake Tana, or the Sobat. | Egypt | According to Ethiopia no longer effective as it was not ratified and its Ethiopian rights were not mentioned. |
| 1906 | London | Great Britain and Congo | Congo agreed not to construct any work on or near the Semliki or Isango. | Sudan and Egypt | According to Congo no longer effective with end of colonial rule. |
| 1906 | London | Great Britain, Italy, and France | The three states committed themselves to the preservation of the integrity of Ethiopia and reconfirmed the 1891 and 1906 Agreements. | Ethiopia, Egypt, and Sudan | According to Ethiopia no longer effective with end of colonial rule. |
| 1925 | Rome | Great Britain and Italy | Great Britain obtained from Ethiopia the concession to build a dam on Lake Tana; the hydraulic rights of Egypt and the Sudan were recognized. | Egypt and Sudan | The League of Nations never ratified the agreement. |

Table 2.12: (Continued)

| Year | Name | Parties | Description | Affected | Status |
|---|---|---|---|---|---|
| 1929 | | Egypt and Great Britain | The agreement allocated 48 billion m³ of water to Egypt and 4.0 billion m³ of irrigation water for the Sudan. | Mainly Egypt | Replaced by the 1959 Agreement. |
| 1929 | | Great Britain (on behalf of the Sudan, Kenya, Tanganyika, Uganda) | No work of any kind could be undertaken on the Nile or on the equatorial lakes without Egypt's consent. | Egypt | Egypt sees it as valid. The equatorial states see it as not valid. |
| 1934 | London | Great Britain (on behalf of Tanganyika) and Belgium (on behalf of Rwanda and Burundi) | Rwanda and Burundi agreed not to construct any dam on the Kagera River and not to damage the flow of the river. | Egypt and Sudan | According to equatorial states no longer effective with the end of colonial rule. |
| 1949 | Owen Falls Agreement | a. Great Britain/Egypt b. Great Britain/Egypt | Egyptian supervision of water discharges at the dam. Egypt took the responsibility for any damages resulting from the rising of Lake Victoria. | Egypt; water rights; Uganda; hydropower rights | Still valid. |

**Table 2.12:** (Continued)

| Year | Agreement | Parties | Purpose | Parties | Status |
|---|---|---|---|---|---|
| 1950 | Owen Falls Dam Exchange of Notes | Great Britain/Egypt | To secure the cooperation of Uganda for Egyptian data collection in Lake Victoria | Egypt and Sudan | Still valid. |
| 1959 | Nile Water Agreement | Egypt and Sudan | Construction of the Aswan Dam; Egypt would receive 55.5 billion $m^3$ and Sudan 18.5 billion $m^3$ | Egypt and Sudan | Still valid. |
| 1977 | Kagera Basin Agreement | Burundi, Rwanda, Tanzania, and Uganda (joined in 1981) | Multipurpose development of the Kagera basin; hydropower, agriculture, trade, tourism, fisheries | Rwanda, Burundi, Tanzania | Valid; difficulties in implementation. |
| 1967 | Nile Hydro-meteorological Survey | Egypt, Kenya, Sudan, Tanzania, Uganda | To survey Lakes Kioga, Victoria, and Albert; to measure water balance in Lake Victoria catchment | Egypt, Kenya, Sudan, Tanzania, Uganda | Still valid. |

*Sources:* Sayed, 1960; Krishna, 1998; Ahmed, 1990; Allan, 1990; Collins, 1990a; Okidi, 1990; Kliot, 1994

present also (Ahmed, 1990: 22). However, because these accords in the Nile basin in fact subjected all the basin states except Sudan to Egypt and its agricultural needs the upstream states' approach to this matter was different. They argued that the accords represented the colonial period and were no longer in effect. Indeed, a month after Sudan announced its independence (February 2, 1956), the Ethiopian government stated that it was upholding its right to use the water within its borders. Since then the Ethiopian government has repeated this statement in several international forums (Shahin, 1986: 18; Allan, 1990: 180; Collins, 1990a: 166; Said, 1993). Kenya has expressed a similar position, as have Tanzania and Uganda. In 1961, when Tanzania (formerly Tanganyika) declared its independence, Julius Nyrere, the president of the country, announced that he did not recognize the 1929 agreement, whereby no development could be undertaken on the equatorial Nile without Egyptian approval. Kenya and Uganda also announced their nonrecognition of this agreement. Egypt responded laconically that the accord was, in fact, still in effect (Okidi, 1990: 203–4). In the 1970s and 1980s the upstream states' water requirements grew, and therefore the issue of allocating Nile water arose, as well as the old dispute concerning colonial accords. In 1977 Ethiopia announced at a UN conference that it intended to utilize the water of the Blue Nile and made similar statements at the end of the 1970s and in 1981 at a UN conference on developing countries. These declarations mentioned the irrigation of 3.8–3.9 million hectares in the Blue Nile basin, as well as several million more hectares in the basins of the Sobat, Akobo, and Umo tributaries (Waterbury, 1979: 78). The equatorial states also stated their intention to utilize Nile water.

Egypt was caught in a dilemma. On the one hand, it could not ignore the rights of all the riparian states to use the Nile water, and it wished to create a positive image as a cooperative country. On the other hand, Egypt could not forgo the water, which was crucial for its existence, and it insisted on the principle of territorial unity of the entire basin, which gave Egypt the right to use the river water. Egypt's response to Ethiopia's statement of intent was therefore twofold. First, it threatened military action: in 1978 President Anwar Sadat said that the Egyptian army would attack any state that seized Egypt's water (Waterbury, 1979: 78). In 1990 Egypt again warned Ethiopia not to utilize Nile water, and included Israel in its warning, stipulating that Israel should not aid Ethiopia in implementing its plans (*Maariv*, July 1, 1990). On July 7, 1991, the Egyptian minister for irrigation warned that if Ethiopia cooperated with Israel in diverting the Nile waters, Egypt would consider this a *casus belli* (interview with al Bian, July 7, 1991). On the other hand, Egypt was prepared to offer Ethiopia 2 billion m$^3$ of water during the drought, and to undertake that all water added to the basin through development projects would be divided among Egypt, Sudan, and Ethiopia (Shahin, 1986).

Collins claims that Egypt should not fear Ethiopia's development plans since they will not injure Egypt or Sudan; rather, they may even increase the Nile's flow in these countries (Collins 1990b). For example, storing water in the Ethiopian mountains, and not in Lake Nasser, will decrease the rate of seepage and evaporation. But even if Egypt acknowledges this, it will not be willing to be dependent on another country for Nile water.

Egypt rejected the equatorial states' request, claiming that it needed clearer data about the White Nile's discharge and the climate in the region. Because Egypt feared that these states would exploit Nile water unilaterally without agreement, it founded an organization, Undugu, several years ago whose official purpose is to have the ministerial level representatives of the Nile basin states meet and discuss Nile issues, agriculture and resource development, and to promote economic, technological, and scientific cooperation (Ahmed, 1990). However, the actual purpose of this group is to enable Egypt to supervise and control water in the upstream states. Its members—Egypt, Sudan, Uganda, Zaire, Central African Republic, Rwanda, and Burundi—are not linked economically; they all trade with the West only and no other connections among them exist (Allan, 1990: 181). To date, the only accomplishment of this organization is its decision to conduct a meteorological survey in the Nile basin.

On the face of it, the situation in the Nile basin is explosive because of the dispute about the river water, but this is actually not the case. Despite the large water requirements of these states, they are not as dependent on the Nile as Egypt and Sudan, and they lack the resources to develop large water projects. Even if population growth and drought spur them toward greater development efforts, another decade or two will pass before they succeed in realizing these plans.

## Relations among the Nile Basin Riparian States

As mentioned, the relations among the Nile basin riparian states are characterized by persistent political turbulence. So long as the war between the central government of Ethiopia and the tribes in the south continues, the moment of truth between Egypt and Ethiopia will be delayed, and Egypt will be able to continue benefiting from all the water without sharing with Ethiopia. When the war ends, the problem of water division will arise again; then Egypt will have to share not only with Ethiopia, but also with the new state of Eritrea.

Sudan's instability has a direct effect on Egypt, which is deeply interested in everything that occurs in Sudan. For many generations Egypt has promoted the concept of the "united Nile valley," based on the ancient historical connection between Egypt and Sudan. In light of this attitude, Egypt ruled Sudan by direct military control, and later through Britain, which governed both states (Waterbury, 1979: 43).

This rule sparked the enmity of the Sudanese, whose struggle for separation of the two states culminated in the Mahdi's revolt. Ill will continued even after Sudan gained independence and became even greater during the dispute over the construction of the Aswan dam, when Numeiri was in power (until 1985) and in 1987. Matters reached a climax on June 26, 1995, with an unsuccessful attempt to assassinate Mubarak, the president of Egypt. In spite of this tension a unity agreement was signed in 1987 between the two states. The relationship between Sudan and Egypt can be characterized, therefore, as ambivalent: on the one hand they are close, and on the other, they evince hostility and suspicion. This ambivalence is expressed in the Sudanese party structure. In the 1940s and 1950s Sudan had two political parties: one supported the Nile valley unity idea and the other opposed it. Egyptian attitudes have been affected by the civil war in Sudan. Egypt sees itself as having a direct connection with this war and its outcome.

The Sudanese civil war has been in progress essentially since Sudan declared its independence. The south wishes to secede from the Arab Muslim north, which holds most power in the state. In 1972 the Sudanese ruler Numeiri signed an agreement with the rebels to stop the war, but it erupted again in 1982 with greater ferocity, in part because of the imposition of Islamic law throughout the country, against the will of the non-Muslim south. The Southern People's Liberation Army (SPLA) demands political autonomy for the south and an equal portion of the nation's resources, including the oil discovered in the south and the Nile water.

The utilization of Nile water is one of the issues over which the war broke out, because at the heart of the development plans for increasing the river's discharge stands the Sudd region in the south. The southern inhabitants oppose these plans, especially that for the Jonglei Canal, because they do not consider the needs of the local residents, who need the swamp water to survive, and because their chief goal is to supply more water to northern Sudan and to Egypt (Krishna, 1988; Collins, 1990a).

On the one hand Egypt is harmed by this, because according to the agreement signed with Sudan, any additional water created by the development projects will be evenly divided between the two countries. On the other hand, Egypt is using the excess water that Sudan is not using, among other reasons, because of the civil war. When the war ends, Sudan will begin to use all the water it is entitled to use. Moreover, any accord signed between north and south Sudan will be based on an equal division of the nation's resources, including a consideration of the needs of the south—a measure that will be disadvantageous to Egypt. Egypt may even have to forgo some of the water it currently uses to the benefit of southern Sudan.

Nonetheless, Egypt would like to see an end to the civil war, because it promotes instability in the entire region. For example, the north Sudanese government is helped by Libya in its war against the rebels in the south, to Egypt's dismay, because Egypt fears that Libya, its old enemy, will acquire control over its water resources and will endanger its stability. Iran is also interested in a weak Sudan, having discovered its inherent advantages. In the early 1990s Khartoum became a center for fundamentalist Iranian–Islamic training (Figure 2.6). Islamic terror radiates from there to Egypt, Somalia, Ethiopia, and even to Kenya and Israel. Tension between Sudan and Egypt has therefore grown, and is likely to lead to an explosion as in 1995 (see above).

In an attempt to bring the Sudanese civil war to an end, Egyptian President Mubarak visited Sudan in March 1988. Egypt would also like Ethiopia to halt its aid to the rebels in the south, as this aid feeds the war. For this purpose, Egypt arranged a meeting in 1987 between the president of Ethiopia and the prime minister of Sudan, but nothing came of these efforts.

The tension between Sudan and Ethiopia stems from a wide range of factors—political, military, religious, and others. The Ethiopian government assists the south Sudanese rebels (who are Christians, like the Ethiopians, and animists). Sudan, which requested that this aid be stopped, supported the Eritrean and Tigre rebels in their war against the government, which helped the Tigre rebels to overthrow the Addis Ababa government in 1991. Sudan hoped that this event would stop Ethiopia from aiding the rebels in the south, but this hope was in vain; the Tigre people cooperate with the south Sudanese people and they will probably continue to grant them aid in the future (Figure 2.6).

According to Waterbury (1978), Egypt suffers from a Fashoda complex, meaning a profound Egyptian fear that instability in the upper Nile basin will impede the flow of the water in the river. The name Fashoda comes from a situation faced by France and Britain in 1898. The two countries were about to go to war because a French expedition wished to explore the sources of the Nile and proposed building a dam on the White Nile, north of the point where the Sobat emptied into it. The Brit-

*Figure 2.6:* Geopolitical Circles in the Nile Basin

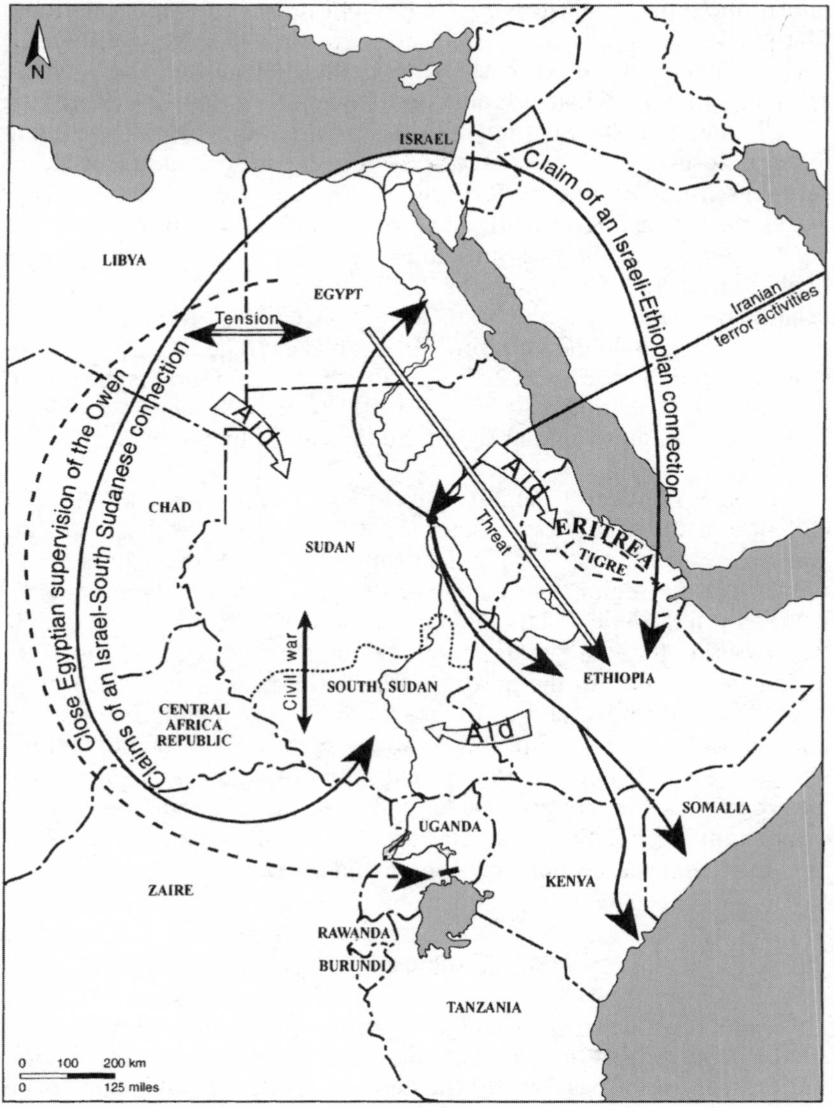

ish and Egyptians were concerned that such a dam would give the French the power to destroy Egypt through flood or drought (Naff and Matson, 1984: 143).

Egypt had good cause for such fears in the 1980s, when Cuba sent an army to Ethiopia, when Ethiopia considered the possibility of uniting with Sudan, and when the revolutions in Zaire took place (Zaire being located close to the Nile sources). Civil wars, which caused waves of refugees; interference by foreign powers, such as Libya, the Arab world, the US, and the USSR; and drought and famine transformed the region into one of the most unstable in the world. Therefore, Egypt is likely to take action if it believes that its water resources are imperiled because of instability in the basin states or because of foreign intervention in the region. In the meantime, Egypt makes frequent efforts to promote peace in the region. However, in the short term Egypt is the principal beneficiary of this instability because water distribution problems will arise once more among Egypt, Sudan, and Ethiopia when stability returns.

As noted, political instability is one of the factors delaying the construction of water development projects on the Nile. Yet these projects could serve as catalysts for political solutions and for the restoration of stability to the region. For example, Ethiopia would transfer water to Eritrea from the Nile and its tributaries, and Eritrea would give Ethiopia free access to the Red Sea. In return, Ethiopia would cease aiding south Sudan in its war with the north. In return for transferring much more water to north Sudan and to Egypt, north Sudan would recognize the political rights of the south. But solutions such as these cannot be realized in the 1990s because to plan and implement major projects like these demands much time. As at least ten years will be required for their completion, even if they were started today all the countries of the region might expect a water shortage around 2000.

## Conclusions

The factors that determine the fair division of international river water are the geography of the drainage basin; its climate and hydrology; past and present use of basin water (historical rights); economic and social needs of the basin riparians; the degree of dependency on the river water; the cost of alternative projects for water use; the existence of resources other than water; the nonwasteful use of basin water; and the possibility of providing compensation for damage caused (Table 2.13).

I observed above how dependent the basin state economies are on the Nile, because agriculture contributes 21 percent or more of the GNP in these states. (In the Western world, agriculture contributes only 3–5 percent of the GNP.) This fact makes the situation along the Nile unique, and it cannot be compared with international rivers in the Western world.

Table 2.13 summarizes the geographical factors, water utilization, and socioeconomic factors in the Nile basin states. A considerable section of the river's course lies in Egypt and Sudan, compared with other states, such as Ethiopia. Yet Egypt and Sudan contribute nothing to the river water while other states, principally Ethiopia, contribute most. The Egyptian climate is arid, and Sudan is arid and characterized by savannahs. In the other states, by contrast, the climate is tropical or savannah, and they enjoy ample rainfall. In northern Ethiopia there is a monsoon climate, but in recent years the climate there has also become arid. Sudan and Egypt, and recently even Ethiopia, are therefore more dependent than the others on river water.

Egypt has historical rights to use Nile water since the start of human civilization. Sudan also has historical rights, less than Egypt but more than the upstream states, which began using Nile water only recently. Egypt and Sudan are the only users of the river water.

All the basin states are dependent on agriculture, which is their principal source of income. Egypt is less dependent on agriculture than the others because it has other sources of income, but it is more dependent on river water than the others.

All the countries in the region are considered to be developing states in socioeconomic terms. In all of them the natural growth rate is high and they cannot match it with agricultural development, and they all import a large part of their food.

This discussion has not considered the possibility of desalination in the Nile basin countries, or enlarging the recycling of sewage water, or increasing the pumping of groundwater in the Nile valley and its surroundings. The potential for such activities indeed exists. But desalination is not a viable solution in the countries under discussion because of their great poverty and their inability to finance and maintain desalination plants in general, still less for the needs of agriculture. The recycling of sewage water does not come up for consideration for both social and economic reasons (in these countries there is great opposition to reuse of sewage water). Only Egypt moved to realize these options in the 1980s and 1990s, particularly the use of groundwater; but they are expensive for that country also, so no marked changed in the foreseeable future is to be expected.

Assuming that the annual discharge of the Nile at the Aswan Dam is 84 billion $m^3$ (as it was before the 1960s), and that about 10 billion $m^3$ of this water evaporates, the total supply available is about 74 billion $m^3$

Table 2.13: Criteria for Water Allocation in the Nile Basin According to Helsinki Convention

| Country | A. Share in Area of Nile Basin (%) B. Water Contribution to the Nile (%) | Climate | Past and Present Utilization | GNP per Person ($) 1995 | Other Resources and Potential |
|---|---|---|---|---|---|
| Egypt | A - 12 B - 0 | Desert | Historical rights; at present consumes about 60 billion m$^3$ of 80% of all consumers | 790 | Heavily dependent on Nile but has other resources such as Suez Canal, tourism, and industry. |
| Sudan | A - 63 B - 1 | Desert 50% Savannah 50% | Historical rights; at present about 13–16 billion m$^3$ or about 18.5% of all consumers | 340(1991) | Heavily dependent on Nile |
| Ethiopia | A - 10 B - 84 | Desert 20% Savannah 80% | No historical rights; at present consumes only 1% (less than 0.6 billion m$^3$) | 100 | Highland farming |

**Table 2.13:** (Continued)

| | | | | |
|---|---|---|---|---|
| Zaire | A - 0.7<br>B - 10 to White Nile | Tropical 60%<br>Savannah 30%<br>Semiarid 10% | 120 | Minerals, oil, hydroelectric power |
| Kenya | A - 1.7<br>B - 30 to White Nile | Savannah 50%<br>Tropical 50% | 280 | Tourism, minerals, hydroelectric potential |
| Tanzania | A - 3.7<br>B - 18 to White Nile | Tropical | 120 | Hydroelectric potential, minerals |
| Uganda | A - 7.7<br>B - 12 to White Nile | Tropical | 240 | Hydroelectric power, tourism |
| Rwanda | A - 0.7<br>B - 15 to White Nile | Tropical | 180 | - |
| Burundi | A - 0.5<br>B - 15 to White Nile | Tropical | 160 | - |

Tropical countries consumers only

} 1.7 billion $m^3$

of water; but the demand in 2000–2005 will be about 90–142 billion m³. Egypt will need about 70–75 billion m³, and Sudan about 32 billion m³. Egypt is willing to allocate to Ethiopia 2 billion m³ but Ethiopian needs are estimated between 6 billion m³ (Waterbury, 1994) and 30 billion m³ (Jovanovic, 1985). Equatorial states will need about 5 billion m³. The deficit will therefore stand at about 16–68 billion m³.

Clearly, this situation cannot long continue, and it will have to be changed gradually toward the twenty-first century. However, as we see in Tables 2.8 and 2.9, a water shortage is to be expected in the downstream states (Sudan and Egypt) as that time approaches, and therefore it seems likely that they will oppose any change in the status quo of the division of Nile water. One might hope that the worsening water shortage will encourage Egypt and Sudan to adopt a cooperative rational use of the Nile waters, including development of the Sudd area, and more efficient use of water in their own territories. In such circumstances all the countries in the region would benefit from the water even after a redistribution and a cutback in water to the upstream states (Allan, 1990; Abebe, 1995; Whittington et al., 1995).

Then how can the Nile water be more fairly divided? One alternative is by development projects in southern Sudan (Rogers and Lydon, 1994). Another, or together with the first, is by development projects on the plateaus of Ethiopia (Whittington et al., 1995). Above all there must be careful use of water within countries and cooperation among the countries on development projects.

According to Whittington (1995), Sudan and Egypt will reduce activities on the Aswan dam in Egypt and the Jebel Awliya Dam in Sudan, where evaporation is especially high, and will agree to build a series of dams in Ethiopia where evaporation is low. He estimates that the immediate gain will be about 6 billion m³ of water; in addition, Sudan and Egypt will concede some of their water (about 2.5 billion m³ each), and thus about 10–13 billion m³ of water will be available for Ethiopia. Sudan will lower the water it uses from 18.5 to about 15.5 billion m³ and Egypt from 55.5 to 52.5 billion m³. Transfers of energy and the introduction of market mechanisms, together with an increase of recycling, will bring about a reasonable solution to the expected shortage.

The problem is that we return to a starting point that assumes that considerations of national security and of prestige will decline in importance, and Egypt will acquiesce in regarding Ethiopia as its water reservoir.

In the Sudd region there is enormous unrealized discharge potential. If the three plans that Hurst proposed are implemented—the Jonglei Canal, drainage of the Mashar swamps and of the Bahr el-Ghazal region, and the Sobat River and tributaries project, the Nile's discharge will increase by about 10–20 billion m³ annually. An additional 5–10 billion m³ may be added to the flow by improvement and elevation of the dams in Sudan and by construction of dams in Ethiopia, and another 15 billion m³ by recycling and redraining water in Egypt. A total of an additional 35–45 billion m³ of water could be added, which would almost cancel the deficit expected by 2025 (Rogers and Lydon 1994).

Most experts assume that hardship will impel this kind of decision making; I believe that the likelihood that nothing will change is greater than the likelihood of regional cooperation. Powerful Egypt, which is in need of water, will continue to maintain the status quo. For a long time to come Sudan will be stuck in its social and religious quagmire and there will be no development in the south. Neither Egypt nor Sudan will furnish Ethiopia anything more than very small quantities of water, only about 1–2 billion m³.

If the redistribution of water does not take place, it is not impossible that war between the upstream and downstream states may ensue. However, the likelihood of this occurring is very slight because of the grave weakness of the upstream states and Egypt's strength. But Egypt and Sudan may expect a water shortage even if they are not forced to share the water with others.

*Chapter 3*

# Geopolitics of the Euphrates and Tigris Drainage Basin

## Introduction

The Euphrates is an international river that flows in Turkey, Syria, and Iraq. The Tigris is an international river flowing through Turkey, Iran, and Iraq and forming the border between Syria and Turkey and between Syria and Iraq for a short distance.

The Euphrates is about 1,875 miles long, including about 41 percent in Turkey, 24 percent in Syria, and 35 percent in Iraq (Table 3.1). The Tigris is about 1,164 miles long, with about 21 percent in Turkey, 77 percent in Iraq, and 2 percent only in Syria (namely, a 22-mile section, which is the Syrian-Turkish border, and a 5-mile section, which is the Syria-Iraq border).

Iran is a minor partner in the system. Within Iraqi territory is a small portion of the Tigris' tributaries, the Great Zab and the Little Zab, and the entire drainage basin of another tributary, the Karun River. The Shatt al Arab (southern half) is shared between Iraq and Iran, and the border between them runs down the middle of the river, according to a 1975 agreement.

The Tigris and the Euphrates have entirely separate drainage basins, but because their last section is united; Turkey, Syria, and Iraq (the principal riparians) share the Euphrates and Tigris water; and formerly water was transferred from basin to basin, it is usual to discuss the two rivers as a single system.

The hydropolitical system of the Tigris and the Euphrates would allow special arrangements for using their water. For example, one state could use the water of one of the rivers and allow another state to use the other river's water. For this purpose the three states would be obliged to negotiate and find ways of using the rivers' water in common.

73

**Table 3.1: Euphrates-Tigris System: Length of Rivers and Basin Areas within Riparian States**

| River | Riparian States | Basin Area (miles square) | % | Length of River (miles) | % |
|---|---|---|---|---|---|
| Euphrates | Turkey | 48,262 | 28 | 769 | 41 |
| | Syria | 29,344 | 17 | 444 | 24 |
| | Iraq | 68,340 | 40 | 662 | 35 |
| | Saudi Arabia | 25,482 | 15 | waddies | 0 |
| Total | | 171,428 | 100 | 1,875 | 100 |
| Euphrates tributaries | | | | | |
| Khabour | Turkey | 1,158 | 23 | 28 | 13 |
| | Syria | 3,861 | 77 | 162 | 87 |
| Total | | 5,019 | 100 | 187 | 100 |
| Balikh | Turkey | 386 | 25 | 50 | 50 |
| | Syria | 1,158 | 75 | 50 | 50 |
| Total | | 1,544 | 100 | 100 | 100 |
| Tigris | Turkey | 17,375 | 12 | 250 | 21 |
| | Syria | 386 | 1 | 27 | 2 |
| | Iraq | 112,741 | 78 | 885 | 77 |
| | Iran | 14,286 | 9 | | |
| Total | | 144,788 | 100 | 1162 | 100 |
| Tigris tributaries | | | | | |
| Great Zab | Turkey | 2,737 | 35 | 137 | 27.5 |
| | Iraq | 1,274 | 65 | 362 | 72.5 |
| Total | | 4,012 | 100 | 500 | 100 |
| Little Zab | Iran | 1,158 | 20 | 44 | 20 |
| | Iraq | 4,595 | 80 | 175 | 80 |
| Total | | 5,753 | 100 | 219 | 100 |
| Adhaim | Iraq | 1,930 | 100 | 187 | 100 |
| Diyala | Iran | 888 | 10 | 156 | 48 |
| | Iraq | 7,954 | 90 | 169 | 52 |
| Total | | 8,842 | 100 | 325 | 100 |
| Total Euphrates and Tigris | | 343,317 | | | |
| Shatt al Arab | Iran\Iraq | | | 113 | |
| (Karun | Iran | 34,750 | 100 | 500 | 100) |

*Sources:* Ionides 1937, Ali, 1955; Beaumont 1978; 37; US Army Corps of Engineers, 1991.

But relations between Turkey and Syria and between Turkey and Iraq are tense, and the relations between Syria and Iraq are hostile.

Like Egypt in the Nile basin, Iraq has a 5,000-year-old historical right to use the water of these rivers. Iraq is also dependent on the two rivers more than the upstream riparians because most of its territory has a desert climate, while the two other states have large areas with different climates, and they also have alternative water sources at their disposal. Moreover, Iraq is a downstream state and Turkey, the upstream state, has complete control over the sources of both rivers and therefore has the advantage in ability to use their water.

## Topography

The source of the Euphrates is two tributaries in the Armenian mountains of eastern Turkey: the Kara Su, which rises close to the city of Erzurum, and the Murat, rising close to Mt. Ararat. The Keban dam was built at the point where these two tributaries meet in Turkey (Figure 3.1). From there the river flows through the Anti-Taurus mountains, before exiting into the Jezira plain in Syria. Here three tributaries join it: the Sajur, which begins in the Gaziantep area in Turkey, the Balikh, which empties into it close to the town of Raqqah, and the Khabur, which empties into it close to the town of Dayr az Zawr. From there to the Persian Gulf no water is added to the river. Because the Euphrates is a flood river, which passes through the basalt mountains of Turkey and the chalk and gypsum region of the Jezira heights, it carries much silt and salt.

The origin of the Tigris is likewise in the Armenian mountains, very close to the Murat, the tributary of the Euphrates noted above. The Tigris does not twist along its course like the Euphrates, but flows directly to the Mesopotamian plain, eventually joining the Euphrates to form the joint river, the Shatt al Arab. The Tigris flows parallel to the Zagros mountains and collects many tributaries on its way, which drop down into it perpendicularly from the hills. The large ones are the Great Zab, which originates in Turkey, and the Little Zab, the Adhaim, and the Diyalah, which originate in Iran. Close to where the Shatt al Arab empties into the sea it is joined by its largest tributary, the Karum, which originates in Iran.

Despite the fact that the Iraqi plains (Mesopotamia) are technically not a delta, they function as a delta in every way—in their soil (the Euphrates and Tigris silt), their flat landscape, the nature of their rivers, and the way they are formed.

It is possible that thousands of years ago the Persian Gulf coast was close to settlements now located inland, on the northern Iraqi plains,

*Figure 3.1:* The Euphrates and Tigris Rivers—Annual Discharge and Water Projects

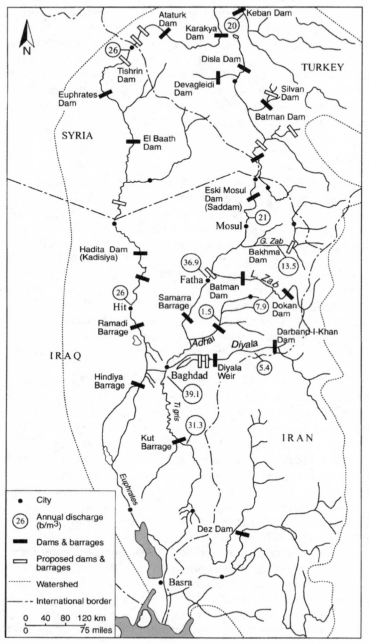

such as Samara and Hit, but in the course of time the Euphrates and Tigris deposited much silt on the sea floor and pushed the sea southward. This process is still going on. Before the new system of dams was built on the Tigris and Euphrates and their tributaries, which slowed the process, the delta advanced about 140 feet a year. In doing so it sometimes left port cities without any sea. Basra was a principal port in the Middle Ages, but today it is far from the sea and access is difficult. The modern port of Fao is silting up and the Iraqis have built a new oil port about 25 miles southeast of it. As the delta expanded southward a giant plain was formed, about 500 miles long and with an average width of 125 miles. This is a very flat plain; Baghdad is just 125 feet above sea level, yet it is about 438 miles from the Persian Gulf, which indicates that for every kilometer of plain there is an incline of only five millimeters!

### Flow Regime

The sources of the two rivers are located in a similar climate, namely a Mediterranean-mountainous climate, where most of the precipitation falls in the winter, first as rain and later as snow, which lies on the mountain peaks until the thaw from March to May. In the summer hardly any rain falls and the rivers receive their water from several springs only. In the winter, on the other hand, the rivers flood (Figure 3.2). At the end of October the first rain falls, and after one or two months, "the little overflow" or "the first overflow" starts in Iraq. In the cold winter months the precipitation becomes snow in the mountains, and therefore in December, January, February, and March there is no significant change in the rivers' flow and the little overflow continues. When the snow melts with the warming of the air in the region, the water level starts to rise. This is the period of the big overflow, which lasts from March until the beginning of June (Figure 3.2). In the months of the *hamsin* (very hot, dry days), March, April, and May, the snowmelt increases and the overflow turns into a heavy flood (Ali, 1955: 30). The rivers lose a large quantity of water on their way due to seepage, evaporation, and human use of water.

The topographical difference between the two rivers creates a difference in their flow regimes. The Tigris flows straight from the snow-capped mountains to the Iraqi plains, while the Euphrates twists in its path and travels over a long distance until it arrives there. Therefore, the main danger of flooding for the residents of the plain, especially of Baghdad, is from the Tigris and not the Euphrates. In the days of the *hamsin* a flood of the Tigris can reach the outskirts of Baghdad within

*Figure 3.2:* Monthly Discharge of the Euphrates (1950–1960) and Tigris (1931–1966)

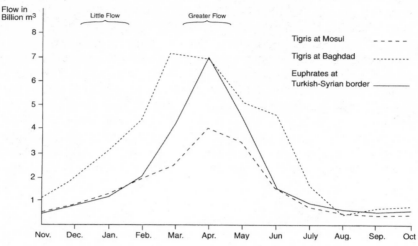

24 hours, while a flood of the Euphrates will reach Iraq only within 10 days, during which time its flow weakens.

The Euphrates flow regime is described in Table 3.2 and Figure 3.2. The little overflow occurs in November-February, and the big overflow in March-June, while in the summer months the quantity of water decreases. At the end of the summer, in September and October, the flow slows.

In the summer months, however, when the demand for water is at its

**Table 3.2: Average Yearly Flow in the Euphrates-Tigris and Tributaries 1931–1966 (billion m³)**

| | | | |
|---|---|---|---|
| Tigris at Mosul[a] | 21.048 | Euphrates at Keban (Turkey) | 20.1 |
| Great Zab | 13.520 | Euphrates at Yusuf Peshe (Syria) | 30.0 |
| Little Zab | 7.950 | Euphrates at Hit (Iraq) | 25.97 |
| Tigris at Fatha | 36.931 | Euphrates at Nasiriya (Iraq) | 14.1 |
| Adhaim | 1.550 | | |
| Tigris at Baghdad | 39.108 | | |
| Diyala | 5.400 | | |
| Tigris at Kut | 31.334 | | |

*Sources:* Brawer and Karmon 1968: 28; Ubell 1971: 6–7; Beaumont et al., 1988: 356; Bilen, 1994: 103; Kolars, 1994.

[a] According to Bilen (1994), Tigris at Mosul is 23.2 billion m³.

peak, there is no water in the river. In summer, therefore, demand for water in Iraq exceeds supply.

The flow regime of the Tigris is presented in Tables 3.2 and 3.3 and in Figure 3.2. The flow data are collected at the four places where the Tigris receives water from its tributaries—Mosul, Fatha, Baghdad, and Kut. Table 3.2 demonstrates the great importance of these tributaries in the flow of the Tigris basin, because they provide more than 50 percent of the discharge. However, just as the discharge of the Tigris increases from tributary to tributary, it rapidly decreases along its source owing to the intensive use of the river water. Because the Tigris tributaries are short and fall from the mountains, they carry much silt with them, and in the flood periods they endanger the plain dwellers, who have been subject to repeated floods throughout history. This danger has been averted by construction of a system of dams and barrages.

The Tigris and Euphrates unite and form the Shatt al Arab near the town of Qurna. The joint river's length is 112 miles and it is about 0.6 miles wide. The final tributary, the Karun, empties into the Shatt al Arab. The Karun has a wide drainage basin and an average annual discharge between 20 and 25 billion $m^3$ of water. Before the construction of the new dams during the 1970s and 1980s, the average annual dis-

Table 3.3: Discharge of the Euphrates-Tigris Rivers by Country (billion $m^3$ and percentage)

| | Turkey | Syria | Iraq | Saudi Arabia | Iran | Total |
|---|---|---|---|---|---|---|
| Total Tigris-Euphrates and tributaries | 58.5 | 1.7 | 15.0 | — | 6.0 | 81.2 |
| Percentage | 72.0 | 2.0 | 18.5 | — | 7.5 | 100.0 |
| Euphrates | 30.0 | | | | | 30.0 |
| Tributaries | — | 1.7 | | | | 1.7 |
| Khabur | | 1.5 | | | | |
| Balikh | | 0.2 | | | | |
| Total | 30.0 | 1.7 | | | | 31.7 |
| Percentage | 95.0 | 5.0 | | | | 100.0 |
| Tigris | 21.0 | | | | | 21.0 |
| Tributaries | 7.5 | | 15.0 | | 6.0 | 28.5 |
| Total | 28.5 | | 15.0 | | 6.0 | 49.5 |
| Percentage | 58.0 | | 30.0 | | 12.0 | 100.0 |

*Sources:* Brawer and Karmon 1968: 28; Ubell 1971: 6–7; Beaumont et al., 1988: 356; Bilen, 1994: 103; Kolars, 1994.

charge of the Shatt al Arab when it empties into the Persian Gulf was
about 20 billion m³.

**Discharge**

The Tigris discharge is greater than that of the Euphrates. The average annual discharge of the Tigris near Baghdad is 1240 m³ a second
(39.1 billion m³), while the average annual discharge of the Euphrates
near Hit is 710 m³ a second (25.9 billion m³) (Table 3.3).

The total discharge of the Euphrates, as understood by hydrologists
today, is between 30 and 32 billion m³ (Bakour and Kolars, 1994: 128–
129), but it changes from year to year (Figure 3.3). The smallest annual
discharge ever measured was 14.9 billion m³ annually, and the largest
was 56.4 billion m³ annually (Kolars and Mitchell, 1991: 97; Bilen,
1994: 96).

The Tigris also varies in its discharge from year to year (Figure 3.3).
The average annual figure at Kut is 31 billion m³. The largest annual
discharge ever measured was about 58.7 billion m³, and the smallest
(measured in Kut in 1989) was about 16.86 billion m³.

It is difficult to determine the average annual discharge of the two rivers together because of the large annual variation (Table 3.3). There
have been years in which about 68 billion m³ were measured in the two
rivers, and years in which the amount was about 84.4 billion m³. The
average is about 74–81 billion m³ (Ubell, 1971: 3; Ali, 1955: 301; Kolars and Mitchell, 1991; Beaumont et al., 1988: 364). Such variation
makes it difficult to determine a fair division of the rivers' water among
the three riparians.

Another difficulty in such a decision is that in the Tigris and Euphrates basins, unlike the Nile basin, the discharge of water has not been
satisfactorily measured, and the behavior of the rivers and their tributaries is not yet entirely clear. The many dams on the two rivers make it
difficult to calculate the amount of water available in each state. Because the Tigris basin has had very few measurements made, there are
large differences among researchers' evaluations, and all should be considered with great caution.

## Meeting Points Between Hydrology and Politics in the Tigris and Euphrates Basins

The portions of the Tigris and Euphrates basins located within each riparian state are presented in Table 3.1

Turkey has the major share of the discharge of the Tigris and of the

*Figure 3.3:* Euphrates and Tigris Discharge (1938–1980)

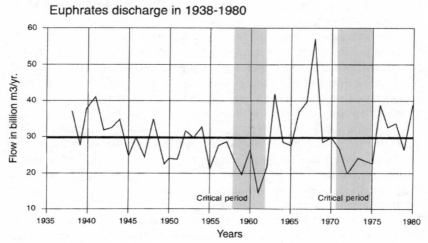

Euphrates discharge in 1938-1980

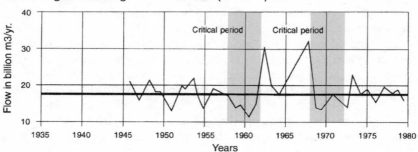

Tigris discharge in 1946-1979 (in Cizre)

Euphrates. Iraq has nothing of the Euphrates discharge, but has the principal share of the discharge of the Tigris tributaries. Syria has nothing of the Tigris discharge, but has the chief share of the discharge of the Euphrates tributaries (the Khabur and the Balikh), and it uses their water. Turkey contributes 72 percent of the total discharge. Iraq contributes 18.5 percent, and Syria's contribution is no more than 2 percent (Table 3.3). If we regard the Karun as part of the Tigris and Euphrates system, then Iran is in third place and contributes about 7.5 percent.

If we fix the division of water according to the proportions of discharge contributed by each state, Turkey and Iraq have the main rights to exploit the water of the Tigris, and Turkey and Syria have main rights

to exploit the water of the Euphrates. However, the division is not determined only according to discharge; Iraq has historical rights to use the
water of the two rivers.

A fair division of the water must be accomplished according to the
needs of the states. Turkey and Syria are greatly in need of hydroelectric
power. In Syria this situation could change because gas and oil have recently been discovered there, which would enable Syria to employ thermal energy instead. Turkey has no sources of energy apart from hydroelectric. Turkey and Syria need water for irrigation to reclaim large
areas of land for their growing populations. Until recently, Iraq needed
water for irrigation, but this situation could soon change because Iraq
has large amounts of oil, which could be used to boost industry and so
curtail agriculture.

A fair division of water would allocate about 40 percent to Turkey,
about 50 percent to Iraq, and about 10 percent to Syria. This distribution
based on discharge, historical rights, and existence of other resources
requires cooperation among the riparians, which would ensure not only
an equitable division of the water but also its quality.

However, in reality the three states do not cooperate, and the upstream states (Turkey and Syria) make use of their advantage over the
downstream state (Iraq). Turkey is an upstream state in the drainage of
the two rivers. Syria is a downstream state of the Euphrates relative to
Turkey, and an upstream state reletive to Iraq. (Iran has a certain advantage in the two tributaries of the Tigris, the Diyala and the Little Zab,
which originate in its territory, but it has no intention of establishing
water projects or using these tributaries owing to the very difficult topography at their sources.) Iraq is a downstream state of the Tigris and
the Euphrates. But it has another advantage; in case of need, it can
transfer water from the Tigris to the Euphrates and back again. (In fact,
Iraq is now completing construction of a project to transfer water from
the Tigris to the lower Euphrates.)

From here on I will deal with reality and not theory. I will consider
unilateral use of water, lack of cooperation, and unfair distribution, all
of which create tension and disputes and in the future could lead to violent conflict.

## Water Projects in the Euphrates and Tigris Basins

### Water Projects prior to the 1950s

According to written accounts, Euphrates water was used as long as
5,000 years ago. On the river banks, one of the oldest and most impor-

tant civilizations on earth arose. The Euphrates was first used in the north: the earliest settlement in the region, of the tenth century BCE, is located at Muraybit in Syria (Saleh, 1985: 70).

In Mesopotamia the civilizations of Sumer, Akkad, Babylonia, and Assyria were founded. They were based on wise use of the river water, including control of the flood water and efficient irrigation practices. According to one estimate, about 20 million people inhabited the Mesopotamian plain at the height of these civilizations (Cressey, 1960). They were the first to use the wheel to raise water and gravity to carry it to the fields. One of the wonders of Mesopotamian civilization is the Naharwan canal, built in the sixth century BCE. Through this canal, 188 miles long and 98 feet wide, water was transferred from the Tigris to the plains of the Diyala river for irrigation. The Nimrod dam, built on the Tigris, blocked the natural flow of the river and diverted the water into the canal (Ionides, 1937: 147). In the same era regulatory and diversion dams were likewise built on the Diyala and the Adhaim.

In the time of the Mesopotamian civilizations the Habbaniya and the Abu Dibis depressions were used for irrigation and for storage. A system of canals connected the two rivers and, owing to slight height differences (a few inches), water could flow freely from river to river. It is no wonder that the earliest maps in the world were found in this region, because only through precise measurement and mapping could water be transferred from the Euphrates to the Tigris and vice versa (Sasson, 1995; Bakour and Kolars, 1994: 125–129).

The Mesopotamian farming civilization began to decline after the tenth century CE because of a weakening of central government, which was no longer capable of administering the drainage and irrigation systems and preventing salination of the land. By the twelfth century, large areas of the land of Mesopotamia were no longer worked because of salination.

With the Mongolian invasion into the plain in the twelfth century, and again in the thirteenth century, the canals and the fields were abandoned, and the area that is today Iraq became a mass of swamps, salty soils, and deserts. Some historians claim that the absolute ruin that struck the region with the Mongolian invasion was the most destructive blow known in human history. Through that single action an entire geographical region was destroyed and left as wasteland for eight centuries or more (Beaumont et al., 1988: 362).

Real efforts to rehabilitate the Mesopotamian plains began only in the twentieth century, with the construction of the Hindiya barrage on the Euphrates (1911–1914). With the discovery of oil, electrically powered pumps were used to pump the river water and the irrigated agricultural land was extended considerably.

The use of Euphrates and Tigris water in Iraqi territory from the start of the civilizations that flourished there until today—notwithstanding the discontinuities due to economic, political, and social conditions in the Mesopotamian plains—gives Iraq historic rights over the water. These are available to Iraq in any and all of its attempts to claim its just portion of river water from the upstream states (Rogers and Lydon, 1994).

One of the striking factors about the dam and lake system of Iraq is the volume of storage capacity. Lake Habbaniya and Lake Abu Dibis hold is about 46 billion m³; the capacity of the Tharthar depression, between the Tigris and the Euphrates, is about 30 billion m³ (Table 3.4). With this reservoir, water is transferred via canals from the Tigris to the Euphrates to regulate the growing water shortage that has developed due to the development projects of Syria and Turkey (Bilen, 1994). In 1958 a canal was built to direct excess water from the Tigris to the Tharthar depression and prevent flooding in the low lying areas of Baghdad.

**Water Projects from the 1950s until Today**

From the 1950s onward many water projects were founded on the Tigris and the Euphrates. At the beginning of the 1990s construction was still at its height. However, there is no cooperation among the states, and each state has built its own projects, especially multipurpose ones for electricity, irrigation, flood prevention, and storage. The projects of the upstream states have upset the plans of the downstream states, which have been obliged to adjust accordingly. In fact, some of the projects initiated by the downstream states in the mid-1980s were undertaken to solve problems of overuse of the river water in its upper section. A vicious circle was thereby created in which the damage caused was greater than advantages gained.

Table 3.4 shows the large extent of development projects in all three states, and the storage capacity of each state is enormous (taking account of the dams and the depressions that have been completed and those planned). Turkey's storage capacity on the Euphrates is about 90 billion m³ (the actual storage capacity used by Turkey is about 47. 6 billion m³). Syria's capacity is 14 billion m³, and that of Iraq is about 100 billion m³ (including the salty depressions and storage dams) (author's calculations based on Bilen, 1994; Kolars, 1994; Rogers and Lydon, 1994). The states do not trust one another, and therefore they attempt to satisfy their own water needs within their own borders. In doing so they harm each other and violate the Helsinki and ILC agreements on the fair and reasonable division of water. When Turkey real-

**Table 3.4: Water Projects in the Euphrates-Tigris Basin (Technical Data)**

| Project | River and Country[a] | Years of Construction | Storage Capacity (billion m³) | Sizes of Dam[b] | Purposes |
|---|---|---|---|---|---|
| **Barrages in Iraq** | | | | | |
| Habbaniya Lake | Iraq | Natural depression | 32 | C 166 | Flood control, irrigation in the dry season |
| Abu Dibis Lake and barrage | E, Iraq | Natural depression Barrage built in the 1950s | 14.4 | A 46 B 1968 C 70 | Flood control, irrigation in the dry season, connected to Habbaniya Lake |
| Hindiya barrage | E, Iraq | 1911–1914 | None | A 25 B 817 | Raising water to feed the Hilla, Musaib, Elhosaniya, and Beni Hassen canals |
| Diyala barrage | Diyala, Iraq | 1927–1928 | None | A 40 B 1400 | Diversion of water to irrigation canals |
| Kut barrage | T, Iraq | 1934–1943 | None | A 34 B 227.0 | Diversion of water to shatt el Jaref |
| Lake Tharthar | T, Iraq | 1950s | 30 | A 23 B 1650 C 1042 | To prevent floods in Tigris transfer from Tigris to Euphrates (second stage) |
| Ramadi barrage | E, Iraq | 1954 | None | A 33 B 685 | Flood control and direct water to Habbaniya Lake |
| Samara barrage | T, Iraq | 1958 | None | A 33 B 826 | Diversion of water to Lake Tharthar |

**Table 3.4 (Continued)**

| | | | | | |
|---|---|---|---|---|---|
| Falluja barrage | E, Iraq | 1985 | None | — | Diversion of water to irrigation canals |
| **Dams** | | | | | |
| Dokan Dam | Little Zab, Iraq | 1959 | 0.63–0.75 | | 400 MW hydropower, water storage, and irrigation |
| Darbandikhan Dam | Diyala, Iraq | 1961 | 5 | A 393 B 420 | Hydropower, flood control, and storage |
| Keban Dam | E, Turkey | 1965–1935 | 30 | A 6923 B 3598 C 262 | 120 MW hydropower |
| Tabqa Dam | E, Syria | 1965–1973 | 12 | A 197 B 15088 C 247 | 800 MW hydropower, irrigation |
| Karakaya Dam | E, Turkey | 1976–1988 | 9.6 | A 482 C 116 | 1800 MW hydropower |
| Haditha (Kadisiya) Dam | E, Iraq | 1979–1990s | 17 | — | 600 MW hydropower, storage, and irrigation |
| Eski Mosul (Saddam) Dam | T, Iraq | 1983– | 30 | A 154 B 11808 | 750 MW hydropower, storage, and irrigation |
| al-Ba'ath Dam | E, Syria | 1983–1986 | 0.9 | A 49 B 2460 | 81 MW hydropower, storage, and irrigation, improvement of fishing |
| Ataturk Dam | E, Turkey | 1983–1990 | 49 | A 577 C 2680 | 2400 MW storage and irrigation |

**Table 3.4 (Continued)**

| | | | | | |
|---|---|---|---|---|---|
| Batama Dam | Little Zab, Iraq | 1989 | | A 689 | Hydropower and storage |
| Tishrin Dam | E, Syria | under construction | 1.3 | A 164 B 3280 | 630 MW hydropower and control |
| **New Canals** | | | | | |
| "Third" River | E, T, Iraq | 1992 | | | Drain marshes, irrigation, drainage |
| "Fourth" River | E, Iraq | 1992 | | | Drain marshes, irrigation, drainage |
| "Fifth" River | | | | | |

*Sources*: Ionides, 1937; Cressey, 1960; Beaumont, 1978: Naff and Matson, 1984; Ockerman and Samano, 1985; Saleh, 1985; Kolars, 1986; Beaumont et al., 1988; Kolars, 1994; *Middle East and North Africa*, 1996; North, 1993.

[a] E-Euphrates.
T-Tigris.

[b] A = height (ft); B eq length (ft); C = size of Lake (square miles).

In Turkey about 20 more dams are under construction or in planning on both rivers. In Syria 10 more dams are under construction on the Euphrates and tributaries. In Iraq 9 more dams are under construction or in planning on both rivers.

izes its own carrying capacity, which will take many years to accomplish, the two downstream states, Syria and Iraq, will be affected. Turkey's actions are in violation of clause 7 in section 2 of the Helsinki Accords, which explicitly states: "The states of the basin will not prevent the other riparians from using the water." Syria also is in violation of this clause. Turkey's projects can be presented differently, as being of great advantage to the downstream countries. Now it is possible to store water from high-flow years for low-flow years (Bilen, 1994).

Another problem that arises because of storage on such a large level is the high rate of evaporation in the large reservoirs. In Turkey, evaporation has already apparently reached 3–4 billion $m^3$ a year or more, and in Syria it stands at about 1 billion $m^3$ (about 0.63 billion $m^3$ at the Tabqa Dam and the remainder at other projects). In Iraqi reservoirs the evaporation is even greater because of the desert climate, amounting to about 4.5–5 billion $m^3$ annually. The evaporation in all of the countries reaches about 9–10 billion $m^3$ annually. Moreover, the evaporation rate will continue to rise, because the projects have not been completed and are continuing apace: Turkey plans for twenty-one dams on the Tigris and Euphrates of which some are complete. Syria is planning to construct more dams on the Khabur and on the Euphrates, and Iraq is planning to build additional dams on the Tigris and the Euphrates (Kolars, 1994).

## Supply and Demand of Water: Turkey

Although, there are no precise figures on the discharge of the two rivers together, the estimate is about 81 billion $m^3$ annually. This estimate will be used as a basis for analyzing supply and demand for water in the riparian states of the two rivers.

Turkey has abundant water in absolute terms, and also relative to other Middle East countries. Its water supply is estimated at about 110 billion $m^3$ (Turkey, 1995: 3). According to other sources the supply is 80 billion $m^3$, including 50 percent from the Tigris and Euphrates (Beaumont et al., 1988: 84). In the 1980s Turkey used about 25 billion $m^3$ (Pope, 1990: 14).

More than 100 dams have been built throughout Turkey for producing electricity and for irrigation. The largest of them are the Hirfanli Dam on the Kizil-Irmak River, which created a lake of 123.5 square miles, a dam on the Sayhan River that created a lake of 35 square miles, and the Sariyar Dam on the Sakarya River, which created a lake of 31 square miles. Some of the dams supply drinking water to Ankara, Istanbul, and other cities. A few are multipurpose.

In the 1960s the area of cultivated land in Turkey amounted to about 25.7 million hectares (64.2 million acres), but apparently only 12 percent of it is irrigated (Beaumont and McLachlan, 1985: 61; Beeley, 1985; Dewdney, 1981: 220). In the 1980s the irrigated area was about 8.5 million hectares (21 million acres) (Kolars, 1994: 48). Turkey nonetheless supplies all its own food requirements and is even left with a large quantity for export. Most of the irrigated land extension was in the western part of the state, while the eastern part was neglected.

In the 1970s Turkey embarked on the rapid development of the east, with the southeast Anatolia project. The Turkish government has many reasons for undertaking this project, which will use large quantities of water from the Tigris and Euphrates. So far Turkey has not used these rivers' water at all.

### The GAP Project (Guneydogu Anadolu Projesi)

GAP, initiated in 1965, is Turkey's largest and most ambitious development project in the southeastern part of the state. The development region (Figure 3.4) covers 28,520 square miles (9.5 percent of the total area of Turkey), including six regions (Si'irt, Diyrbakir, Mardin, Adiyaman, Urfa, and Gaziantep). Most of the development area borders Syria and some of it borders Iraq. Five and a half million people inhabit the six regions (as of 1991): 50 percent Kurds, about 40 percent Turks, and 10 percent Arabs (Toepfer, 1991). In 1980 about 68 percent were farmers and the remainder were industrial workers (17 percent) and service workers (15 percent) (Turkey, 1989, 1990; Kolars and Mitchell, 1991; Toepfer, 1991).

The project is intended to transform the southeastern part of Anatolia, an area of plains and hills with a semiarid climate, into the "bread basket" of Turkey by irrigating millions of hectares. Other goals are to advance the economically and socially weak population and bring it closer to the west; to lift the region out of a state of chronic developmental backwardness directly into the twenty-first century by producing ample electricity, which will be used to industrialize the region (factories for edible oils, leather, meat, flour, cotton, construction materials, etc.); and by paving a new road network connect the region with the western part of the state. The Turkish government hopes in this way to integrate the Kurds into the Turkish core and to attenuate separatist processes there, which have spread into other parts of the country, sometimes in a violent fashion.

The development project includes twenty-one dams on the Euphrates, the Tigris and their tributaries, including about seventeen dams with hydroelectric stations that can produce 8,753 megawatts. This plant will

90

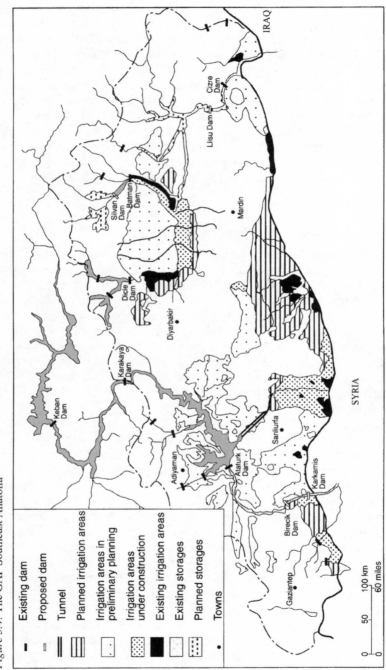

*Figure 3.4:* The GAP Southeast Anatolia

Existing dam
Proposed dam
Tunnel
Planned irrigation areas
Irrigation areas in
preliminary planning
Irrigation areas
under construction
Existing irrigation areas
Existing storages
Planned storages
Towns

Keban Dam
Karakaya Dam
Silvan Dam
Batman Dam
Ilisu Dam
Cizre Dam
Dicle Dam
Mardin
Diyarbakir
Adiyaman
Atatürk Dam
Sanliurfa
Karkamis Dam
Birecik Dam
Gaziantep

SYRIA
IRAQ

0    50    100 km
0         60 miles

increase the production of electricity in Turkey by 70 percent, and will save the country much import of oil for electricity. The dam's water will irrigate about 1.7 million hectares (4.2 million acres), an addition of about 20 percent to the irrigated territory of the state. About 55 percent of the land to be irrigated is intended for cereals and for planned grazing, and the rest for industrial crops (mainly rice, cotton, sugarcane, and oilseed), fruit, and vegetables (grapes, oranges, and pistachio nuts, which will be the main branch of the entire project). These crops are intended for the domestic population and for export (Kolars and Mitchell, 1991).

The project involves extensive land reform, which has already begun, and the resettlement of a large population from extensive areas that will be flooded. About 170,000 residents are being moved from the Ataturk reservoir flood area, about 15,000 residents have already been moved from the Karkaya region, and 25,000 residents from Keban region. These residents will be settled in new villages (*Newspot*, Jan. 18, 1990).

The total cost of the project is about $21 billion, or $1.5 million per day for about 40 years, since its beginning in 1965. The World Bank partially funded the construction of the Keban and Karkaya Dams. But the Ataturk dam and the other projects are financed by the Turkish government because the World Bank makes its participation conditional on Turkey's consultation with the downstream states on water allocation. Therefore, there have been delays, and Turkey is not keeping to the schedule of the project. Nevertheless, it continues to progress. The main development at present is in the Euphrates basin, while the implementation of the development plans on the Tigris has so far been postponed. It is hard to believe that plans for the Tigris will be executed in the near future, owing to the growing conflict between the central government of Turkey and the Kurds who inhabit the Tigris basin.

## Principal Water Projects in the Euphrates Basin

### Keban Dam

This dam was built on the Euphrates, where its tributaries, the Kara Su and the Murat, join together. Its construction began in 1965 and was completed in 1974, four years behind schedule. The delay was caused, among other reasons, by the fact that the dam was built on a karstic sinkhole that swallowed huge amounts of water, and sealing it entailed enormous expense. The dam is of large dimensions: about 3,600 feet long and about 656 feet high. The lake's carrying capacity, with a surface area of 262 square miles, is about 30 billion $m^3$. The dam is used for electricity production alone and not for irrigation. It produces about

1,240 megawatts of electricity, but it is capable of producing double that figure. The electricity is transferred principally to the Ankara and Istanbul regions.

### The Karakaya Dam

This dam is located south of the Keban Dam. It was begun in 1967 and completed in 1988, three years after the planned date. The dam is intended for electricity production only and its production capacity is 1,800 megawatts. The reservoir dam is 88 miles long, and it reaches the Keban Dam.

### The Ataturk Dam

This is the largest and most costly of the GAP dams (Kolars and Mitchell, 1991: 38–41, 193). It has been described as the fifth largest dam in the world (Jansen, 1990: 11). It is multipurpose and intended for irrigation and electricity production. Its production capacity is 2,400 megawatts of electricity and irrigation of 5 million hectares. It is located about 112 miles south of the Karakaya Dam, close to Bozova village. Construction began in 1983 and was completed in 1993, including the tunnels that carry the water from the lake to the irrigation region (Sunliurfa Tunnels). The dam's lake stores about 48.4 billion $m^3$ of water with a surface area of 338 square miles. The construction of the dam cost $3 billion (Kolars and Mitchell, 1991: 31).

The filling of the lake has created political problems, which reflect the difficulties of the entire project. In January 1990 Turkey stopped the flow of the Euphrates in order to fill the dam's reservoir. The stoppage lasted one month, from January 13 to February 13, allowing the reservoir to accumulate 1.5 billion $m^3$ of water. (In spring 1990, with the snowmelts, an additional 5 billion $m^3$ of water were added [*Newspot*, May 31, 1990].) In the period before the flow was cut off, from November 23, 1989, until January 13, 1990, Turkey increased the discharge of the river from 500 $m^3$ per second to about 750 $m^3$ per second to compensate Syria and Iraq for the interruption of flow and allow them to store water and use it as they saw fit. However, Syria and Iraq could not use this excess water, and when the flow was cut off they suffered a water shortage. Syria's power station at the Tabqa Dam produced only 12 percent of its capacity, and throughout Syria there was even a shortage of drinking water. Due to the electricity shortage, the pumping of groundwater in the coastal plain and in the Damascus basin was stopped, and therefore water was in short supply in this part of Syria too. Similarly, damage was caused to the winter crops of the Euphrates valley. In Iraq the winter crops along the Euphrates valley also suffered. The Iraqi and Syrian governments insisted repeatedly that Turkey renew the river's flow, but Turkey not only disregarded these demands, it even made clear to Syria that if Syria did not fulfill several geopolitical conditions, the water cutoff would last longer than a month. During 1993–1994 the construction of the dam was completed and the reservoir filled up as a result of heavy rains and snow during the years 1991–1993.

### Sunliurfa Tunnels

These are two tunnels to direct the water from the Ataturk Dam to the irrigation region. They therefore form a single organic unit with the dam. Each tunnel is 25 feet in diameter and 15 miles long. Together, they will discharge 328 $m^3$ of water per second. The flowing water will produce 50 megawatts of electricity at the Sunliurfa power station.

Two main canals extend from the tunnels: The Sunliurfa tunnel irrigates 48,000 hectares and the Haran Canal irrigates about 1 million hectares. The area in question stretches from Lake Ataturk through Mardin in the east, to the Syrian border in the south (Figure 3.4). It will be the largest irrigation project of its kind in the world. (As of 1998, this part of the project had not yet been completed.)

### The Birecik and Karkamish Dams

These dams are intended for electricity production and for irrigating land close to the Syrian border (near the ancient city of Karkamish) and will be used for electricity production and for irrigation. Construction has begun in Birecik Dam, and the idea that Syrians would build a small dam in their territory was rejected (Kolars, 1994: 65; Turkey, 1995: 19–21).

Two additional small dams are to be built south of Gaziantep, and a small dam on one of the Euphrates tributaries, near Adiyaman. Aside from the dams, an irrigation system will be built on the Euphrates for land reclamation, and a supporting infrastructure will be developed for another four irrigation projects that will be fed by Euphrates water. The Adiyaman-Gosku-Araban project is an irrigation project to be supplied by water from the Ataturk Dam. It will irrigate 71,000 hectares in the area between Adiyaman and Gaziantep. The Adiyaman-Kata project will be combined with the Adiyaman-Gosku-Araban project, but it will also have a power station to produce 196 megawatts of electricity. The Suruc-Baziki project will irrigate 0.15 million hectares between the Ataturk Dam and the Syrian border. The Gaziantep project is intended to irrigate 8,900 hectares close to the Syrian border, west of the Euphrates River.

The carrying capacity of the dams is 47.6 billion m$^3$ of water. The evaporation and seepage rates will be very high, and the water quality will be adversely affected. Building the dams will cause indirect damage to the downstream states if Turkey decides to speed the implementation of the water project and interrupts the river's flow.

Suppose that in order to irrigate 1 hectare in the semiarid Urfa region, about 10,000 m$^3$ of water are needed annually; then, about 1.1 billion m$^3$ of water annually will be needed to irrigate 11 million hectares (with the completion of all the Euphrates projects). Moreover, to these data add 3–4 billion m$^3$ of water annually to compensate for losses through evaporation and seepage in the large reservoirs. In other words, in the Euphrates projects about 14–15 billion m$^3$ of water will be utilized.

If we subtract about 2 billion m$^3$ from this number (water returning to the river's course), the total amount of water that Syria and Iraq will lose is about 12–13 billion m$^3$, or about 40 percent of the average annual flow of the river. According to Turkish sources, this is the amount that Turkey will eventually use (Istanbul Chamber of Commerce, 1989; *MEED*, Jan. 19, 1990). However, some western sources claim that the amount will reach about 50 percent of the total flow of the Euphrates and perhaps more as a result of the large volume of the reservoirs (Bakour and Kolars, 1994: 128–129; Kolars, 1994: 36; Allan, 1985). The downstream states will certainly not accept this. Therefore, verbal reactions, if not others, may be expected from the basin states.

At the close of the 1980s the question of the amount of water that Turkey would release at its Syrian border became the focus of a dispute between Turkey and the other basin states, and between Turkey and the United States, which feared negative developments in the region. Turkey continues to state that it will allot Syria and Iraq 500 m$^3$ of water per second, which is about 15.5 billion m$^3$ per year (*MEED*, 1990: 23; Waterbury, 1994: 55). According to the most optimistic estimate available, Turkey will release 625 m$^3$ per second, which is about 19.7 billion m$^3$ per year (Allan, 1987: 29; Turkey, 1995).

### GAP—Intermediary Geopolitical Appraisal

All of the projects built so far have been completed at least a few years behind schedule: the Keban Dam four years, and the Karakaya and Ataturk Dams three years to date; the construction of Karkamish Dam has not begun, nor has the Tigris project been started. These delays affect the expected time for possible conflicts between Turkey and its neighbors; as the completion of the GAP project is delayed, so is the conflict. It is possible that this conflict will not occur at all, for example, if Turkish enthusiasm about the project cools, or if Iraq—with its plentiful oil reserves—makes necessary changes in its economic structure and develops its industrial and services sectors while cutting back on agriculture. Of course, a worst-case scenario exists, namely that one or two dry years will occur (for example, a flow of 15 billion $m^3$ only, as in 1974). In such a situation Turkey will use all the water and is likely to leave Syria and Iraq with insufficient water. There is no doubt that such a situation would lead to the outbreak of a conflict.

## Water Projects on the Tigris (Figure 3.4)

### The Dicle-Kralkizi Project

This project includes, the Kralkizi Dam and the Dicle Dam. The Kralkizi Dam is intended to produce 90 megawatts of electricity, and the Dicle Dam 110 megawatts. The Dicle Dam will also be used to irrigate 0.12 million hectares on the right bank of the Dicle tributary (east of Diyarbakir).

### The Batman Dam

This planned dam will generate 185 megawatts of electricity and irrigate 37,744 hectares on both banks of the Batman River (between Batman and Silvan).

### The Garzan Dam

This dam will be located on the Garzan tributary and should produce 90 megawatts of electricity and irrigate 60,000 hectares of land between Silvan and Si'irt.

### The Ilisu Dam

This large dam will be built 25 miles northwest of the point where the Tigris meets the Syrian border and is intended to produce about 1,200 megawatts of electricity. It is not intended for irrigation.

### The Cizre Dam

This is located in the Silopi-Nusaybin-Cizre region, near the junction of the Turkish border and the Syrian-Iraqi border, and is intended for production of 240 megawatts of electricity and irrigation of 0.12 million hectares of land.

The projects will supply a total of 5–7 billion m³ (5 billion m³ for irrigation and in addition 2–4 billion m³ to replace water lost to evaporation minus 2–3 billion m³ of recycled water, which is about 35 percent of the total Tigris discharge of 18–20 billion m³ where it enters Iraq. Altogether, the Tigris and its tributaries are projected to irrigate about 0.56 million hectares. The projects will create about 2,215 megawatts of electricity. The Tigris projects will not begin to be implemented until after 2000 (Toepfer, 1991; Bakour and Kolars, 1994: 128).

In light of the growing hostility between the Kurds and the central government in Turkey, it is doubtful that it will be possible to implement this project, located in the heart of the Kurdish region.

## Supply and Demand for Water: Syria

The quantity of surface water in Syria, aside from the Euphrates, is 2.4–4 billion m³ (Gischler, 1979: 114; Beaumont et al., 1988: 84). The main water sources, excluding the Euphrates, are the following international rivers: the Khabur, a Euphrates tributary; the Orontes; the Afrin, an Orontes tributary; the Yarmuk; and the rivers which flow within Syria only, the Barda and the Waj in the Damascus basin, the Sin and the Kabir on the coast, and a few other small rivers (Figure 3.5). Syria also has access to the Tigris along a very small section of its course, about 27 miles, and it pumps water from this area to irrigate about 0.15 million hectares (Tishrein, Nov. 12, 1989; Mar. 8, 1995). This plan, which Iraq certainly will not approve, is likely to create additional tensions in the basin.

Besides the surface water, Syria has groundwater estimated at 1.6 billion m³. This water is pumped from 30,000 wells, half of them in the Damascus region, the Orontes basin, and the Aleppo Plateau (Gischler, 1979: 114). In Syria the area irrigated by groundwater is larger than that irrigated by rivers (Allan, 1987: 31), but the heavy pumping causes salination in all of the wells at the sites listed.

The storage capacity of the water projects in Syria is estimated at about 14 billion m³, including principally (about 12 billion m³) Lake Assad formed by the Tabqa Dam (Figure 3.5). In the meantime, the construction of the al Baath Dam has been completed, and this capacity will grow larger still because Syria is constructing and planning dams on the Yarmuk, the Orontes, and the Khabur (the Smali Dam) and reservoir projects in the Akkar coastal plain, and it plans to raise the Tabqa Dam another few feet. (According to Tishrein, Oct. 22, 1987, storage capac-

*Figure 3.5:* Irrigation Areas and Water Projects in Syria

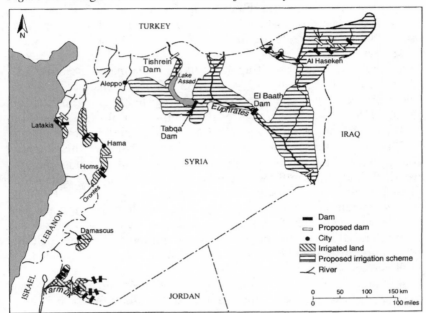

ity resulting from the raising of the dam will amount to 13.4 billion m³.) Similarly, Syria is building another dam on the Euphrates called "Sixth of Tishrein," about 50 miles from the Turkish border. In addition, a dam is planned on the Euphrates, in the eastern part of the state, for electricity. The clamor for water in Syria for electricity and irrigation stems from urgent, growing needs in food supply and industry.

**Irrigation**

Agriculture has an important place in the Syrian economy, which will be maintained for many years to come because of the low socioeconomic level of the farmers in Syria and because of the urgent need for food, which is ever increasing with the rapid growth of population.

Of Syria's 18.5 million hectares (46 million acres), only a small portion—according to one estimate, 6.5–8.8 million hectares (16–22 million acres)—is useful for agricultural purposes (Gischler, 1979: 113; Beaumont, 1985: 6). In 1957 about 0.4 million hectares were irrigated. Since then, the irrigated areas have been expanded by 54 percent, and in 1990 the irrigated area stood at 0.660–0.693 million hectares according to official data (*Syrie et le Monde Arabe*, 1987; Syria, *Statistical Abstract*, 1990; Sadik and Barghouti, 1994: 8). In fact, the total irrigated area is less, because considerable land has been lost through erosion, salination, agrarian reform, and urbanization (Manner and Sagafi-Nejad, 1985: 263).

The irrigated area in the Euphrates basin is estimated at about 0.37 million hectares (Bourgey, 1974: 343, 350; Syria, *Statistical Abstract*, 1990). The Syrians planned to extend the irrigated land by an addition of 0.6–065 million hectares after the completion of the Tabqa Dam (Naff and Matson, 1984: 91). In 1983 it was decided to limit the plan to 0.35 million hectares only, and Kolars estimates that even this is ambitious in light of the few achievements on the ground. It is possible that eventually only 0.24 million hectares will be irrigated. This means that about 2.4 billion $m^3$ of water will be used (Kolars, 1994: 50). The lack of development is due in large part to soils with high gypsum and salt content, which are unfit for agricultural use, and the lack of professional manpower, as well as the high cost of reclaiming land for agriculture, which currently swallows about a quarter of all the funds budgeted for public projects in Syria.

How much Euphrates water does Syria use? Here too estimates vary widely. According to one source, Syria uses 3 billion $m^3$ for irrigation and local domestic use (Naff and Matson, 1984: 91). But according to a Syrian source, in the 1970s Syria used 2.31 billion $m^3$ of water, and by the end of the 1980s it was using 4.79 billion $m^3$ to irrigate 0.126 million hectares for domestic use and for industry in the region (*al Qabas*, Mar. 12, 1990). According to this, 35,220 $m^3$ are required to irrigate 1 hectare of land (which seems rather high, because the 2.31 billion $m^3$ included water for domestic and industrial use), in which case Syria would need about 21 billion $m^3$ of water to realize all its plans to irrigate about 0.6 million hectares, and about 10 billion $m^3$ for 0.3 million hectares. Despite this being an exaggerated figure, it demonstrates how high the expected demand for water is in Syria.

It seems that to realize the entire plan of irrigating all 0.6 million hectares, Syria will need 6 billion $m^3$ of water (10,000 $m^3$ per hectare), in addition to the amount it will need to irrigate existing fields, for domestic use, and for industry. I assume that the basis for assessing demand will be about 6 billion $m^3$ for irrigation, and an addition 1–2 billion $m^3$ in evaporation and domestic use ( a total of about 8 billion $m^3$! One can assume that Syria will regain about 2 billion $m^3$ of water from Turkey's irrigated fields, and therefore Syria's total demand in the year 2000 will reach about 6 billion $m^3$ (Table 3.5).

According to Kolars, at the end of the development period demand will reach about 12 billion $m^3$ of water, minus recycled water, so net consumption will total 8 billion m³ (Kolars, 1994: 86). Bilen presents many other data and estimates from various experts who have tried to assess the demand for water in Syria (Bilen, 1994). Their data fluctuate between 0.2 million hectares, meaning 2 billion m³ of water, and 0.8 million hectares, meaning 8 billion m³ of water; this is in addition to seepage and evaporation. It also has been estimated that in year 2025 Syria's demand will fluctuate between 5 and 10.7 billion m³ (Rogers and Lydon, 1994: 307).

If Turkey meets its responsibilities and allocates about 15 billion m³ annually to its neighbors, then Syria will be able to obtain all the water it will need (although the quality of water will probably drop due to the many development projects in Turkey). Syria will face no problem, but Iraq will get only 4–7 billion m³ of water on a many-year average.

Syria will be able to realize all of its plans in the Euphrates valley, grandiose though they may be, but if it does so it will face a serious geopolitical problem: Iraq will not agree to the loss of most of its Euphrates water. Iraq may have no choice but to acquiesce to Turkey's actions, but it is hardly conceivable that it will do the same regarding Syria (*Middle East International*, Feb. 16, 1990; Kolars, 1994: 80).

This problem will not arise if Syria's and Turkey's plans turn out to be overly ambitious and impractical. However, even if Syria and Turkey do not implement their plans, the Euphrates's flow at the entrance to Iraq will decrease due to evaporation, seepage, and growing demand on the part of riparians.

**Electricity**

Syria needs Euphrates water for electricity production for the same reasons as Turkey—to avoid importing other energy sources, including oil. At the beginning of the 1980s about 30.5 percent of all Syrian electric power was hydroelectric, but there were times when the rate reached 43.7 percent and even 60 percent. The Tabqa Dam produces 720 megawatts of electricity, and the al Baath Dam 81 megawatts of electricity, while the Sixth of Tishrein Dam is planned to produce 630 megawatts (*Syrie et le Monde Arabe*, 1982; *MEED*, Jan. 1990, Feb. 23, 1990).

According to forecasts, demand for electricity in Syria will double by 2000, but the additional electricity will apparently be from thermal stations. Syria is converting to thermal power stations because of forecasts of future water shortages, disappointment with the dams and a wish to prevent too great a dependency on them, and the discovery of new oilfields in the eastern part of the state. As mentioned, when the water level in Lake Assad dropped in 1990, after Turkey blocked the Euphrates's flow, the dam's yield fell to a mere 10 percent of its generating capacity, which caused serious damage to the Syrian economy and to the supply of electricity to cities in particular (*MEED*, Jan. 19, 1990: 8). The al Baath thermal station, is already working in close proximity to the Tabqa Dam, producing 500 megawatts. Apparently, it was built near the dam to take advantage of the already existing electricity grid and cooling system. Moreover, Syria's gas and oil sources are located not far from there.

**Domestic and Industrial Consumption**

In the mid-1970s the demand for water in the domestic sector in Syria was about 0.4 billion m³ (Gischler, 1979: 114). In the coming decade consumption will probably reach 1.5–1.9 billion m³ (Rogers and Lydon, 1994). Today there is already a water shortage in some cities in the Damascus basin because of years of drought and overpumping from the basin's wells (*al Yawm al Usbu'a*, Dec. 19, 1989). Because of the water shortage for domestic needs, which until now has been met by well water, there will be a need in the future to use Euphrates water for urban domestic use.

**Conclusion**

If Turkey completes all the projects planned for the Euphrates, and if pressure is placed on Syria by Iraq to ensure it receives the water it deserves, the amount of water reaching Syria will drop by about 40 percent (Jansen, 1990: 11). Therefore, a water shortage for domestic needs, electricity production and then for agriculture will be felt. Some estimate the shortage at about one billion m³ while others claim that it will be even more severe, reaching over 2–3 billion m³ per year in the near future.

**Supply and Demand for Water: Iraq**

At the entry point to Iraq the total discharge of the Tigris and Euphrates, prior to the new projects, is about 75 billion m³ (Table 3.2). In addition, Iraq has groundwater, and it is known that in the 1970s this water was used to irrigate 20,000 hectares of land. In the northeastern strip of the country, the Kurdistan mountains, rain and snow fall, and widespread agriculture exists there, comprising about a quarter of all Iraqi agricultural lands.

**Irrigation**

In the early 1960s the agricultural area of Iraq irrigated by river water was estimated at 6.0 million hectares (Ali, 1955: 46; Ubell, 1971), in the 1970s at 7.6 million hectares, and at the beginning of the 1980s at 5.9 million hectares. But there is an even lower estimate of 2.5 million hectares (Adams and Holt, 1985: 195; McLachlan and Nasser, 1986; Gleick, 1993: 262). For the distribution of these areas see Figure 3.6. This decrease is explained by the salination of the soil on the Mesopotamian plains, which continuously depletes Iraq's agricultural land.

However, all these estimates are based on false data provided by Iraq. It is also possible that there is confusion between data on the total of cultivated land in Iraq and data on agricultural areas in the plains. I will attempt to overcome this difficulty and assess the land irrigated by the river water by calculating the quantity of water that was available to the farmers, and the amount of land that can be irrigated with that water.

Each hectare in Iraq is irrigated with 13,000 $m^3$ of water annually according to Ubell, or with 15,950 $m^3$ according to another source (Okerman and Samano, 1985: 192). There is evidence that in the Euphrates basin 1.23 million hectares were irrigated with 16–17 billion $m^3$ of water in the 1960s. To enlarge the territory in the Euphrates even slightly, to about 1,500,000 hectares, 20–24 billion $m^3$ annually would be needed. However, such a quantity is unavailable today, and will remain unavailable in the future. Moreover, if Syria and Turkey carry out their plans upstream, one may assume that the quantity available today will continue to decrease. There are already reports that irrigated land is steadily diminishing. According to these reports, Iraq has used only 13 billion $m^3$ of water recently; in other words, irrigated land has dwindled to only 0.9–1 million hectares!

In the past, various sources reported irrigation of about 3.0 million hectares. According to the irrigation data presented above, this implies the use of 40–48 billion $m^3$ of water for irrigation in the Tigris basin, accounting for 77–90 percent of the river's discharge (43–52.6 billion $m^3$).

However, there are also reports stating that to maintain a sound ecological system for the river, at least 15 billion $m^3$ of water annually should run off to the sea. Evaporation of the water of the rivers and irrigated areas in Iraq is greater than in the other partner countries to the river basins. This evaporation causes high water salinity, which has become the scourge of the Mesopotamian plains. The only way of handling this problem is proper drainage and flushing, and much water is required for this. If, to that end, Iraq indeed uses 15 billion $m^3$, an average of only 25–33 or perhaps 38 billion $m^3$ of water is left, and Iraq can

irrigate 2.4–2.8 million hectares at most in the basin of the Tigris and
its tributaries. This means that there has been no expansion of irrigated
areas in the Tigris basin either. This assessment is confirmed by the
daily *al Qabas*, in which it was claimed already at the end of the 1980s
that only 90 percent of the discharge of the two rivers was used: 14–15
billion m³ from the Euphrates and 32–38 billion m³ from the Tigris, to-
taling 52–53 billion m³ out of a volume of 60 billion m³ of available
water (*al Qabas*, 13 March 1990). According to an American source,
the amount in fact used is 41 billion m³, to which must be added 6–7
billion m³ of water returned to the river course (US Army Corps of Engineers, 1991).

Despite this reduced estimate, one should not disregard repeated reports of the building of dams, diversion dams, and irrigation canals in
the basins of the Tigris tributaries, the Diyala, the Adhaim, and others.
Owing to the lack of reliable data, we must assume that there, at least,
irrigated agricultural lands have been added.

**Conclusion**

Despite reports that 6.0–7.6 million hectares were being irrigated in
the 1950s and 1960s, one must assume that these are exaggerated data,
and in Iraq about 4.0 million hectares are irrigated (0.9–1 million in the
Euphrates basin, 2.0–2.4 million in the Tigris basin, and an additional
0.2–0.3 million hectares in Diyala and elsewhere), and for this 52 billion m³ of water are used (14 billion m³ from the Euphrates and about
38 billion m³ from the Tigris). If we add to this the water earmarked for
draining the basin, namely about 15 billion m³, we attain a discharge of
about 67 billion m³, which is the minimal discharge in the two rivers.

These estimates of irrigated land in Iraq allow us to assess what is
likely to happen in the future (Table 3.5). Regarding the Tigris, if in the
not too distant future Turkey uses 3.5–7 billion m³ from the river and
Syria uses only about 0.5 billion m³, and if at least 15 billion m³ of
water must be left in the Tigris for drainage and on account of evaporation, but that 3–4 billion m³ of returning water will enter from Turkey,
then Iraq will be obliged to reduce the amount of Tigris water it uses
from 32–38 billion m³ to about 30–35 billion m³. If, in addition, some
Tigris water will have to be transferred to the drying Euphrates River
bed, then the cutback will have to be greater still. These figures are very
close to the conclusions of Bakour and Kolars (1994: 128).

As for the Euphrates, if Turkey allocates only 15 billion m³ to Iraq
and Syria, and Syria uses only 6–8 billion m³ (and not the 12 billion m³
planned), then Iraq will receive only 7–9 billion m³ of water (and not
17 billion m³ as in the 1950s or even the 13 billion m³ it has obtained

in the recent past)—sufficient to irrigate only 0.5–0.6 million hectares in the Euphrates basin. Needless to say, this will necessitate closure of several hydroelectric power plants along the riverbed. Moreover, damage will be incurred not only to irrigation and hydroelectric production but to the river flow generally, which will have serious ecological implications.

The solution would be to transfer water from the Tigris to the Euphrates, but this would involve a cutback in the irrigated land in the Tigris basin. The minimum required for irrigating the Tigris basin is estimated currently at 32–38 billion $m^3$ annually. If about 6 billion $m^3$ are transferred to the Euphrates basin, only 26–32 billion $m^3$ will remain in the Tigris, and in the future 24–28 billion $m^3$, which will enforce a considerable reduction in irrigated land. The reduction will grow greater if in addition the quantities of water for domestic use and industry rise.

Despite future irrigation problems Iraq is likely to encounter with Euphrates water, this has not prevented the government in recent years from implementing a canalization project: three large canals in the southern region of the state, one of them 350 miles long, called Third River, and another southward called Fourth River (Figure 3.6).

The reasons for a project of this kind are debatable. Some claim that it is a military move intended to drain the marshes in the southern part of the state, thereby allowing the Iraqi army access by motorized vehicles to the former marsh areas, to suppress the rebellious Shi'ites in the Basra region. The army cannot attack by air because of UN regulations. Other possible reasons are that the project is intended to facilitate oil prospecting and extension of agricultural land in the marsh area; or that draining the marshes is the result of, among other things, the worsening shortage of Euphrates waters. One way or another, the rivers in Iraq are undergoing changes in the far south also (North, 1993).

**Electricity**

About 50 percent of the electricity produced in Iraq in the 1970s (1,300 megawatts) was generated by hydroelectric power stations. After the Kadisiya (Hadita), the Eski-Mosul (Saddam), and other dams are completed, electricity production will rise by an additional 6,000 megawatts (see Figure 3.6). On the Euphrates alone there are four power stations, which will soon produce about 40 percent of all the electricity in Iraq (*al Qabas*, Jan. 29, 1990).

Even if these data are exaggerated, as other data indicate (*Middle East and North Africa Yearbook*, 1990), it is clear that significant damage is projected for electricity production in Iraq if the Euphrates dries up. But unlike Syria and Turkey, Iraq has plentiful oil and actually does

*Figure 3.6:* Iraq—Land Uses

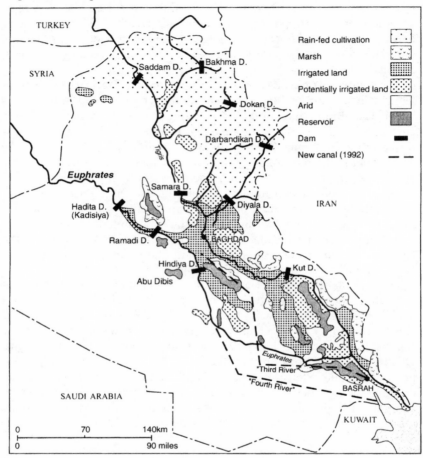

not need hydroelectric power stations. It can therefore solve the problem by transferring to thermal electricity production without difficulty. (As for extravagant spending, the $2–5 billion that Iraq spent on constructing the dams for hydroelectric electricity production pale in comparison with the sums it expended in its war in the gulf and its war with Iran, which have been estimated at hundreds of billions of dollars.)

### Domestic and Industrial Consumption

According to Gischler's estimate, about 0.5 billion m³ of water are taken up by domestic consumption, and about 2.24 billion m³ are consumed by industry, which Rogers estimated at 3.5 billion m³ in 1990 (Rogers and Lydon, 1994: 306). Presumably, with the growth in the population and the enlargement of the big cities, the domestic and industrial demand for water will reach 5–6 billion m³. This amount will have to be deducted from the quantity earmarked for agriculture.

## Supply and Demand for Water in the Riparian States: Conclusion

If Turkey completes its GAP program and Syria even partially completes its own projects, it will be necessary to calculate whether a shortage of water in the Euphrates and Tigris may be expected and whether the shortfall may be balanced in one river at the expense of the other.

Such a calculation may be made in two time spans: one is from the present situation to the final situation on realization of all the projects in Turkey and Syria (without stating the target year); the other is estimating demand for water each decade from the present to the year 2040, when the development programs of the Euphrates and Tigris lands are expected to be completed.

By this method we can estimate when the crisis will take place, namely, when demand for water will exceed supply (Table 3.5).

Table 3.5 shows that until 2010 there will be surplus water in the Euphrates and the Tigris, because the projects will take longer to implement than expected.

In 2010 a shortage of water in the Euphrates may be expected, and this will oblige Iraq to transfer surplus water from the Tigris to the Euphrates. Between 2020 and 2030 a situation may arise in which there will be a shortage of water in the Euphrates and the Tigris, owing to the great demands in their three riparian states. In fact, an emergency situation will be felt already around 2020, because the 4 billion m³ of water that will remain as surplus in the two rivers will not suffice for the drainage of the Euphrates and Tigris basin into the sea.

An amount equal to at least 10–20 percent of the rivers' discharge, namely 8–10 billion m³, is needed to drain the river of the salts and the great quantity of sewage that accumulates from about 30 million inhabitants of the Iraqi plains. The failure of drainage action will turn the rivers of Iraq into a stinking and salty sewage system.

It may be asked whether the many existing reservoirs in the three states will not help to postpone the shortage. The advantage of the reservoirs is the prevention of seasonal crises that occur in a single year, or the adjustment of the distribution of water between good years and bad years, but they cannot solve the chronic cumulative water shortfall.

**Table 3.5:  Demand and Supply of Water in Euphrates-Tigris Basins (1995–2040) (billion m³)**

|  | 1995 | 2000 | 2010 | 2020 | 2030 | 2040 |
|---|---|---|---|---|---|---|
| **Euphrates** | | | | | | |
| Turkey | 3 | 4-6 | 10 | 12 | 15 | 20 |
| Syria | 1-2 | 2-3 | 6 | 8 | 10 | 12 |
| Iraq | 14-17 | 14-17 | 14-17 | 14-17 | 14-17 | 14-17 |
| Total demand | 18-22 | 20-26 | 30-33 | 34-37 | 39-42 | 46-49 |
| Supply | 30 | 30 | 30 | 30 | 30 | 30 |
| Balance | +12 +8 | +10 +4 | -3 | -4 -7 | -9 -12 | -16 -19 |
| | | | | | | |
| **Tigris** | | | | | | |
| Turkey | 0.5 | 1 | 2 | 3 | 5 | 7 |
| Syria | 0.1 | 0.1 | 0.2 | 0.3 | 0.4 | 0.5 |
| Iraq | 32-38 | 32-38 | 32-38 | 32-38 | 32-38 | 32-38 |
| Total demand | 33-39 | 33-39 | 34-40 | 35-41 | 37-44 | 40-46 |
| Supply | 50 | 50 | 50 | 50 | 50 | 50 |
| Balance | 17-11 | 17-11 | 16-10 | 15-9 | 13-6 | 10-4 |
| | | | | | | |
| **Euphrates + Tigris** | | | | | | |
| Turkey | 3.5 | 5.7 | 12 | 15 | 20 | 27 |
| Syria | 1-2 | 2-3 | 6.2 | 8.3 | 10.4 | 12.5 |
| Iraq | 46-55 | 46-55 | 46-55 | 46-55 | 46-55 | 46-55 |
| Total demand | 50.5-60.5 | 65-65 | 64.2-73.2 | 69.3-78.3 | 76.4-85.4 | 85.5-94.5 |
| Supply | 80 | 80 | 80 | 80 | 80 | 80 |
| Balance | +30 +20 | +27 +15 | +15.8 +6.8 | +10.7 +1.7 | +3.6 -5.4 | -5.5 -14.5 |

*Notes:* Iraqi demands based on 1980s use. The table is based on the author's interpretation from available data and the progress of the development projects.

## Economics and Society for the Euphrates and Tigris Riparians

The three principal riparians in the Tigris and Euphrates belong to the Third World, albeit to its more advanced countries, as the socioeconomic data in Table 3.6 demonstrate: high population growth and great dependency on agriculture. There are, nonetheless, differences among the three countries.

### Turkey

Food production matches population growth (Table 3.7) in Turkey, an intensively agricultural state, but the agricultural sector is on the decline. At the end of the 1980s, 40 percent of the working population were farmers. Turkey is the largest wheat producer and the largest food exporter. It has a large amount of agricultural land, estimated at about 8.5 million hectares, including about 1.7 million hectares in Anatolia.

Table 3.6: Euphrates and Tigris Riparians: Basic Socioeconomic Data

| Country | Population | | Population Growth (%) | | GNP per Person 1993 | Agriculture as Percentage of GNP | |
|---|---|---|---|---|---|---|---|
| | 1995 | 2010 | 1980-1992 | 1992-2005 | | 1965 | 1993 |
| Turkey | 61 | 80 | 2.3 | 1.9 | 2120 | 34 | 15 |
| Syria | 15 | 24 | 3.3 | 3.3 | 1160[a] | 29 | 30 |
| Iraq | 20 | 34 | 3.6 | 3.8 | 1950[a] | 18 | 16[a] |

*Source:* World Bank, *World Development Report*, 1994; Population Reference Bureau, 1996
[a] - 1989

Table 3.7: Index of Food Production per Person (100 = 1987) by Country [a]

| Country | 1987 | 1988 | 1989 | 1990 | 1991 | 1992-1994 |
|---|---|---|---|---|---|---|
| Turkey | 100 | 105.2 | 94.9 | 102.5 | 101.4 | 101 |
| Syria | 100 | 125.7 | 77.4 | 96.6 | 91.3 | 88 |
| Iraq | 100 (1981) | - | - | 90 | - | 85 |

*Sources:* World Resources Institute, 1988/9; 1994/5; 1996/7, World Bank 1993
[a] - The food production covers all edible agricultural products that contain nutrients

The plan for irrigating lands in southeast Anatolia ensures the continuation of agricultural development in the state. The rate of food production will not merely match the natural growth rate of the population, but Turkey will in fact be able to augment its food exports (Figures 3.6, 3.7, 3.8).

Turkey is also in the midst of rapid industrialization. It has steel plants, many customers, an abundance of water sources, and hydroelectric energy sources. Tourism is also advancing (Figure 3.7). Turkey can therefore cut back its agriculture and its use of Tigris and Euphrates water for this purpose without affecting its use for hydroelectric energy production.

## Syria

Syria has a large agricultural potential. But it does not use this potential and has become a food importer instead of a food exporter (Table 3.8). The reasons for this are a clumsy and corrupt bureaucracy, ignorance of the farmers, years of drought, and the water shortage caused

*Figure 3.7:* Natural Resources in the Euphrates-Tigris Countries

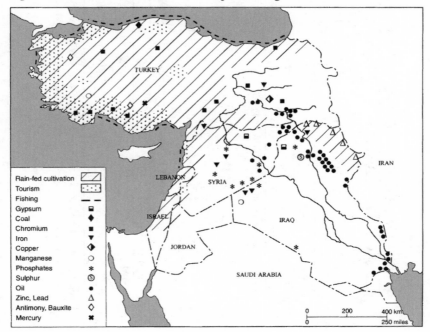

*Figure 3.8:*  Geopolitical Circles in the Euphrates-Tigris Basin

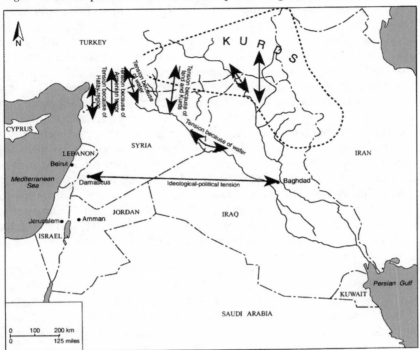

**Table 3.8: Grain Imports by the Tigris and Euphrates Riparians (thousands of tons)**

| Country | 1974 | 1990 | 1993 | 1995 |
|---------|------|------|------|------|
| Turkey | 1276 | 3177 | 2107 | 2243[a] |
| Syria | 339 | 2091 | 1131 | 733[b] |
| Iraq | 870 | 2834 | 1552 | 1222 |

*Source:* World Bank, *World Development Report,* 1994; FAO 1996.
[a] Turkey exported in 1995 3,710,000 tons
[b] Syria exported in 1995 1,790,000 tons

by population growth and Turkey's water projects (Table 3.7). Syria has not implemented its plans to expand its agricultural land, and there has also been a slowdown in food production in the country generally (Table 3.8). The forecasts for the future are not optimistic: food imports will continue to grow and Syria's agricultural sector will continue to shrink.

The rate of food production does not match the natural growth rate, as data concerning food imports (Table 3.8) confirm. For many years Syria, which is not densely populated, was a food exporter, but as a consequence of its population growth it was forced to import food. There has likewise been a decrease in the volume of cotton and wheat production and a freeze in agricultural development generally (*Mideast Market*, May, 16. 1988: 15; *Middle East and North Africa Yearbook*, 1996).

Syria is less developed than Iraq and Turkey and more dependent on agriculture. Although oil and gas have been discovered in Syria, the industrial sector is backward and the potential for its development not great (Figure 3.7). Syria's economic situation worsened in the 1980s because of high expenditure on defense, the drop in oil prices, the reduction in aid from the Arab world and the USSR, and a faulty bureaucracy and ruling system. The water shortage in the Euphrates contributed to the country's difficulties and led to a cutback in electricity supply to the towns and a delay in agricultural development. However, in 1991, after the Gulf War, Syria did receive renewed aid from Arab states as well as from the Western countries.

In conclusion, Syria is the weakest of the three states, and in another ten to fifteen years it will grow relatively weaker, because the other two states have many economic resources that will enable them to develop, while Syria does not. Syria will find it difficult to diminish its agriculture, and reduce its water consumption, and to develop industry instead.

### Iraq

Iraq has great agricultural potential, but it does not exploit it because of soil salinity (causing 20–30 percent of the land to be abandoned in recent decades), excess bureaucracy, unsuccessful reform, ignorance among the farmers, and wars.

Food production apparently matches population growth in Iraq, but the data concerning the food production growth cannot be regarded as current (Tables 3.6, 3.7, 3.8) because they relate to the time of the Iran-Iraq war, when all the country's resources were on a war footing. In consequence of the Gulf War (1991), Iraq is probably in an even more difficult situation than Syria in this respect.

Iraq became an importer of food from the United States at the end of the 1980s, surpassed only by Saudi Arabia among the Middle East countries in its rate of import (*MEED*, July 2, 1990: 4–5; Table 3.8). According to another source, about 80 percent of the food consumed in Iraq at the end of the 1980s was imported (*Economist*, Sept. 8, 1990). In Syria and Iraq food imports constitute a considerable proportion of overall imports. In the 1980s a regression in Iraqi agriculture became evident, which caused a growth in the share of food imports out of total imports, but there are no reliable figures.

Iraq has oil and manpower for developing very advanced industry (including military, nuclear, chemical, and other industries). After the Gulf War the economic infrastructure of the state was destroyed, including transportation, water projects, power stations, and industrial projects. The state is torn by civil war and stricken by partial famine and epidemics, and all government systems have essentially collapsed. A large number of the oil fields are under international supervision, and the oil income will be used in coming years for reparations to states harmed in the Gulf War. However, all this considered, Iraq is rich in oil (Figure 3.7), and it could develop its industrial sector when the government stabilizes. Iraq can therefore increase its food imports and trim its agricultural sector, and hence its water needs.

## Relations and Agreements on Water among the Tigris and Euphrates Riparians

Lack of cooperation among the states and absence of mutual consideration in developing water projects naturally bring about serious crises. The first of these erupted in 1974, when Turkey filled the Keban Dam reservoir and Syria filled the Tabqa Dam reservoir at the same time. As 1974 was a dry year, the flow of the Euphrates in Iraq stopped. The Arab League's attempt to mediate did not work, and Iraq called up its army and concentrated it on the Syrian border; Syria hastily released about 200 million m$^3$ of water from the Tabqa Dam.

A second crisis, less serious than the first, occurred in 1983, when the level of the Tabqa Dam reservoir dropped, and Syria blamed Turkey for it. The most recent crisis, in the winter of 1990, was discussed above in the section on the Ataturk Dam.

However, not only has the quantity of water that each state receives raised controversy, but so has the quality. Due to the increased use of Euphrates water in Turkey and Syria, fertilizers, toxins, and effluents enter the water, and Iraq, the downstream state, receives very low-quality water.

Despite the repeated and varied protests of Syria and Iraq concerning Turkey's plans, Turkey continues to promote the GAP program, but has also initiated coordinating meetings among the three riparians. In 1990 the fifteenth such meeting took place, but it did not accomplish anything (*Middle East International*, Feb. 16, 1990: 12; *Newspot*, June 18, 1990). To gain time, Turkey proposed that the three states conduct a joint survey of the agricultural and water potential in the Euphrates region, to determine how much water should be allocated to each state (*MEED*, July 20, 1990: 23). Another of Turkey's proposals was to examine the inefficiency of water use in Syria and Iraq, as compared with the economical use and efficiency in Turkey (*Newspot*, June 28, 1990: 1). Turkish President Ozal visited Syria in 1987, as did the Turkish foreign minister. Turkey, wishing to prove to the countries of Europe that it was worthy to join the European Community, adopted a position of compromise in 1990, declaring that it was ready to sign agreements and to cooperate, and even brought up the Peace Pipeline concept; but in fact, as we have seen, Turkey acts without any cooperation with or consideration for its neighbors, because the development of the Anatolia region is of utmost importance to it. A claim repeatedly made by the Turkish government is that the Euphrates and Tigris are Turkish, not international rivers, and therefore Turkey is not obliged to obey the accepted laws concerning international rivers (Tekeli, 1990: 211; Frankel, 1992: 7; Waterbury, 1994: 57; Turkey, 1995: 13).

During the crisis of the early 1990s it became clear that water issues play a political, not just an economic, role. During this crisis, Turkey promised that if Syria acceded to its political demands, Euphrates water would resume its flow. If Syria did not, Turkey warned, the interruption of the flow would long continue. What were Turkey's demands? First, that Syria stop supporting the Kurdish underground operating against Turkey from behind the Syrian borders; and second, that Syria cease aiding the Armenians training in the Beqáa in Lebanon for acts planned against Turkish diplomats throughout the world (*MEED*, Jan. 19, 1990; *Middle East International*, Feb. 16, 1990; Turkey, 1995). Hints of Turkish intentions to link political pressures with water issues have been raised in the past (*Briefing*, Feb. 27, 1982; *Economist*, Dec. 16, 1989: 56).

The relationship among the three states is very intricate. They are connected not only by water rights, water division, and water quality, but also by complex historical and political factors (Figure 3.8).

Syria and Turkey are divided on the question of the Hatay region (Alexandretta). In 1939, on the eve of the Second World War, France transferred this region from Syria to Turkey, and Syria wants it back (Jansen, 1990: 11–12; Turkey, 1995).

Tension between the two is furthermore linked to the Kurds, who live in all three countries. Turkey oppresses this minority, as does Iraq. Syria, on the other hand, which has only a very small number of Kurds—who do not pose a political danger—supports the Kurdish-Marxist guerrilla movement. Syria has an interest in aiding this movement because one of the targets of the guerrilla group is the GAP (Waterbury, 1994: 55).

Turkey and Syria have conflicts also over the issue of the right to use the Kwik River, which rises in Turkey and then flows through the Aleppo plateau in Syria. Its water is used for drinking by the residents of Aleppo, but Turkey also uses the water, and reduces the amount remaining for Syria. Syria, on the other hand, completely exhausts the Orontes water, leaving Turkey only polluted water. Another historical conflict between Turkey and Syria is linked to the mutual land requisitions that occur on either side of the border (*al Yawm al Usbu'a*, Dec. 18, 1989).

In contrast to the tense relationship between Syria and Turkey, that between Iraq and Turkey was correct, and even good, prior to the gulf crisis. The two states had a common interest in keeping the Kurds down, they were linked by close trade relations, and, above all, Iraq exported its oil through Turkey (about 60 percent of all Iraq's oil exports) and sold oil to Turkey, as well as importing many products from it. During the years of the Iran-Iraq war, Turkey was one of Iraq's only gateways to the outside world, which made the relations between them even closer.

After Iraq invaded Kuwait, Turkey took sides in the conflict and joined the coalition that formed against Iraq. Turkey provided a base for the warplanes that attacked targets in Iraq, and at the time of writing (1998) Turkey still aids the U.S. Air Force and the UN units in their defense of the Iraqi Kurds. After the current crisis is solved relations between the two states will probably return to their former condition.

As for Syria, despite its identity of interest with Iraq regarding Turkey's development of the Euphrates, these two states are mired in deep ideological conflict, and personal hatred exists between the leaders of the two countries. During the Iran-Iraq war Syria unconditionally supported Iran against its Arab "sister." In the 1991 Gulf War Syria once again aligned with the enemies of Iraq, and even participated in the fighting against it.

As a result of these complicated relationships, so far no formal agreements on dividing water among them have been signed. During the British and French mandates in Syria and Iraq, the powers agreed that there was a need to create a committee to study the water situation and to solve problems that might arise concerning the use of Euphrates water. There is also a protocol that France and Turkey signed in 1930 regarding coordination between Syria and Turkey on the utilization of the Euphrates.

In 1946 an agreement was signed between Turkey and Iraq, in which it was decided that Turkey would report to Iraq on all activities to be conducted in the Tigris and Euphrates basins. It was also decided that

Iraq was authorized to build dams within Turkey to increase the flow of the Euphrates within Iraq's borders (Caelleigh, 1983: 121).

As for new agreements among Turkey, Syria, and Iraq, in recent years diverse information has been gathered on the existence of overt or secret agreements: one source claims that Turkey has undertaken to allocate 19.7 billion m³ of water annually to Syria (*Middle East*, Oct. 1987: 27; Waterbury, 1994: 55). According to another source, Turkey has undertaken to allocate about 15.5 billion m³ of water annually to Syria and promised to provide Syria and Iraq with about 60 percent of Euphrates water (*al Yawm al Usbu'a*, Dec. 18, 1989; Waterbury, 1994: 57).

In 1990 Turkish sources published information on an agreement that Iraq would receive 58 percent of the amount released by Turkey (*MEED*, July 20, 1990). It is not clear how Turkey could promise a specific amount to Iraq without involving Syria in the decisions.

Conflicting information emerged from a meeting of representatives of the three states. It was stated that Syria demanded 13 billion m³, Turkey 14 billion m³, and Iraq 18 billion m³. Naturally, such a distribution is not possible, for the Euphrates does not hold sufficient water to satisfy the wishes of all the states together. The Euphrates discharge is about 30 billion m³ and the total demands of the states amount to 45 billion m³.

In 1994 the Jordanian water commissioner spoke before participants at the Nineteenth Conference of the Center for Arab Studies at Georgetown University in Washington, D.C., and among other things he stated that in 1990 two provisional agreements had been signed concerning the Euphrates waters. One was between Turkey and Syria, in which Turkey undertook to release 500 m³ of water per second (15.5 billion m³ annually), for Syria. The second agreement was signed the same year between Syria and Iraq, and it determined that Syria would receive 58 percent of the water and Iraq 4.2 percent (figures precisely the reverse of those published in *MEED* in 1990).

In the same lecture, the water commissioner reported that immediately upon signature of the agreements, Turkey released 700 m³ water per second from the Euphrates and not 500 m³ as it had promised. This meant that Turkey released about 22 billion m³ of water per year to the downstream states. Was this a one-time gesture? Perhaps the decision was to release such a large quantity as long as there was no demand in the GAP project. Clearly, as long as Turkey's consumption does not exceed 8 billion m³ a year, there is no obstacle preventing it from releasing about 22 billion m³ of water annually, for the Euphrates discharge is about 30 billion m³ of water and Turkey's reservoirs contain 47 billion m³, which ensures supply even in the rare dry years. At the present stage it is important for Turkey to produce electricity, and it does so while simultaneously releasing the amount of water required by Syria and Iraq. These circumstances may change, as stated, between 2010 and 2020 when the demand for water in Turkey rises, and it will be met at the expense of its neighbors.

For how many years can Turkey be generous toward its neighbors should the latter suffer from long periods of drought? On the assumption that Turkey will need 10–20 billion m³ of water annually, it is assured of all the required amount even if it suffers a repeat of the most severe drought it has ever experienced (in that drought Turkey received about half its average rainfall for two years). In such a case Syria would win two to three years' grace by virtue of the reservoirs in Turkey, and then the shortage would be felt in Syria, to say nothing of Iraq, which would be left without Euphrates water as early as the second year of drought (in spite of its own reservoirs).

The fears of Syria and Iraq concerning the Euphrates in Turkish hands are chiefly psychological since at present Turkey indeed has the option of closing off the flow of water for a long period. Were it not for this fear by Arab states from a non-Arab upstream state, the reservoirs would in fact be a blessing for the three states.

## Principles for Fair Water Division in the Tigris and Euphrates Basin

In considering how to allocate the river water fairly, one must review all the relevant factors in water distribution: the relative contribution of each state to the rivers' flow, each state's climate, each state's historical rights to water use, alternatives to water use, other resources within each state, wasteful use of water, as well as the possibility of developing water projects without harming the other riparians. These factors are represented in Table 3.9.

However, the picture presented in the table highlights the difficulty of adopting a position on the allocation of water to Iraq. On the one hand, Iraq has a high income from oil, and therefore its dependency on water could decrease, particularly as its use of water for irrigation is extremely wasteful. One might advise Iraq, therefore, to reduce its agriculture and develop its industry, thereby easily solving its water problem without harming its economy. On the other hand, other data indicate that in socioeconomic terms it is a developing country, and its population is highly dependent on water. Moreover, Iraq has clear historical rights to water use, and a desert climate. Besides its dependency on agriculture, Iraq is highly dependent on hydroelectric power produced by the rivers. If the country seems to be freeing itself from its depen-

Table 3.9: Criteria for Water Allocation in the Euphrates-Tigris Basin

| Criteria | Turkey | Syria | Iraq | Others |
|---|---|---|---|---|
| Share in area of Euphrates (%) | 28 | 17 | 40 | 15 Saudi Arabia |
| Share in area of Tigris (%) | 12 | 1 | 78 | 9 Iran |
| Water contribution, Euphrates (%) | 87 | 13 | - | - |
| Water contribution, Tigris (%) | 100 | - | - | - |
| Water contribution, Tigris tributaries (%) | 27-37 | - | 39-46 | 24-27 Iran |
| Climate | Mostly Mediterranean | 90% arid or semiarid | 70% arid | |
| Present utilization (billion m$^3$): | | | | |
| Euphrates | 1-3 | 4 | 14-19 | |
| Tigris | 0.5 | 0.1 | 37-42 | |
| GNP per person 1993 | 2120 | 1160 | 1950[a] | |
| Other resources and potential | Industry, minerals, tourism, agriculture, except in the east | Oil, agriculture other than the Euphrates basin | Oil and gas | |

a - 1998

dency on agriculture, and developing its industry, following the Gulf War this process will certainly be delayed, and the population will continue to engage in agriculture for many years. Even agricultural development could be held up for many reasons, and even regress, so that agriculture would be fairly backward in this country.

What conclusions should we draw from this paradoxical state of affairs? Does a fair division of water mean that Iraq must be considered a large consumer of water, or should it be told to seek alternatives to water in industry and in oil?

Turkey is a country blessed with natural resources and water, with developed agriculture, and developing industry, and in the future it will be an industrialized country. It is not highly dependent on the river water, and its dependency on water will diminish still further. Nor does Turkey have historical rights to use the water. However, Turkey is the primary contributor to the river's flow; it still has a high rate of population growth and a large population, and it wants to develop the resources that will allow it both to feed its growing population, and to export food. Although Turkey is a developed country the eastern part is backward and requires energetic development. This is necessary to connect the region's population, which is mostly Kurdish, to the western part of the state and to integrate it with the rest of the country; in so doing, the Turks hope to mitigate the nationalist ferment among the Kurds. Therefore, the agricultural development plan is crucial. Equally crucial is hydroelectric power, as Turkey has neither oil nor gas. Turkey, therefore, does have the right to utilize the rivers' water. The question is the quantity it should be allotted. As the owner of the water sources Turkey is entitled to request a quantity equal to that of its two neighbors, that is, about a third of the rivers' flow, or perhaps even a half.

Syria is trapped in a grave economic situation. It has no financial reserves despite the recent discovery of many energy sources in the country. From a socioeconomic perspective, Syria is a developing country, and it cannot eliminate agriculture. It is dependent, therefore, on Euphrates water, both for agriculture and for hydroelectricity, and more than the other two states, which are rich in other resources. Its proven oil potential will apparently suffice for about ten years, and then Syria will need thermal electricity and hydroelectricity (*Middle East and North Africa Yearbook*, 1996).

If the three states were to sit around the conference table, imbued with goodwill to conclude their water distribution dispute fairly, they would probably come up with the following agreement. The Euphrates would be divided principally between Turkey and Syria, most of the Tigris water would go to Iraq, and a small part of it would go to Turkey. Thus, each riparian would receive its fair share. In the spirit of the Helsinki and ILC Accords, particularly the section on concentration of the other riparians, Turkey would postpone the development of the Tigris and only develop the Euphrates. Turkey should be content with utilizing the Tigris for electricity only, allowing Iraq to use all the water for its needs; this would compensate Iraq for conceding the Euphrates, and it could even transfer water from the Tigris to the Euphrates, where water will be lacking. Such a division, of course, would obligate Iraq use its water more economically. For its part, Syria would receive all the Euphrates water that Turkey allotted it, would exploit the Balikh and the Khabur, and would draw a small quantity of water from the Tigris. If Syria did not have to allocate water from the Euphrates to Iraq it would not suffer a water shortage.

Such a solution meets the Helsinki principles, at least for the next fifteen years, but will the Middle Eastern states accept it? In reality, the three states do not cooperate and are not abandoning their ongoing grandiose plans for irrigation and dams. This increases the seepage and evaporation of water, impairs water quality, and reduces the total amount of water available for distribution. If development continues, it is possible that in the years 1995–2010 a serious conflict will erupt among the countries over water distribution in the two rivers, or one or two of the states will be forced to curtail their projects because of the wastage involved. In the meantime, there are delays in implementing the water projects in all three countries, for varying reasons, hence the water shortage.

The water problem in the Tigris and Euphrates basin also is connected with what takes place in the Yarmuk basin. What Turkey as an upstream state on the Euphrates does to Syria, Syria as an upstream state on the Yarmuk does to Jordan. Any arrangement in the north, in the Tigris and Euphrates basins, will set a precedent for arrangements in the south, in the Yarmuk basin.

*Chapter 4*

# The Jordan-Yarmuk Basin: Conflict over Little Water

## Background

The Jordan is the smallest of the rivers so far considered in this book. However, it provides the clearest illustration of the term hydropolitics generally, and in the Middle East especially.

The drainage basin of the Jordan extends over an area of 6,315–6,820 square miles, depending on the sources (UN, *Register of International Rivers*, 1978; Naff and Matson, 1984; Salik, 1988). The states sharing the basin are Israel, Jordan, Syria, and Lebanon. Recently the Palestinian people have joined them (Figure 4.1). Before 1967, 53.9 percent of the drainage basin was located within the Jordanian kingdom, 29.6 percent in Syria, 10.4 percent in Israel, and 1.6 percent in Lebanon (UN, *Register of International Rivers*, 1978).

The northern drainage basin is situated mainly in Israel, and the Jordanian kingdom has no share in it. Lebanon has no part of the southern drainage basin. Eighty percent of the area of the Yarmuk drainage basin is in the territory of Syria, which also controls most of its sources. The Jordanian kingdom, by contrast, has very little of the Yarmuk but has historical rights to the use of its water. Until 1967 Israel had a minute part of the Yarmuk basin. This situation changed after the Six Day War.

The chief water source of the Jordan basin countries is rainfall. Syria alone receives water also from a source outside its borders, the Euphrates, which rises in Turkey, and some water from the Tigris and the Orontes. The annual water potential in each of the reparian countries is: Lebanon, 3.8–8.8 billion $m^3$; Jordanian kingdom, approximately 0.85 billion $m^3$; Palestine (including water entering from Lebanon and Syria), 1.5–2 billion $m^3$; Syria (with the Euphrates), about 30 billion $m^3$ (Gischler, 1979; Beaumont et al., 1988).

119

*Figure 4.1:* Jordan River Basin and Palestine Aquifers

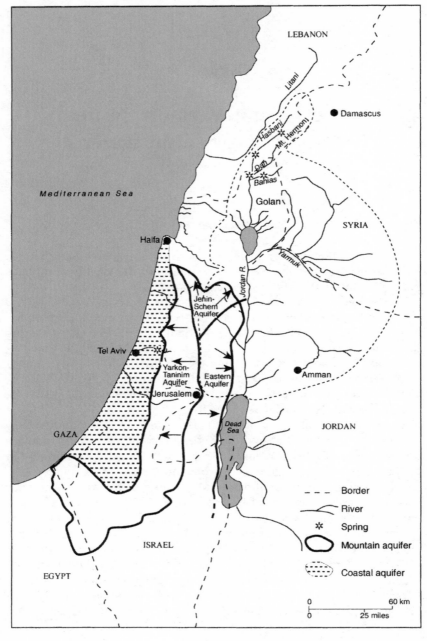

Lebanon by virtue of its climate is not dependent at all on the Jordan basin for supplying its water needs. Syria enjoys alternative water sources in the north, but the south of the country suffers from lack of water. Israel, the Palestinians, and the Jordanian kingdom are greatly dependent on the water supply from the Jordan-Yarmuk basin. All the basin states have population increase rates among the highest in the world. The need for water is growing constantly, and the exploitation of water from the Jordan river with all its tributaries has almost reached the maximum. As if this were not enough, a considerable part of the basin lies in a semiarid or desert region, and the river's discharge varies markedly from year to year.

From 1948 to the mid-1990s a state of war existed between Israel and the Arab states in the river basin. In this period many development projects were executed unilaterally by the river partners, especially Israel, Syria, and Jordan (see Figure 4.2). In 1993 a declaration of principles was signed between Israel and the Palestinian people, with the goal of a peace agreement between them eventually.

In 1994 Israel signed a full peace agreement with the Hashemite kingdom of Jordan, and many of its clauses concern water. Since 1993 the parties have been engaged in the search for ways of a new and rational distribution of the meager waters of the Jordan River. Negotiations between Israel and Syria and Lebanon are ongoing, but at the time of writing no conclusion has been reached.

In previous chapters we dealt with drainage basins: that of the Euphrates and the Tigris, including all of Iraq, northern Syria, and eastern Turkey; and that of the Nile, including Egypt, most of Sudan, and the principal part of Ethiopia. Turning to the Jordan River basin we encounter a unique situation, stemming from its physical and political structure. This obliges us to exceed the limits of the drainage basin to address several additional water issues linked to it.

One of these is the groundwater of the central mountain spine in all Palestine, namely, the western highland aquifer. This aquifer constitutes a part of the political unit known as the "West Bank" (Judea and Samaria), and also a part of Israel (see Figure 4.1). Water problems on the Israeli coastal plain and in southern Israel also influence the complex of questions connected with the Jordan basin, since Israel's National Water Carrier transfers Jordan water to the drainage basin of the Mediterranean Sea. The Gaza Strip is not physically attached to the West Bank, nor to the Jordan basin, but it is one Palestinian unit. Therefore, any solution concerning the supply of water to the Palestinians must necessarily consider the needs of the Gaza Strip too, which has hardly any water sources of its own. A similar situation exists in the Jordanian kingdom also. There too the Jordan River is the major water supply, and

*Figure 4.2:* Water Projects on the Jordan River

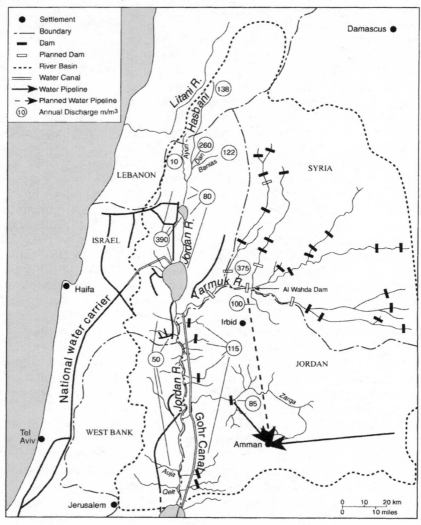

is complemented by additional sources (mainly desert groundwater). A consideration of the Jordan basin must therefore include the entire Jordanian kingdom. The share of Lebanon in the Jordan basin is negligible; and of Syria only the southwestern area is included in it. The discussion, therefore, must concern the water regimes of Israel, the Jordanian kingdom, and the Palestinian people, and also the southern Syrian water regime and that of a tiny area of Lebanon. It should be realized that the water shortage in the region is a chronic problem and the dispute over the Jordan water is complicated and difficult to solve; this is so despite agreements already concluded in the past, and despite negotiations on further agreements (Sexton, 1990; Uri Sagi, interview, September 1995).

## The Jordan Flow Regime

The chief sources of the Jordan are: the Hatbani (Snir) River, the Banias (Hermon) Spring, and the Dan Spring (see Figure 4.1). The Hasbani rises in Lebanon, about 19 miles north of its border with Israel. Its chief springs are the Hasbaya and the Wazzani. The latter springs rise in an area that until 1967 was within Syria. The Hasbaya Springs rise in Lebanon. The Dan Spring, the most important of all the upper Jordan tributaries, rises in Israeli territory (within the Green Line). This is a karstic spring, affected directly by the quantities of rainfall on Mt. Hermon. Consequently, its flow is more or less constant (Table 4.1). The Banias too is a karstic spring. It rises in a cave on the Golan Heights, territory that passed into Israeli hands in 1967. Before 1967 the area belonged to Syria, and the source was 0.6 miles east of the border with Israel.

Three and three-quarters miles south of the Israeli–Lebanese border, 256 feet above sea level, the three streams unite to form the Jordan River. Before the construction of the National Water Carrier the river flowed southward and entered the Hula swamps and afterwards Lake Hula (the lake and the swamp were drained in 1959). In the Hula Valley, one of the Jordan's tributaries enters the Jordan; this is the Ayun, which originates in Lebanon, west of the Hasbani. In addition, spring waters and floodwaters from both sides of the Jordan Valley, from the upper Galilee, and from the Golan Heights also enter the river (Table 4.1).

The section from the Jordan's exit from the Hula Valley to its entry into the Kinneret is a narrow gorge, and the water descends down dozens of waterfalls from about 230 feet above sea level to 689 feet below sea level. The current at the entrance to the Kinneret is suddenly arrested, and at this point it creates a small delta, which is traversed lengthwise by a series of streams.

The Kinneret is actually a continuation of the Jordan, and the many tributaries of the river empty into it. The lake is 12.5 miles long, 5.6 miles wide, and 64 square miles in area. It is the only sweet water lake in the world at such a low altitude (689 feet below sea level).

The origin of the lower Jordan is at the southwestern end of the Kinneret. The Jordan does not exit due south of where it enters the Kinneret

**Table 4.1: Jordan-Yarmuk Drainage Basin and Discharge**

| | Area of Basin (miles²) | Riparian Countries | Per country (miles²) | Per country (%) | Length of River (miles) | Average (m³) | Discharge (%) |
|---|---|---|---|---|---|---|---|
| Hasbani (Snir) | 237.0 | Lebanon | 232 | — | 14.3 | 138 | |
| | | Israel | 5 | — | 4.3 | — | |
| Banias (Hermon) | 67.5 | Syria[a] | 46 | — | 4.3 | 122 | |
| | | Israel | 21.5 | — | 1.9 | — | |
| Dan | 9.5 | Israel | 9.5 | — | 5.6 | 260 | |
| Ayun | 20.0 | Lebanon | 18.5 | — | 5.0 | 8–10 | |
| | | Israel | 1.5 | — | 5.0 | — | |
| Eastern rim springs (Golan Heights) | 357.0 | Syria | 357 | — | — | 34 | |
| Western rim springs (Galilee) | 295 | Israel | 297 | — | — | 12 | |
| Floods on both rims | | Syria and Israel[b] | — | — | — | 80–100 | |
| Hula Valley (springs) | | Israel | — | — | — | 90 | |
| Hula Valley (rain) | | Israel | — | — | — | 60 | |
| Sea of Galilee (springs) | | Israel | — | — | — | 50 | |
| Sea of Galilee (rain) | | Israel | — | — | — | 70 | |
| Total Jordan North Basin (Mediterranean climate) | 988.0 | | 988 | 100 | | 926–946 | 100 |
| | | Lebanon | 250.5 | 25 | — | 146–148 | 16.0 app. |
| | | Syria | 403 | 41 | — | 196–206 | 21.0 app. |
| | | Jordan | — | — | — | — | — |
| | | Israel | 334.5 | 34 | — | 582–592 | 63.0 app. |

**Table 4.1: (Continued)**

| | | | | | | | |
|---|---|---|---|---|---|---|---|
| Less evaporation in the Sea of Galilee | | | | | | 250–300 | |
| Total available water in the Sea of Galilee | | | | | | 626–696 | |
| Yarmuk (semiarid climate) | 2625 | Syria | 2369 | 90.24 | 22.5 | 374 | 79 |
| | | Israel | 17 | 0.66 | 7.5 | — | — |
| | | Jordan | 239 | 91 | 2.5 | 101 | 21 |
| Eastern rim south of the Yarmuk (semiarid and arid climate) | | | | | | | |
| Arab | 103 | Jordan | — | — | — | 35 | — |
| Zigleb | 41 | Jordan | — | — | — | 13 | — |
| Al Jurum | 79 | Jordan | — | — | — | 13 | — |
| Yabis | 48 | Jordan | — | — | — | 5 | — |
| Kufrinja | 43 | Jordan | — | — | — | 13 | — |
| Rajib | 32 | Jordan | — | — | — | 7 | — |
| Zarqa | 1313 | Jordan | — | — | — | 85 | — |
| Shueib | 69 | Jordan | — | — | — | 11 | — |
| Kafrein | 68 | Jordan | — | — | — | 13 | — |
| Husbun | 23 | Jordan | — | — | — | 5 | — |
| Others | 565 | Jordan | — | — | — | 20 | — |
| Total eastern rim | 2384 | Jordan | — | — | — | 220 | — |
| Western rim south of Sea of Galilee (semiarid and arid area) | | | | | | | |
| Tavor | 81 | Israel | — | — | 9.4 | 6 | |
| Harod | 70 | Israel | — | — | 12 | 8 | |
| Tirza | 127 | West Bank | — | — | 23 | 16 | |

**Table 4.1: (Continued)**

| | | | | | | |
|---|---|---|---|---|---|---|
| Auja | 104 | West Bank | — | 17.5 | 10 | |
| Qelt | 69 | West Bank | — | 15 | 4 | |
| Others including springs | 304 | Israel and West Bank[c] | — | — | — | |
| | | | | | | |
| Total western rim | 757 | — | — | — | 54 | |
| Total southern basin | 5766 | — | 5766 | 100 | 749 | 100 |
| | | Lebanon | 2369 | 41.0 | 374 | 50 |
| | | Syria | 319 | 6.0 | 19 | 2.5 |
| | | Israel | 2623 | 45.0 | 321 | 43 |
| | | Jordan | 455 | 8.0 | 35 | 4.5 |
| | | West Bank | | | | |
| | | | | | | |
| Less evaporation | | | | | −40 | |
| Total available water in the mouth of Dead Sea (natural flow) | | | | | 1335–1405 | |

*Sources:* Karmon, 1956; Ben Aryeh, 1965; Nimrod, 1966; Khourie, 1981; Naff and Matson, 1984; Jordan, 1986; Paldi, 1987; Gilad, 1988; Salik, 1988;

[a] Up to 1967
[b] Syria 50%; Israel 50%
[c] Israel 50%; West Bank 50%

because the Yarmuk delta pushes it westward (Ben Aryeh, 1965). Just over six miles south of the Kinneret the Yarmuk joins the Jordan. The Yarmuk basin is divided principally between Syria and Jordan—most of it in the former. For 25 miles it serves as a border between the two countries, and for ten miles it forms the border between Jordan and Israel. The Yarmuk is fed by springs and floodwater.

After leaving the Kinneret, the Jordan flows within the lisan marls formation in the Jordan Valley, between the Kinneret and the Dead Sea. The river is on average three to nine feet deep and 90–174 feet wide, varying by season. The Zor strip, some 100 feet below the Ghor strip, is covered with thick plant growth. The Ghor strip expands widely on both sides of the Zor, and this is the most settled area today. The Zor strip cuts into the Ghor area in a system of twisting mixed badlands ("Katara"), which reach a height of up to ninety feet.

From the mouth of the Yarmuk to the Dead Sea, the Jordan receives scores of tributaries, from the Judean and Samarian hills and from the east Jordan hills, the Irbid plateau region, the Ajlun Hills, Amman, and the Moabite plateaus to the east. The largest of the tributaries from the west are the Tabor, Harod, Bezek, Tirtsa, Auja, and Qelt streams. The largest tributaries from the east are the Arab, Ziqlab, al Jurum, Yabis, Kufrinja, Rajib, Zarka, Shueib, and Kafrein streams (for their discharge see Table 4.1).

The distance between the Kinneret and the Dead Sea is 62 miles, while the river's length in this section, because of meandering, is 120 miles. From its origin in the heights of Mount Hermon, about 9,184 feet above sea level, to its termination in the Dead Sea, 1,312 feet below sea level, the River Jordan's total length is 206 miles.

## Climate

All the riparians of the Jordan-Yarmuk basin, excluding Lebanon, have large tracts situated in an arid or partially arid climate; the remaining areas, which have a Mediterranean climate, suffer from water shortage for long periods in the year. The desert comprises 85 percent of the area of Jordan, about 60 percent of the area of Israel and the West Bank, and 65 to 70 percent of the area of Syria. There is no desert in Lebanon, however, and only about 30 percent of its area is located on the edge of the semiarid climate zone.

Rain in the Jordan basin (except for the Hermon region) falls very infrequently, and varies in quantity from year to year, from winter to summer, and from month to month in the winter season. Between 1987 and 1990 a drought struck the Jordan basin states, and the flow in the

Jordan basin subsequently dropped by more than 50 percent. In good years the flow increases very quickly and returns to the normal level.

### The Northern Drainage Basin

Mount Hermon is the principal water source of the upper Jordan's tributaries. The amount of water that falls on the mountain in the form of rain and snow has been estimated at about 50 inches per year. Because it consists of karstic rock, the mountain's drainage system is mostly subterranean, and the water erupts as karstic springs. The Awaj and Zabdani Springs flow eastward (their discharge is about 500 million $m^3$ of water, and they supply water to the Damascus basin). The springs feeding the Hasbani drain westward, toward Lebanon (the annual discharge of the Hasbani is 117–138 million $m^3$) and the Banias and Dan Springs flow toward the Israeli border. In all, the Jordan system receives about 440 million $m^3$ of water from Mount Hermon (Gilad, 1988: 39). Mount Hermon also feeds the Yarmuk; about 60 percent of the Yarmuk's sources, which have been estimated at about 240 million $m^3$ of water, come from the Hermon aquifer. The rest of the Yarmuk water is from rainwater (Burdon, 1954; Colton et al., 1984). The Jordan's discharge at its exit point from the Hula Valley has been estimated at about 660 million $m^3$ (Paldi, 1987: 25).

### The Kinneret (Sea of Galilee)

The Kinneret is the largest and most important sweet water reservoir in Israel. More than 900 million $m^3$ of water flow into it per year (Salik, 1988). According to the Kinneret Administration, the figure is about 610 million $m^3$ net after evaporation. The Jordan and its tributaries pour between 580–600 million $m^3$ of water per year into the Kinneret on a multiyear average. The spring water that originates beneath the bed of the Kinneret has been estimated at about 50 million $m^3$ (Avnimelech et al., 1978: 104; Gilad, 1988); the spring water and floodwater that flows directly (not via the Jordan) into the Kinneret basin stands at about 135 million $m^3$ (including water from the Yarmuk and from cloud seeding).

The volume of water that evaporates from the Kinneret is 270–300 million $m^3$ per year (Salik, 1988). The total carrying capacity of the Kinneret is 3,985 million $m^3$ (Gal, 1987: 9; according to the Kinneret Administration, about 4,131 million $m^3$), but the operative carrying capacity of the Kinneret today is about 680 million $m^3$ of water, which is based on a spread of only 13 feet. The operative carrying capacity of the Kinneret may be increased by lowering the minimum water level; if it drops an additional 6.5 feet the operative capacity increases to 1 billion m³ of water, but this endangers the water quality. But even this is not a particularly large carrying capacity, a fact that greatly reduces the Kinneret's ability to serve as a long-term national and international water reservoir as water needs continue to grow. The Kinneret will certainly not be able to serve as an international reservoir for Israel, Jordan, Syria, and the Palestinians (in an era of peace).

### The Southern Drainage Basin

South of the Kinneret a new drainage system begins, which is completely different from the northern drainage system (Table 4.1).

The Jordan's flow as it exits the Kinneret southward was measured in the past (1921–1945) at about 675 million m³ per year, but by the 1990s, owing to pumping by the National Water Carrier and irrigation in the Kinneret region, the flow is much smaller: only about 69 million m³ (annual average) of water drains from the Kinneret into the Dead Sea, including about 24 million m³ of saline water diverted from the Kinneret into the southern Jordan through the salt water carrier, 6 million m³ of sewage water, and the sweet water that supplies the settlements south of the Kinneret (Kinneret Administration, 1995). Only once every several years, when rain falls abundantly, is the Degania Dam opened and the excess water flows into the southern basin. This happened in the winters of 1980, 1981, and 1987; and in the winters of 1992 and 1993 the flow was about 262 million m³ each year (Kinneret Administration, 1995).

### The Yarmuk

The area of the Yarmuk's drainage basin is 2,626 miles square, mostly located in Syria. The average annual discharge is 475 million m³ of water, but it changes markedly from year to year. For example, in 1928–1929 the river's discharge was 874 million m³, and in 1927–1928 it was 271.4 million m³ only (Ben Aryeh, 1965: 77). The discharge also changes from the summer season to the winter season. In summer it includes only water from springs, and reaches 175 million m³; in winter it also includes rainwater, reaching 300 million m³. The Yarmuk empties into the Jordan River six miles south of the Kinneret, and from there the Jordan flows as a united river to the Dead Sea. Along its course it collects tributaries from either side of the valley (Figures 4.1 and 4.2; Table 4.1). Most of the water entering the Jordan in winter flows to the Dead Sea and is lost. Storage is needed to save this water. Such storage would become possible through the erection of a dam on the Yarmuk upstream, in the Maqarin region, or by diverting the Yarmuk into the Kinneret so that the latter would serve as a reservoir for both rivers.

In 1933, before the dams and canals on the Jordan River were built and before water was pumped from it, the Jordan carried about 1.2 billion m³ of water to the Dead Sea. In 1988, which was a dry year, only 60–100 million m³ reached the Dead Sea. Presently, in an average year about 200 million m³ of poor quality water enters the Dead Sea, the rest of the Jordan water having been used by the population of the region (Salik, 1988: 107; Israel, Water Commissioner, 1995).

## Aquifers Common to the Jordan Basin and Its Surroundings

Groundwater complements the surface water of the Middle Eastern countries (see Chapter 7 for a detailed discussion, and Figure 7.1). Here I shall survey the groundwater aquifers in Syria, the Jordanian kingdom, and Palestine. In hydrographic and political terms these aquifers constitute an integral part of the Jordan basin. The groundwater of Lebanon is negligible in this respect.

### Syria

Some of the Syrian groundwater is common to both Turkey and to Iraq. For this reason it is difficult to determine exactly the total amount of groundwater in Syria. It is assessed at 1.4 billion m³ (Arad, 1988). Of this water the significant element for the Jordan basin is the Yarmuk aquifer (included in the Yarmuk discharge), and the Hermon aquifer, which is common to Syria, Lebanon, and Israel and supplies water to the major springs of the Jordan river, such as the Dan. This aquifer appears in the water discharge balance of the upper Jordan.

### The Jordanian Kingdom

The water reservoirs in the highlands of the Jordanian kingdom north of the Dead Sea form an integral part of the Jordan basin. The water that rises in the Zarqa springs and other streams is included in the river's water balance.

The Arava aquifers lie in the southern part of the kingdom. This groundwater is common to Israel and the Jordanian kingdom and is not connected to the Jordan basin (Figure 4.4). The Arava aquifer extends from the Dead Sea to the Eilat–Aqaba region. It is divided into: northern and southern aquifers. The total amount of usable water is estimated at 40–70 million m³ (Zohar and Schwartz, 1991; Gvirtzman and Benvenisti, 1993).

East of Aqaba is another international aquifer, the al Disi basin. This basin may be part of a larger underground water body, called the Saq, which reaches as far as Kuwait, and is perhaps connected to the Tabuq aquifer in Saudi Arabia. The potential of this reserve is estimated at 280 million m³, and it is used by Jordan and Saudi Arabia. The Jordanian kingdom uses about 100 m³ of it annually. Of this, 12 million m³ are carried to Aqaba and the rest is pumped for irrigation of Bedouin lands in the Wadi Ram area and to supply Amman. Saudi Arabia pumps about 3 million m³ of this water annually (Murakami, 1995: 184–194; Gross and Soffer, 1996).

The Jordanian kingdom also has national aquifers: the Azraq basin, in the northeast, which supplies water to Amman, and the al Jafar basin in the southeast.

It is estimated that the potential of the kingdom's groundwater reaches 530 million m³; of these, 300 million m³ are replenishable and 230 million m³ are fossil water (Murakami, 1995; Shatanawi and Al Jayousi, 1995; Gross and Soffer 1996) .

**Palestine**

Groundwater forms a significant part of the water potential of Palestine. A small part is national, and most is international. Israel's national aquifers are in Galilee, on the Carmel and on the Mediterranean coast. Their yearly supply is about 562 million m³ (according to the Israel, Hydrological Service, 1993), about 35 percent of Israel's water potential if one discounts returned water and salty water, or 30 percent of the potential if these categories of water are included in the overall balance. During the last century the Israeli coastal aquifer has been overexploited. In recent years efforts have been made to prevent further deterioration in the quality of its water, so the volume of pumping from it has been reduced from the previous 400 million m³ to 245 million m³. This has been accomplished by changing the water source of entire towns to water pumped from the western side of the highland central aquifer (Gvirtzman, 1994: 90). About 40 million m³ of the water in the Kinneret basin is from groundwater common to Israel and Syria (according to the pre-1967 borders). The most important aquifers are three separate water bodies (with great geopolitical significance, as we shall see), located in the central highland backbone of Palestine, which includes the mountains of Judea and Samaria (the West Bank). Together these water bodies are known as the central highland aquifer. The potential of this aquifer is assessed at 600 million m³ (or more), constituting about 40 percent of the total high-quality water of Israel. It is highly sensitive in political terms, as it is located on either side of the Green Line separating Israel and the West Bank.

The central highland aquifer stretches from the foot of the Carmel in the north to the Beer Sheba region in the south (Figure 4.1). It is about 81 miles long and about 22 miles wide, and its depth is 1,40–3,298 feet below surface. The rock structure that allows water to seep and collect in it is a mixture of limestone and dolomite that geologists call "Judean composite." Penetration of water is possible wherever this structure is found on the surface. About 25–30 percent of the rainwater falling on the Judean mountains infiltrate into the aquifer, 3–5 percent flows off in streams, and the rest evaporates (Gvirtzman, 1993). Over this aquifer lives a population crowded into the cities of Nablus, Jenin, Jerusalem, Hebron, Ramallah, and hundreds of smaller settlements. Their sewage, if not treated properly, is easily liable to penetrate into the central highland aquifer and pollute it.

There are separate water bodies making up the central highland aquifer. The western aquifer, also known as the Yarkon-Taninim, yields 340–360 million $m^3$ of water annually. This is the best water in all Palestine. At present all this water is pumped in a system of springs on both sides of the Green Line. In the past most of this water rose in Israel, at the Rosh Ha'ayin Springs (220 million $m^3$) and the Taninim Springs (100 million $m^3$). Some water (about 40 million $m^3$) drained to the sea (Gvirtzman, 1993: 88).

The northern aquifer, also called Nablus-Gilboa (or Jenin-Nablus) yields a total of about 140 million $m^3$ of water. Pumping takes place on two stories: the lower story gives about 70 million $m^3$ and the upper about 68 million $m^3$. In the past, before dozens of wells were drilled down to this aquifer, the water emerged in a series of springs in the Bet She'an valley in Israel, and only a small amount of water, 18 million $m^3$, drained to the Wadi Fara' springs on the West Bank (Gvirtzman, 1994: 88).

The third aquifer is the eastern. At present about 100 $m^3$ of water are pumped from it. A considerable part of its water rises as springs, including those of Wadi Kelt, Jericho (18 million $m^3$), 'Ujah (10 million $m^3$), Fashha (40 million $m^3$ of salty water), Ein Gedi, etc. It is estimated that the potential of this aquifer is greater than the amount drawn from it today.

These three water bodies constituting the central highland aquifer are the most important water source in all Palestine, accounting for about 40 percent of the entire water potential and yielding the best quality water in the country. This aquifer is on both sides of the Green Line, so its water is international, claimed by Israel and by the Palestinians. The protection of the quality of this water and prevention of pollution are of great importance and carry geopolitical implications. The source of the water of this aquifer is largely in West Bank territory. Drilling to pump it may be done only in places of water accumulation, and these are not to be found everywhere on the West Bank. For example, water cannot be pumped in a strip 6–9.5 miles wide on the section of the highlands between Mount Hebron and the Bet She'an valley. Places of water accumulation lie close to the Green Line, so drillings are performed on either side of this line (Gvirtzman, 1995). This fact is of central importance in the final determination of the border between the state of Israel and the Palestinian people, and in the agreements on the use of the water of the aquifers.

## Supply and Demand for Water in the Jordan Basin

### Introduction

An evaluation of the demand for water in the states of the Middle East is problematic, as it is not clear how this may be done. One is faced with a number of alternatives: an evaluation may be based on the data of the various governments and their development plans (some of them extremely grandiose), and added to this the domestic and industrial water consumption forecast for the future. One may construct a real demand assessment based on full use of the agricultural lands in the state and according to the range of crops currently grown on them; to this might be added the forecast demand for water for drinking and industry. One may construct a theoretical demand model based on the assumption that water is a commercial commodity and therefore is saved in every possible way. Using this model one calculates agricultural, domestic, and industrial consumption. Each of these approaches has advantages and disadvantages.

I shall assess demand by using official figures, which constitute a basis for political and economic decisions by the states concerned. Only in the absence of such figures will I make my own calculations. In my evaluation I shall refer to conventional sources of water exclusively, on the assumption that nonconventional solutions such as desalination, import of water, or serious transformation in the water regimes of states are extremely costly and will require much time to implement. I shall examine all the Jordan basin states in turn, checking each one's supply of water (surface and groundwater) and the demand for water. After that will I be in a position to make an overall evaluation.

**Supply of Water: Lebanon**

Apart from a small section in the northern valley, Lebanon is entirely located in a Mediterranean climate with plentiful precipitation and snow in the mountains. An estimate of the water potential in the state varies between 3.8 billion m³ (according to Gischler, 1979) and 4.8–5 billion m³ (according to Glieck, 1993 and Allan, 1996a: 5). Beaumont, Black, and Wagstaff estimate the total flow of the water in the Lebanese rivers at 1 billion m³ (Beaumont et al., 1988: 84), but this figure is unacceptable, as the average flow of the Litani alone is 600–700 million m³; moreover, in addition to the Litani, the Orontes, Awali, Damur, and other rivers flow in Lebanon, and in most of them the discharge is high in summer as well as winter.

**Demand for Water: Lebanon**

The water consumed by irrigation in Lebanon (about 50,000 hectares) did not exceed 0.245 billion m³ in the mid-1960s (Beaumont, 1985: 6–7), and in the mid-1970s it reached 0.647 billion m³. In 1981 consumption for irrigation dropped, according to Beaumont, owing to the civil war, to 0.425 billion m³. According to Kally, in the mid-1980s, 85,000 hectares were irrigated with 800 million m³ of water. He claims that Lebanon can extend its irrigated territory to about 200,000 hectares, which would require, among other things, 1.5–2 billion m³ of water; even if we add domestic and industrial consumption, which does not exceed 0.5 billion m³ of water per year, Lebanon will still have a large volume of excess water (Gischler, 1979: 104; Kally, 1986: 37; Glieck, 1993; Allan, 1996a). In a new publication based on a series of updated estmates, different from the above, the authors mention a need for 3.1 billion m³ in Lebanon in 2030, compared with 1.5 billion m³ in 2000; that is, in about 30 years Lebanon will have exhausted its water (Israel, *Development Options*, 1996).

**Supply of Water: Syria**

Although two-thirds of Syria's territory is located in an arid or partially arid region, Syria is blessed with much water. The Euphrates and its tributaries, the Balikh and the Khabur, contribute 24–26 billion m³ of water to the state. The Orontes River also flows in Syria (about 1.5 billion m³) and the Barada and Awaj Rivers flow in the Damascus basin (about 0.5 billion m³). Similarly, Syria has subterranean and other water sources (about 1.4 billion m³). Syria's total water potential stands at 29–32 billion m³ of water (Rogers and Lydon, 1994; Allan, 1996a). Yet it should be remembered that Turkey and Iraq are partners with Syria in using the Euphrates. Taking account of Turkey's development plans to use about 20 billion m³, it can be assumed that Syria's water potential will reach 13–14 billion m³ in the year 2010, and if we also consider Iraq's needs, the potential declines to 5–10 billion m³ only. The carrying capacity of Syria's dams amounts to 12–13 billion m³, a large volume of the state's water potential demand (see Chapter 3).

These calculations, even if reliable, concern the state as a whole. However, regarding water sources, it is incorrect to treat Syria as a single geographical unit, and is preferable to separate it into regional divisions. The water supply of southern Syria should be examined apart from that of northern Syria. Note that this situation may change if Syria lays a water pipeline from the Euphrates to the Damascus basin and the Yarmuk basin. In such a case the computation of the supply of water of southern Syria would change entirely, as would the geopolitical status of the Jordan basin. There are signs that the Syrians are contemplating such a pipeline, as an alternative to the idea of carrying water from Turkey to southern Syria, one that Syrians have rejected out of hand (personal conversation on October 26, 1995, with Professor Kolars, after his return from a visit to Syria). The water potential of southern Syria is based on a total of 600 million m³ of water in the Damascus basin: 0.5 billion m³ of surface water and a further 100 million m³ of groundwater (*MEED*, Oct. 13, 1989). To this is added the use of 200–250 million m³ of spring water and rainwater from the upper basin of the Yarmuk. The remaining water of the Yarmuk basin is allocated to the Jordanian kingdom.

The overall water potential of southern Syria is estimated at 0.8–0.9 billion m³. Syria claims that it also has water rights to the Banias, the Hasbani, and the Kinneret. According to its calculations, the water potential of southern Syria amounts to 1.0–1.1 billion m³. If in fact Syria were to succeed in transferring between 250 million m³ and 1 billion m³ water from the Euphrates to the south of the state, all the water problems of southern Syria and of the Jordanian kingdom would be solved. Israel would then be free of some of its anxieties over water and could move forward in its negotiations with Syria.

### Demand for Water: Syria

Most of the demand for water in Syria is for irrigation. Syria's irrigated territory has been extended, and with it Syria's water requirements (Table 4.2).

According to Gischler, Syria used about 93 percent of its water to irrigate its agricultural land, and there was no water left from its water-

**Table 4.2: Irrigated Land and Water Demand in Syria (Various Years)**

| Year | Irrigated Land (million hectares) | Water Demand (billion m³) |
|---|---|---|
| 1957 | 404 | 2–4 |
| 1965 | 567 | 28–5.6 |
| 1976 | 547 | 5 |
| 1986 | 652 | 8 |
| 1991 | 643 | 8–9 |

*Sources:* Cressy 1960; Gischler, 1979; *Middle East and North Africa Yearbook, 1990*; *Syrian Statistical Yearbook, 1991*

abundant regions to transfer to its dry and thirsty regions. Moreover, there is evidence of a growing shortage of water for drinking and for industry in the big cities, principally in the Damascus basin. Because water is not yet transferred from region to region, it is possible to analyze the demand for water in the Yarmuk basin separately, but first we should consider the country in its entirety.

By the end of the 1980s Syria had a water shortage of 1 billion m³, and the state desperately needed additional water (*al Hayat*, July 1990). As for the future, demand in the whole state will be 11–15 billion m³ in 2025 (Rogers and Lydon, 1994: 306; Israel, *Development Options*, 1996). To solve the water shortage problem, Syria will be obliged to cut back its irrigation plans in the Euphrates region. Theoretically, a revolution in Syria's water policies is possible, allocating more water to industry and private use at the expense of irrigation, but this is unlikely in the near future (Kanovsky, 1985a; Syria, 1988).

In the southern part of the state, near the Golan Heights and the Yarmuk basin, there are, according to one estimate, about 43,488 hectares of arable land (Saliba, 1968). To irrigate all this area, 350–400 million m³ of water are needed (according to 10,000 m³ per hectare). In 1996 Syria used 200 million m³ of Yarmuk water for irrigating this area, which is the carrying capacity of the existing dams today in the region. Of the 34,000 hectares of cultivated land in the southern region (irrigated land and grazing, according to Syrian data), there is a plan to irrigate 10,000 hectares in the Dar'a, Abta, Sheikh Maskin, and Tafas regions. These are only some of the settlements that will receive water for irrigation according to the development plan, so exploitation of the water will grow even more intense when it is implemented (*al Ba'ath*, May 9, 1988).

To summarize: In 1996 about 800 million m³ of water were utilized in the Damascus basin and in southern Syria, serving a population of

4.5 million. If this population should double in 20 years it will be 9 million in 2015. This population will consume about 0.5 billion m³ of water in domestic use (calculating 50–60 m³ annual per capita consumption); industry will require about 100 million m³; agriculture, even if it remains at its present scale, will need a further half billion m³ (200 million m³ for the lands of southern Syria and 300 million m³ for the Damascus basin). Thus, water consumption will reach 1.1 billion m³ in 2015.

### Supply of Water in the Jordanian Kingdom

A desert or semiarid climate prevails over most of the territory of the Jordanian kingdom. The country cannot rely on a supply of water from rainfall and it depends on surface water and groundwater. The water potential of the kingdom is indeterminate, as there is uncertainty regarding the future of the Yarmuk as well as unclear information on the volume of desert groundwater in the state.

Previous data maintain that the Yarmuk contributes about 400 million m³ water to the kingdom. In reality, it is able to obtain only about 160 million m³ from the Yarmuk. Until 1993 Jordan's water potential was estimated at 0.8–1.2 billion m³, and some assessed it even at 1.4–1.7 billion m³ (Kally, 1986; Gischler, 1979: 10; Canaan, 1990; *Jordan Times*, 1991; Shatanawi and al Jayousi, 1995: 89; Israel, *Development Options*, 1996).

Publications from 1995 (Table 4.3) estimate the Kingdom's water potential at 1.0 billion m³: 55 percent are groundwater, 40 percent surface water, and 5 percent recycled water. In 1995 the main effort of the Jordanian government was directed at pumping groundwater, including fossil water, and transferring it to the towns, especially Amman. In the two years between 1990 and 1992 the quantity of groundwater pumped increased by 200 million m³ (Shatanawi and al Jayousi, 1995:90; Rozental, Feb. 15, 1995).

Another problem in Jordan is water quality. Because much water is taken for domestic use in the cities, which are rapidly expanding, Jordan's situation with regard to drinking water is not improving. There are several paths that Jordan could follow to increase its water potential. One of these would be to add dams on the eastern tributaries and elevate the existing dams to trap floodwater in the eastern basin of the Jordan (this project was under construction in 1996). Another is repair of leaking pipes, which according to one estimate account for the loss of 44–50 percent of the water in Amman (*al Rai*, Jan. 8, 1990). Irrigation could be economized through the introduction of sprinklers and other advanced means. The problem in not merely a technical matter of intro-

**Table 4.3:  Jordan: Water Potential, Supply, and Demand**

| | Yarmuk | Eastern Tributaries of Jordan River | Groundwater Renewable | Groundwater Fossil | Recycled Water | Total |
|---|---|---|---|---|---|---|
| Potential (1990) | 400 | 207 | 271 | 560 | 45 | 1483 |
| Supply | | | | | | |
| 1990 | 130 | 170 | 190 | 210 | 30 | 730 |
| 1993 | 160 | 241 | 534 | | 48 | 983 |

| Years/Demand | Agriculture | Domestic | Industry | Total |
|---|---|---|---|---|
| 1975 | 375 | 40 | 20 | 435 |
| 1985 | 400 | 150 | 30 | 580 |
| 1990 | 920 | 175 | 35 | 790 |
| 1995 | 889 | 224 | 49 | 1162 |
| 2000 | 1051 | 315 | 63 | 1429 |
| 2005 | 1224 | 398 | 80 | 1702 |
| 2010 | 1419 | 497 | 100 | 2016 |
| 2020 | 1879 | 705 | 150 | 2734 |

| Years/Deficit | |
|---|---|
| 1990[a] | -60 |
| 1995[b] | -179 |
| 2000[c] | -446 |
| 2005[c] | -719 |
| 2010[c] | -1033 |
| 2020[c] | -1751 |

*Sources:*  For supply 1990 and demand 1975-1990: Chezawi 1992; Canaan 1990; Sut al Sha'ab 6.6.89; *al Rai* 8.1.90. For 1995-2020: Shatanawi and al Jayousi 1995: 90; Rozental Mar. 15, 1995 (conference)

[a] Demand minus supply, 1990.
[b] Demand minus supply, 1995, without recycled water.
[c] Demand minus supply.

ducing modern systems, nor is it educational. It seems that in the Jordan valley, modern irrigation means are available to the farmer, but he prefers flood irrigation. In addition, it is estimated that with a reasonable effort at recycling water, which is underdeveloped in the kingdom, Jordan could completely reuse about a quarter of its irrigation water by the end of the 1990s. This issue too involves a psychological obstacle: the people of the region are unwilling to use recycled water. Amending the faulty water pricing policies would also force the population to save water. The Jordanian government is now beginning to grasp the need to adopt water-saving policies and to take steps to increase its water potential. The peace with Israel will increase the potential to some extent, but will not alleviate the gap between supply and demand in the near future. Therefore, the steps listed above are vital.

### Demand for Water in the Jordanian Kingdom

The land suitable for irrigation in the whole country is estimated at 125,000 hectares (Saliba, 1968: 43; Cressy, 1960: 462). Irrigated territories are being expanded at the rate indicated in Table 4.4.

In 1972 only 4.6 percent of agricultural lands in Jordan were irrigated. By comparison, in Israel 41 percent of the agricultural lands are irrigated and in Syria 7.6 percent are irrigated (Naff and Matson, 1984: 28). The greatest potential for irrigation is on land in the eastern Jordan valley, where the irrigable territory is estimated at 36,000 hectares (Shatanawi and al Jayousi, 1995: 92). But 700 million m³ of water are needed for this purpose, and it is unlikely that so much will be found in Jordan.

The irrigated land in Jordan is watered by the Ghor Canal (Abdullah Canal) and the tributaries of the eastern basin. Some land is irrigated by

**Table 4.4: Irrigated Land and Water Demand in Jordan (Various Years)**

| Year | Irrigated Land (thousand hectares) | Water Demand (million m³) |
|------|------------------------------------|---------------------------|
| 1957 | 32.5 | 250 |
| 1965 | 33.0 | 258 |
| 1975 | 36.0 | 375 |
| 1985 | 38.0 | 400 |
| 1991 | 62.5 | 642 |
| 2005 | 70.0 | 1224 |

*Sources:* 1957—Cresey, 1960: 463; 1965—Beaumont 1985: 5–6; 1975—Kalley, 1986: 26; 1985—Kalley, 1986: 32; 1991—Shatanawi and Al Jayousi; 1995; 2005—Israel, *Development Options,* 1996.

wells or directly from the Jordan River (Naff and Matson, 1984: 51; *Jordan Times*, 1991). On the plateaus of Jordan, about 33,000 hectares are irrigated by groundwater (Shatanawi and al Jayousi, 1995).

The principal water shortage in Jordan is felt today in domestic consumption, primarily in Amman, where domestic consumption has steadily grown since the 1970s (Table 4.3).

At the beginning of the 1990s Jordan already suffered a drinking water shortage at a rate of about 50 million m³ (*al Rai*, Jan. 8, 1990). Greater Amman consumed about 39 million m³ of water in 1989, and 80 million m³ in 1995. In Amman there will be a need for 100 million m³ of water in 2000. The water used for domestic consumption in Amman at the beginning of the 1990s was fossil water originating in the underground drainage basins in al Azraq in the eastern desert, and it is obvious that it will not be possible to continue using them forever. According to plans Amman will receive 12–14 million m³ of water from the Talal Dam and more water from the Ghor Canal in the future, and also from Israel (Murakami, 1995; Allan, 1996b).

Jordanian industry consumed about 35 million m³ of water in 1975 and a similar volume in 1990 (Gischler, 1979: 102; Adams and Holt, 1985; *Jordan Times*, Feb. 7, 1991). According to forecasts, industrial consumption in 2005 will reach 79 million m³ (*Sawt al Sha'b*, June 6, 1989; *Jordan Times*, Feb. 7, 1991; Shatanawi and al Jayousi, 1995).

In 1990 demand for water in Jordan already exceeded supply: demand was 994 million m³, and supply was 730 million m³, that is, a shortfall of about 264 million m³ (Table 4.3). Toward 2005, a shortage of 380 million m³ is expected, which will be partly offset by fossil water. While supply will then be about 0.9–1.1 billion m³, including recycled water, demand will reach 1.4–1.6 billion m³ or more (Shatanawi and al Jayousi, 1995; Israel, *Development Options*, 1996).

The outlook for more distant years, for example 2020, speaks of the need for 2.7 billion m³. The potential will then stand at 1.3 billion m³ (including recycled water). There will therefore be a deficit of 1.4 billion m³ of water.

### Supply and Demand of Water: Israel

Israel is located partly in a region of arid and semiarid climate, and partly in a region of Mediterranean climate. However, even in the region of the Mediterranean climate, irrigation is necessary most of the months of the year. Eighty percent of Israel's water sources are located north of Tel Aviv, but only 30 percent of the potential agricultural land is located there.

Israel's actual water potential is much lower than previously estimated (Table 4.5). Basically, it is only about 1.6 billion m³ (excluding recycled sewage water and saline water); in practice, however, Israel each year uses 200–300 million m³ more than the supply and thus creates a growing water deficit. This overexploitation of water has serious implications for the future quantity and quality of water in Israel.

About 60 percent of the groundwater in Israel originates outside the 1967 borders, namely, in Lebanon, the Golan Heights, the Yarmuk, and the Judean and Samarian hills (West Bank). The highland aquifer in the Judean and Samarian hills alone provides 40 percent of Israel's total water potential, not counting recycled water and floodwater (Table 4.5), and this is of great geopolitical significance.

The Jordan River plays a large role in Israel's water potential. The Kinneret basin provided one-third of Israel's water supply. This water is located in an area from 685 feet below sea level to 697 feet below sea level. This sector contains 590–615 million m³ of water. About 400–440 million m³ are pumped into the National Water Carrier, and 87 million m³ are exploited around the Kinneret, 20 million m³ to the salty water carrier and about 26–60 million m³ as overspill (Kally, 1978; Schwartz, 1986; Geffen, 1987). Since its foundation, Israel has adopted a water policy that prefers present development at the expense of the future, and it has thereby brought the water situation almost to bankruptcy.

In 1947 Israel's water consumption was 240 million m³. By 1975 it had risen to 1.730 billion m³, and from then until 1993 the demand for water was stable at 1.793 billion m³. If to this, we add recycled water, we reach the figure of 1.950 billion m³. In 1994 the demand was for 1.857 billion m³, of which 1.18 billion m³ was for agricultural use, and 132 million m³ (7 percent) was for industry (Israel, Water Commissioner, 1995).

Total agricultural land in Israel was estimated at 500,000 hectares, including 240,000 irrigated hectares (41 percent) in 1988. It seems likely that in the coming years this figure will not grow, but will shrink. It will be necessary to cut the amount of water per hectare, which today stands at 6,000 m³ on average. The annual domestic consumption per person in Israel is 70–100 m³ of water. This is more or less the basis for calculating consumption until 2010. In recent decades, demand has exceeded supply by 200–300 million m³ per year (Gvirtzman, 1990: 16; Israel, State Comptroller, 1990: 33). In light of the limited supply and the growing deficit, there is no way to avoid planning demand for the year 2010 to match supply. The forecast demand for 2000–2010 can be found in Table 4.6. This table shows that water consumption by agriculture will undergo significant reductions, both in total and freshwater consumption. Agriculture will receive partial compensation from recy-

Table 4.5: Israel's Water Potential

| Sources | Fresh[a] | Salty[a] | Total[a] | Total[b] | Total[c] | Total[d] |
|---|---|---|---|---|---|---|
| Groundwater | 850 | 232 | 1082 | 1389 | 1149 | 980 |
| Coastal aquifer | 240-283 | | | 395 | 245 | |
| Local aquifer (Carmel, Galilee) | 237 | | | 168 | 237 | |
| Western aquifer | 330 | | | 382 | 360 | |
| Northern aquifer | | | | | 140 | |
| Eastern aquifer | | | | 377 | 100 | |
| Negev and Arava | | | | 67 | 67 | |
| Surface Water | | | | | | 240 salty |
| Utilization in Hula Valley | 122 | | | | | |
| Available from Sea of Galilee | 490 | | | | | |
| Salty Canal | -20 | 20 | | | | |
| Overspill from Sea of Galilee | | | | | | |
| Total of Sea of Galilee Basin | 592 | 20 | 612 | 503 | 600 | 580 |
| Flood Use | 160 | | 160 | | 160 | 145 |
| Reclaimed Sewage | 241 | | 241 | | 114 | 430 |
| Total Water Potential | 1843 | 252 | 2095 | 1892 | 2023 | 2375 |

[a] Israel State Comptroller's Report 1991; Schwartz 1986; Gvirtzman 1990.
[b] Water Commissioner 1994.
[c] Author Calculations, based on Gvirtzman 1993, Water Commissioner 1994.
[d] Tahal to year 2010.

Table 4.6: Water Demand in Israel (1985-2010) (million m³)

| Sector | 1985 | | | 1990 | | | 2000 | | | 2010 | | |
|---|---|---|---|---|---|---|---|---|---|---|---|---|
| | FW | RW | T | FW | RW | T | FW | RW | T | FW | RW | T |
| Agriculture | 1200 | 210 | 1410 | 860 | 380 | 1240 | 820 | 430 | 1250 | 550 | 767 | 1317 |
| Domestic | 420 | - | 420 | 650 | - | 650 | 768 | - | 768 | 970 | - | 970 |
| Industry | 80 | 30 | 110 | [a] | 40 | 40 | 100 | 45 | 145 | 131 | 50 | 181 |
| Total | 1700 | 240 | 1940 | 1510 | 420 | 1930 | 1678 | 476 | 2153 | 1651 | 817 | 2468 |

Source: Israel, State Comptroller, 1991: 46; Israel, Water Commissioner, 1994
Note: FW: fresh water; RW: reclaimed water; T: total
[a] Within domestic use

cled water (sewage and floods). This is about 30 percent of the total potential in 2010. The demand by industry and by domestic consumption will increase. Only sweet water can be used for domestic consumption, and this addition can only be achieved through saving on water consumption by agriculture. Industry can also use recycled water so the addition of water for industry will be chiefly through this means. Between 1985 and 2010 the demand for water in Israel will change only slightly (see Tables 4.5 and 4.6). Israeli water policy intends to direct efforts primarily to recycling sewage water. The amount recycled will constantly rise, and by 2010 will reach about 250 million m$^3$ (in addition to the use of salty water). From 2010 on, the gap between demand and supply will widen continuously, and will have be bridged by desalination. In 2010 it will be necessary to desalinate 80–100 million m$^3$, and thereafter the amounts of desalinated water will continue to increase (Israel, Water Commissioner, 1994).

These calculations are based on the assumption that there will be no transfer of water from the Israeli water regime to the water regimes of neighboring countries. If this assumption proves unfounded it will be necessary to increase the quantities of desalinated water and to alter the above timetable.

Several ways are open for Israel to increase its supply. One of these is to direct excess water to flow into the aquifers. In recent years excess water has been streamed from the Kinneret and from floodwater to the coastal plain aquifer to increase the subterranean reservoir in this sensitive region. In this way, evaporation and brackish water penetration of the aquifer are prevented. From 1983 to 1988, 221–245 million m$^3$ of water were introduced into the coastal aquifer and 150–200 million m$^3$ into the highland aquifer annually. This is a large quantity in itself, but because these two aquifers had a deficit of about 1.6 billion m$^3$ of water due to overpumping, some scientists estimate that 80 percent of the wells in the coastal plain will be closed in the future (*Biosphera*, August 1989; Gvirtzman, 1990). Another way is to divide Israel's water system into two separate systems, one to supply drinking water only and one to supply recycled water from sewage or floods to agriculture and industry. A third course is to use salty water for agriculture. This would require growing crops that could withstand salinity above 400 mg of chlorine per liter.

In addition, water could be saved by a cutback on agriculture and the adoption of measures to reform its structure, for example, by reducing water-thirsty crops (avocado, banana, mango, cotton) and increasing water-saving crops, such as greenhouse crops. Water-pricing policies too would result in savings. At the end of the 1980s only the domestic sector was paying the full cost of water, the equivalent of 53 cents per cubic meter, while the agricultural sector paid only 13 cents; such a low price obviously leads to untold water wastage. Raising water prices would cause a more rational and careful use of water. But this will not be easy to implement, both because agriculture in Israel has symbolic significance as one of the central values of Zionism, and also because the branch has a very strong lobby in the Knesset (Parliament). Because of the water crisis, Israel must change its attitude to agriculture, its "sacred cow." Israeli agriculture has been the proverbial "jewel in the crown" and has enjoyed many achievements; however, Israel is drawing the rope too tightly by using its water to the extreme limit, and the state must ease the tension lest the rope snap.

As for recycling sewage water, this important measure has not yet been exhausted. Until the end of the 1960s, all sewage emptied into the sea from canals or rivers. This water, which was not only unused, in fact polluted the coasts on the Mediterranean, including the bathing beaches of Tel Aviv and Haifa, and still worse it polluted the coastal aquifer. Since the 1960s sewage water has been used, but this source has not yet been fully exploited. In 1996 the sewage water supply was about 300 million $m^3$, but only 200 million $m^3$ were being used. In other words, Israel has an unused potential of 100 million $m^3$ of sewage water (Schwartz, lecture, Nov. 5, 1996). In 1989, 14,000 hectares were irrigated with 144 million $m^3$ of recycled sewage water, and the rest of the recycled sewage water was directed into the coastal reservoir.The construction of purification plants is planned for near the year 2000. These will purify about 350 million $m^3$ of sewage water, equal to about 17 percent of the total projected water supply of Israel in 2000 (Israel, State Comptroller, 1990: 20).

Desalination, is yet another measure. At the end of the 1980s, the cost of desalinated water in Israel was 60–150 cents per cubic meter. This is a high price, which Israeli agriculture cannot afford. Therefore, water in Israel is desalinated only in Eilat, where it is an important water source. Some other small plants desalinate saline water in the Negev. The desalination solution is thus not suitable for conventional agriculture, but it can be applied for domestic and industrial use, and perhaps even for greenhouses, principally in the south of Israel: the cost of transferring water from the north is high and the price of desalinated water will approach and perhaps even match that of ordinary water there. As stated, in 2010 or even sooner Israel will enter the age of full-scale desalination (for desalination, see Chapter 8).

Israel may increase its supply by trapping floodwater. The volume of floodwater in Israel is estimated at about 160 million $m^3$, but in 1990 only about 40 million $m^3$ was trapped in about 120 reservoirs built for this purpose throughout the country. The total capacity of these reservoirs is about 100 million m³. If Israel fills them, it will fully exhaust the possibilities of this source (Shamir et al, 1985: 16; Schwartz, 1986; Israel, State Comptroller, 1990). And lastly, there is importing of water. In recent years the concept of importing water from neighboring countries with surplus water, such as Turkey and the former Yugoslavia, has arisen. For economic and geopolitical considerations, the idea was rejected (see Chapter 8).

### The Gaza Strip Supply

The Gaza Strip has a semiarid climate (annual rainfall is between 7.87 inches in the south and 15.75 inches in the north). The region is poor in resources and in water. The area of the strip is small (139 square miles) and densely populated. In 1996 about 900,000 people lived there, at a density of over 6,475 people per square mile (compared with 531 people per square mile in Israel). The sole water source in the Gaza Strip is groundwater. This is located in a sandy aquifer at a depth of only 33–49.2 feet, and its storage capacity is 45–60 million m³ (Table 4.7). For more than 30 years overpumping of the groundwater has taken place, and its level falls 5.9–7.9 inches each year. This situation has caused the seepage of seawater into the aquifer and a 60-percent salination of the water sources. Today the saltiness of the water is 400 mg of chlorine per liter, and in certain places it is as high as 1,500 mg chlorine per liter (Kahan, 1987:3; Assaf et al., 1993).

### The West Bank Supply

The area of the West Bank is 2,239 square miles, and it is populated by 1.25 million Arabs and about 150,000 Jews (1998). This does not include the inhabitants of Jerusalem (430,000 Jews and 180,000 Arabs) (1998). It is forecast that in 2000 the population of this area will be 2.5 million (Jews and Arabs, including the Jerusalem corridor). In 1967 the water potential of the West Bank was estimated at about 400 million m³. In the mid-1980s it was assessed at 600–650 million m³ (Schwartz, 1988; Assaf et al., 1993). In the mid-1990s it was determined that it is possible to pump more from the eastern aquifer, so the estimate of the water potential of the West Bank has risen (Gvirtzman, 1993, 1995) (Table 4.7).

### Gaza Strip Demand

Of the 120 million m³ pumped from groundwater in Gaza, 88 million m³ are allocated for agriculture and 32 million m³ for domestic and in-

**Table 4.7: Water Supply and Demand in the Gaza Strip and West Bank (in million m³)**

|  | 1995[a] | 2000[a] | 2008[b] Palestinian Demands | 2008[b] Minimum Requirement |
|---|---|---|---|---|
| *Gaza Strip* | | | | |
| Supply | 45–60 | 35–50 | | |
| Demand | 110–120 | 190–200 | | |
| Agriculture | 80–88 | 150 | | |
| Domestic | 30–32 | 40–50 | | |
| Jews | 3.4–4 | | | |
| *West Bank* | | | | |
| Supply | 610–670 | 610–670 | 610–670 | 610–670 |
| To Israel | 455 | 310–360 | 110–160 | 135–195 |
| Demands in West Bank | 200 | 250–300 | 500 | 475 |
| Arabs | 145 | 200–250 | 500 | 475 |
| Agriculture | 105 | | | |
| Domestic | 15 | | | |
| From Israel | 25 | | | |
| Jews | 55 | 50 | | |
| Agriculture | 40 | | | |
| Domestic | 10 | | | |
| From Israel | 5 | | | |

*Sources:* Assaf et al. 1993; Gvirtzman 1993, 1995; Israel, Civil Administration 1993, 1996.
[a] Normal situation
[b] These figures take into account expected Palestinian water needs.

dustrial use. There is no supervision of pumping in Gaza, nor are there water budgets, and anyone can dig a well and irrigate his field. In 1996 there were about 2,300 wells in Gaza, and the agricultural land, including irrigated land, was about 11,000 hectares (68.54 percent irrigated) (Benvenisti, 1987; Benvenisti and Khayat, 1988; Israel, Civil Administration, 1993).

This land included 4,200 hectares of vegetables and strawberries, which consume 34 million m³ of water annually (8,000 m³ for a hectare of vegetables); 5,800 hectares of oranges, which consume 49 million m³ of water (about 8,500 m³ per hectare); and 1,000 hectares of other fruit, which consume 3 million m³ of water (3,000 m³ for a hectare of olives and almonds). These figures illustrate the irresponsibility not only of indiscriminate pumping, but also of choosing water-thirsty crops that are completely unsuited to the poor, semiarid region of Gaza Strip. Since 1967, 17 Jewish settlements have been founded in the Gaza Strip. Their water consumption amounts to 3.3–4 million m$^3$ annually, which they receive from within Israel and from some local wells (Assaf et al., 1993; Israel, Civil Administration, 1993).

According to forecasts, by 2000 the demand for water in Gaza will rise to 200 million m$^3$ (Kally, 1986: 75; Israel, Civil Administration 1993), including 42–50 million m$^3$ required for domestic use (Table 4.7). If Israel adopts the principle that each person in Israel and Gaza should receive the same domestic quota (100 m$^3$ per person annually), the water demand in Gaza will reach 100 million m$^3$.

However, even now some of the drinking water is tainted. The water problem in the Gaza Strip can only grow worse. The solution is the establishment of desalination plants for domestic and industrial water consumption. At the first stage the plan is to desalinate 10 million m$^3$ at five locations at a cost of $320 million. In addition, work is being readied for recycling sewage; by 2000 it is hoped that 15 million m$^3$ will be recycled (Israel, *Development Options*, 1996). It should be noted that the Palestinians claim that the water of the West Bank belongs to them, and that water should be transferred from there to the Gaza Strip.

### West Bank Demand

For its coastal plain Israel uses water from the highland aquifer situated in the West Bank. Hence, this water is of great importance in political considerations determining the final borders between states in the region.

Prior to 1967 the demand for water on the West Bank was small, reaching only 89–100 million m$^3$. Of this, 96 percent was for agriculture and 4 percent was for domestic use. There was hardly any industry in the region at that time (Kahan, 1987: 2). The small demand for water arose from the paucity of deep boreholes in the area and this fact was linked with the low technological, social, and economic level of the population then. The water that was not used flowed from the highland aquifer to the coastal plain, and from the beginning of the twentieth century it was used there by the Jewish settlements for intensive development of agriculture. The Jewish settlement, and subsequently the state of Israel, used the highland aquifer even before 1967 and in this sense the 1967 war did not cause any change.

In 1995 the West Bank consumed about 195 million m$^3$ of water, of which about 115 million m$^3$ was used by the Arab population and about 30 million m$^3$ by the Jewish population. The source of 165 million m$^3$

was in West Bank itself, while 30 million m³ of high-quality water were transferred there from Israel (for drinking, for both populations).

Out of the water potential of West Bank, estimated in 1997 at 670 million m³, 455 million m³ are used in Israel as was the case even before 1967 (Table 4.7). Water consumed by Jews and Arabs from the aquifers are according to the distribution in Table 4.8.

The lands of the eastern part of the West Bank are entirely desert, and its western part is hilly and terraced. Arable land therefore amounts to only 200,000 hectares (out of a total area of 0.58 million hectares in the West Bank). Of this area only about 10,000 hectares are irrigated (in Wadi Fara', the Jordan valley, and several additional places, mostly in valleys).

In reference to the data presented above, the Palestinians demand an increase of their water allocations so as to irrigate 20,000 hectares more and thus to be able to absorb half a million refugees. Two approaches are evident among the Palestinians in regard to their water claims. The maximalist approach puts forward a demand for most of the water potential of the West Bank and the Gaza Strip, namely 560 million m³ (Zarour and Isaac, 1991; El-Hindi, 1990). The minimalist approach accounts only for the needs of drinking, a small amount of industry, and small-scale home agriculture. Its calculations are based on the consumption of between 67–125 m³ per person annually (in various ways). According to this approach, in 1992 the Palestinian population required a total of 134 million m³ of water (by the first alternative) or 250 million m³ (by the second alternative).

Approximately this amount was indeed transferred to them. According to the forecast of population growth, in 2008 the Palestinian population, using the minimalist approach, will consume 380–475 million m³ (Assaf et al., 1993).

**Table 4.8: Water Consumed from the Aquifers of the West Bank (million m³)**

| Aquifer | For Jewish Population | For Palestinians | Total |
|---|---|---|---|
| Yarkon Taninim | 340 (to Israel) | 20 | 360 |
| Nablus-Jenin | 115 (to Israel) | 23 | 138 |
| Eastern Aquifer | 40 | 60–70 | 100–110 |
| Total | 490 | 103–113 | 598–608 |

*Sources:* Assaf et al. 1993; Gvirtzman 1993, 1995; Israel, Civil Administration 1993, 1996.

[a] Normal situation.

[b] These figures take into account expected Palestinian water needs.

## Summary of Supply and Demand in the Jordan Basin

If we compare the conventional water supply of the Jordan basin and the sources close to it with present demand figures and those forecast for the future (to 2010), a very grim picture indeed emerges (Table 4.9). Let us review the situation of each country separately, and then the overall picture.

Lebanon is the only state in the basin that possessed surplus water in 1995 and will enjoy a surplus for a term of 30 years more.

If the agriculture of southern Syria remains at its present levels there will be no problem of water in the region until 2015. But if agriculture expands, a shortage of water may be expected there as early as 2000. The situation may alter if recycled water is used or if water is imported by pipeline from Lebanon or northern Syria.

For many years Israeli water consumption has adapted itself to supply. From 2010 Israel will be obliged to complement the water it lacks by desalination (unconnected with the recycling of sewage water, a process that has already begun). In 2010 it will be necessary to desalinate about 80 million $m^3$ of water. The quantity of desalinated water will constantly increase, and will reach 1 billion $m^3$ in 2040. If the peace agreements cut into Israel's water, it will be necessary to advance the start of desalination.

In 1995 there was a gap of at least 30 million $m^3$ of water between demand and supply in the Gaza strip. The outlook for 2000 envisages a gap of 150–200 million $m^3$. The Gaza Strip is an extreme case, in which no solutions are possible except desalination. At the first stage salty water and sewage water will be desalinated. At the second state it will be necessary to desalinate sea water. The latter project will have to be implemented with international assistance as early as the end of the 1990s.

A strict policy of regulation enforcement by Israel did not allow free use of water in the West Bank. Therefore, there was no gap between demand and supply in 1995. In consequence of the signing of the intermediate agreement ("Oslo-2") between Israel and the Palestinian people, this situation will continue until the signing of the permanent accord. Regarding the more distant future, assuming that the amount of water available to the Palestinian people does not exceed 250–300 $m^3$, and on the basis of various professional Palestinian publications predicting future demands for water, in 2010 a shortage is envisaged at a level of 200–250 million $m^3$ of water.

For the Jordanian kingdom, the forecast for 2005 shows a gap of about 600 million $m^3$ of water between what is required and what exists. This gap will widen by 2010 up to 1.4 billion $m^3$.

Table 4.9: Exploitation of Jordan Rivers and Groundwater in 1994, compared with Johnston Plan and Future Use (million m3)

| Country | Sources | According to Johnston Plan | 1994 | Future Demand (≈ 2010) |
|---|---|---|---|---|
| Lebanon | Hashani | 35 | app. 5 | 5-10 |
| Syria | Yarmuk River | 90 | 200 | 215 |
| | Jordan River | 44 | | 44 |
| Jordan | Jordan River | 100 | app. 10 | |
| | Yarmuk River | 377 | 160 | ± 500 |
| | Western and Eastern Rim | 243 | 241 (Eastern) | |
| | Groundwater and other sources | | 582 | 1500 |
| Israel | Jordan River | 375-450 | 600 | 600 |
| | Yarmuk River | 25 | 25 | 25 |
| | Other sources | | 1470 | 1843 |
| Palestinians | Jordan River | - | ± 20 | 200 |
| | Other sources | - | 140[a] | ±400 |
| | Water to Dead Sea | - | ± 150 | |
| | Jordan Discharge | 1299-1374 | 1299-1374 | 1594 |
| | Other sources | | 2212 | 3473 |

[a] Includes in Israel 1994

From the above figures it may be calculated that in 2005–2010 the total gap between demand for and supply of water of all states of the Jordan basin will reach 1.5 billion m$^3$ (Table 4.9). Such a quantity of water cannot be saved. This gap will necessitate drastic solutions by all states involved. The international community may be mobilized also to assist in light of its desire for social and political quiet in this region of the world.

## Economics and Society in the Jordan Basin States

The countries sharing the Jordan basin differ. Israel is a developed state while the others are developing states (Table 4.10). The Palestinians are

**Table 4.10: Jordan-Yarmuk Basin Riparians' Socioeconomic Data**

|  | Population (million) | | Rate Growth (%) | GNP ($) | Agriculture as % of GNP |
|---|---|---|---|---|---|
|  | 1966 | 2010 | 1990–2000 | 1995 | 1995 |
| Syria | 15.0 | 23.5 | 3.6 | 1120 | 30 |
| Lebanon | 3.7 | 5.0 | — | 2660 | — |
| Israel | 5.5 | 6.9 | 1.5 | 15920 | 3 |
| Jordan | 4.1 | 6.2 | 3.8 | 1510 | 8 |
| Palestinians (West Bank and Gaza) | 2.1 | 3.5 | 3.5 | 1511(WB) 791(GS) | — |

|  | % Working in Agriculture 1993 | Grain Import (thousands of tons) | | | Index of Food Production per Person | | |
|---|---|---|---|---|---|---|---|
|  |  | 1974 | 1990 | 1995 | 1979–81 | 1982–84 | 1992–94 |
| Syria | 28.0 | 379 | 2091 | 734 | 100 | 101 | 88 |
| Lebanon | 11.0 | 354 | 354 | 830 | 100 | 113 | 192 |
| Israel | 3.5 | 1376[a] | 1802[a] | 2370[a] | 100 | 115 | 97 |
| Jordan | 7.6 | 171 | 1578 | 1258 | 100 | 107 | 127 |
| Palestinians (West Bank and Gaza) | — | — | — | — | — | — | — |

*Sources:* World Bank, World Tables, 1993; World Bank, World Development Report, 1994; World Resources Institute, 1995; 1997; FAO, 1996; World Bank Atlas, 1997.
   [a] Includes the Palestinians

now taking their first steps, in difficult initial circumstances. Table 4.10 presents the degree of dependence of these states on agriculture.

Syria is the most dependent on agriculture. This is evident in the number of people employed in agriculture and in its contribution to the gross national product. The dependence of Israel and Jordan on agriculture is less. Regarding Jordan, it should be noted that it depends on large imports of food, which increase in direct proportion to the increase in its population. Lebanon is seeking to rehabilitate itself after a war lasting twenty years, and at this stage data on it are unreliable. Can these states release themselves from their dependency on agriculture? Jordan has some mining, for example, for phosphates and potash, which are exported. But this is not enough to free Jordan from its dependency on agriculture. In the 1980s, the state received income as remittances from its citizens working in the Persian Gulf, but the Gulf War in 1991 adversely affected this source. If the water shortage in Jordan worsens, agriculture will be cut back, but because Jordan lacks other resources, its dependence on foreign aid will grow, or poverty and want will grow. Jordan has no alternative but to adhere strongly to agriculture.

Syria's economic situation is more sound than Jordan's. Syria's national debt is large, its monetary reserves are small, and its dependence on food imports is large and growing; but it has oil, gas, and mines. After the Gulf War Syria received aid from Kuwait, Saudi Arabia, and other countries. However, it is difficult to see how this state will break free of its heavy dependence on agriculture with its unskilled labor force, and its birthrate, which plays havoc with its economy.

Israel has a large, varied industrial sector, enjoys a great deal of foreign aid, and is therefore more flexible than Jordan and Syria in all water issues and can reduce its dependency on agriculture. But Israel's water shortage for agriculture and domestic use should not be underestimated; neither should its national debt, which requires it to fully exploit all its resources, including water, for its economic health. Moreover, despite decreased dependence on agriculture, it remains an important cornerstone of Zionist ideology and of the quality of life in a state so small and so industrialized.

Lebanon does not have natural resources, and the only way open to it to overcome the difficult crisis in which it is entangled is to base itself economically, once more, on the provision of international and regional services, such as banking, tourism, leisure, trade in gold and other items, as it did before the civil war (Soffer, 1992).

In all four states population growth is very rapid, and the growth in agricultural development is not keeping pace. Therefore, the dependency on food imports in these four states is large. In this regard, Jordan and Syria are also in more dire straits than Israel and Lebanon (Table

4.10). Yet all are nevertheless dependent on food imports, especially cereals. Most imports are from the United States; a large portion is food aid. The dependency of the riparians on the United States for fulfilling their cereal needs has grown so much that it represents a potential political weapon in American hands.

Meanwhile, the Palestinians are joining the participants in the Jordan basin. The Palestinians are a very poor population, living in difficult geographical circumstances, and relying to a great extent on traditional agriculture (in the West Bank) and on fruit growing (in the Gaza Strip). Many years will elapse before the population becomes free of its dependence on agriculture. For agriculture to exist water is needed, especially in the Gaza Strip. However, owing to the proximity of Israel, and owing to the capacity of Israel to supply employment, the Palestinians, in an era of peace, may undergo a rapid transition from work in agriculture to industry and services.

## Geopolitics in the Jordan Basin

### Introduction

In the foregoing sections I dealt with the map of the drainage basin, the course and discharge of the river, and the climate prevailing in the different regions of the basin. We gained an acquaintance with the countries located in the Jordan basin, and I mentioned the harsh and belligerent system of relations that existed between Israel and its neighbors for many years. I did not touch on the harsh system of relations existing among the Arab states themselves in general and in the Jordan drainage basin in particular. Nor have I addressed the lines of the international boundaries, which slice across the basin in a variety of directions, or the great interest that the river Jordan elicits in the Christian world for its religious associations. The meshing of all these factors makes the hydropolitics of the Jordan basin extremely complex compared with that of the basins of larger rivers. In the following sections I shall treat hydropolitical issues: old plans to exploit the river, projects already implemented and those earmarked for the future; how the states of the area, world powers and various international bodies are seeking a solution to the intricate situation of the Jordan river, yet supplying drinking water in quantities sufficient for the population of the area and promoting this population.

Many plans were drawn up for using the Jordan-Yarmuk waters. The seventeen most significant of these until the 1960s are listed below, including those that were implemented and those that were not but affected what was done afterwards. In the period prior to the establishment of the state of Israel (1948) eight important plans for water projects were proposed for the Jordan River. Almost all of them envisaged the erection of dams on the Yarmuk and the construction of one or two canals on either side of the Jordan valley for its irrigation. The plans, which treated the basin as an integral system, were rejected out of hand owing to the Israel–Arab conflict. Some of them gave precedence to the Arab side and some to the Israeli/Jewish side. Few plans were completely neutral. From the 1960s the countries put forward new plans, some of which were executed. In the 1990s, following the start of the peace negotiations between Israel and its neighbors, a new wave of plans was published, to which I shall devote a separate section.

### Plans and Projects for Exploiting Jordan Water from 1900 to the Early 1950s

*The Franjieh plan* (1913) was intended mainly for the irrigation of either side of the Jordan valley. In addition, twenty-one hydropower stations were planned. To implement the enterprise, a diversion of the Yarmuk to the Kinneret was proposed, including a western canal along the Jordan carrying about 100 million m³ (Kliot, 1994: 189).

Palestine's water sources aroused international attention, especially from the British, in the 1920s and 1930s. The question of water resources was linked to the general "carrying capacity" of Palestine, and therefore the British treated the issue as one of major political significance. The British determined how many inhabitants the land could absorb according to the volume of water in Palestine, and scarcity of water provided them with another pretext among many to limit the number of Jews in the country. This pretext was also a weapon in the hands of the Arab states in their opposition to *aliya* (Jewish immigration), and in essence this issue has still not been dropped from the regional and international agenda, even today.

*The Rutenberg plan* (1920) treated the entire Jordan basin as a single system. Rutenberg suggested utilizing the differences in altitudes between Mount Hermon and the Dead Sea. He fixed the locations for ten reservoirs and thirteen hydroelectric power stations, with a productive capacity of 413 horsepower. He likewise proposed the irrigation of 0.28 million hectares of land on both sides of the river (Rutenberg, 1920).

Rutenberg's plan was not realized: the British turned it down, principally because it required French–British cooperation in the Jordan basin. It is noteworthy that the Jordanian Ghor Canal that was "born" 40 years later exactly matches the canal proposed by Rutenberg for construction east of the Jordan River. In 1926 Rutenberg put forward an additional plan: to produce electricity at the junction of the Yarmuk and Jordan Rivers. This plan he succeeded in implementing. The power station he established operated between 1932 and 1948, and supplied 173 kilowatt hours (kwh) of electricity. In 1948, during the Israeli War of Independence, the power station was destroyed by the Jordanians (Ben Aryeh, 1965; Kliot, 1994: 189; Wolf, 1995).

*Mavromatis* (1922) produced a multipurpose plan for the whole of Palestine, for irrigation of the Hula valley and both sides of the Jordan valley. In addition, power plants on the Yarmuk and Jordan Rivers were envisaged. To execute the plan a diversion of the Yarmuk to the Kinneret was proposed, including two canals along the valley. This plan was never realized.

*The Henrich plan* (1928) was intended to irrigate about 3,000 hectares in the mouth of the Yarmuk on the east bank of the Jordan. This plan was not implemented.

*The Ionides plan* (1939) was meant to irrigate about 20,000 hectares in the Jordan valley and 10,500 hectares in the Hula valley. Its implementation called for the diversion of the Yarmuk into two canals along the Jordan valley. The plan was never realized.

*The Lowdermilk plan* (1944) proposed integrated development of the Jordan-Yarmuk basin. The Jordan and the Yarmuk would be diverted into canals and pipelines to irrigate about 0.12 million hectares along the Jordan valley, and into one pipeline to irrigate the Mediterranean coast. Hydropower plants were proposed by diversion of Mediterranean seawater to the Jordan valley and the Dead Sea, with the aim of producing a total of 1 billion kwh. The background to this multipurpose plan was to settle about four million Jews in Palestine, in addition to 1.8 million Arabs. The plan, which was fundamentally based in ideology rather than engineering, exerted an extremely powerful influence on the future plans drawn up by the Jews that led to the laying of the National Water Carrier (Lowdermilk, 1944; Jerusalem Media and Communication Centre, 1994: 30; Kliot, 1994: 200; Reguer, 1995).

*The Blass plan* (1944) was an extension of the Lowdermilk plan, including the construction of reservoirs on the Yarmuk (Kliot 1994: 201).

### Plans and Initiatives to Use Jordan Water from 1950 to 1955

The establishment of the state of Israel and the kingdom of Jordan and the creation of the refugee problem in 1948 in the Jordan valley were the driving forces behind the intensive planning for utilization of Jordan water. The Arabs proposed about five plans, some of them entirely ignoring the existence of the state of Israel (Kliot, 1994: 189–197). The overall Arab plan mentions Israel, but allots it only 182 million m³ of water. Other plans, for example, the Macdonald plan and the Main-Clap plan, were integrated programs, based on a broad regional outlook.

*The Main-Clap plan* served later as a basis for the work of Johnston (Main, 1953; Wolf, 1995). In this period Israel proposed three plans, which were various elaborations on the Lowdermilk plan adapted to the altered geopolitical circumstances. The Johnston plan was also drawn up at this time. This plan (or more accurately the Johnston II plan) determined to a far greater extent the development of sources of the Jordan that took place in later years, and it was also the plan that formed the foundation for the water discussions between Israel and its neighbors (Biswas, 1994).

*The Hays-Savage plan* (1948) attempted to implement the Lowdermilk plan. It envisaged diversion of Jordan water to the Negev and diversion of Mediterranean water to the Dead Sea. The Bet Netufa valley would serve as a national reservoir. There would be a hydropower plant on the Hasbani, and diversion of the Yarmuk to the Kinneret. In all, the plan would supply 2 billion m³ for the irrigation of 0.24 million hectares and the production of 165,000 kwh. Fifty percent of the Yarmuk water was to be allocated to Jordan, and the remaining 50 percent and all the Jordan water to Israel.

*The Israeli plan* (1951) was a compromise based on the Lowdermilk and the Blass plans. It called for drainage of the Hula swamps, irrigation of the Negev, and a tunnel from the Mediterranean to the Dead Sea for hydropower.

*The Macdonald plan* (1951) was based on Israeli-Jordanian cooperation. The Kinneret would be used for joint storage, and there would be canals on both sides of the Jordan valley. The project would irrigate 65,000 hectares along the valley.

*The Bunger plan* (1951) was for Jordan and Syria, ignoring Israeli rights as a riparian. The plan proposed the construction of a high dam at Maqarin on the Yarmuk with a storage capacity of 480 million m³. Another small dam was proposed for Addassiya on the east side of the Jordan valley. The implementation of the plan would provide 43,500 irrigated hectares of land in Jordan and about 6,000 irrigated hectares in Syria.

*The Main-Clap (unified) plan* (1953) was an integrated multipurpose plan that ignored the political boundaries. It proposed a dam on the Hasbani for both hydropower and irrigation; dams on the Dan and Banias to irrigate the Galilee; draining the Hula swamps; dams on the Yarmuk River (at Maqarin and Addassiya); and elevating the Deganya Dam at the outlet of the Kinneret to increase the lake's storage capacity. The total use of water was to be 1.213 billion m³, which would allow irrigation of 41,000 hectares in Israel, 49,000 hectares in Jordan, and 3,000 hectares in Syria.

*The Arab plan* (1954). This was meant to irrigate the Jordanian part of the Jordan valley by building the Maqarin and Addassiyah Dams and the Ghor Canals on both the east and the west sides of the valley. There would be a dam on the Hasbani for irrigation in Lebanon, and canals from the Banias for irrigation in Syria. The total water available would be 1.396 billion $m^3$, about 20 percent of it for Israel's use and about 80 percent for the Arabs.

*The Israeli plan* (Cotton, 1954). This was a multipurpose project including the Kinneret as the national water reservoir; a canal would be cut from the Kinneret to the south of the country via Bet Netufa reservoirs. The Litani would be used for electricity and irrigation. The total water available would be 2.354 billion $m^3$, of which 45 percent would be for Syria, Lebanon, and Jordan, and 55 percent for Israel. Irrigation for 0.26 million hectares would be available. (Israel would use about 1.2 billion $m^3$ and would irrigate about 79,000 hectares.)

*The Baker-Harza plan* (1955). This was a Jordanian plan for irrigation and electricity. It envisaged the construction of the Maqarin Dam, storage of surplus water from the Yarmuk in the Kinneret, and canals on both sides of the Jordan valley (within the Jordanian kingdom only).

(The sources for the water projects and plans from 1950–1995 are Ionides, 1953; Doherty, 1965; Kally, 1965; Stevens, 1965; Nimrod, 1966; Blass, 1973; Khourie, 1981; Naff and Matson, 1984; Lowi 1993: 90–92; Kliot, 1994.)

### The Johnston Plan

After several incidents between Israel and Syria over the draining of the Hula swamps and the diversion of the National Water Carrier from the area of the Benot Ya'akov bridge to within Israel, U.S. President Eisenhower sent Eric Johnston to the region in search of an acceptable solution for the division of Jordan water between Israel and the Arabs. Johnston came to the Middle East as an emissary of the president with the rank of ambassador. He held a series of talks with professionals in Israel, Syria, Lebanon, and Jordan, and later, in 1953, he presented Eisenhower with the first version of his proposal. It was based largely on Main's plan of 1953. It underwent some changes, and in 1955 the final version was placed before the president. Israel and Jordan each separately announced agreement with the plan (Nimrod, 1966; Lowi, 1993: 79–114; Reguer, 1993; Drezon-Tepler, 1994; Kliot, 1994).

The Johnston plan received de facto recognition from the United States, which had initiated it, and from Israel and Jordan, which saw it as a basis for water distribution between them. Subsequently, the Americans helped each of them implement separate water plans in the spirit of the agreement. Syria and Lebanon, on the other hand, never considered themselves committed to the plan. It received recognition by water experts in all the Arab countries, but never won official ratification because of the Arab states' refusal to recognize Israel (Saliba, 1968: 75).

These are the main points of the Johnston plan: A dam would be built in the upper sector of the Yarmuk, at Marqarin, to trap 400 million m$^3$ of water for irrigating the Jordan valley. A diversion dam (barrage) would be at the confluence of the Yarmuk and Jordan Rivers, near the village of Addassiya in the eastern Jordan valley. This dam would divert Yarmuk water into the Jordanian Ghor Canal. The Kinneret would be a reservoir for the Jordan River and for the floodwater from the Yarmuk, which would be diverted to it, and would provide Israel and the Jordanian kingdom with water. A connecting canal would link the Kinneret and the Ghor Canal, transferring 100 billion m$^3$ of water to the Jordanian kingdom, including 85 million m$^3$ of fresh water and 15 million m$^3$ of salt water (55 million m$^3$ would be transferred in the summer season). A canal connecting the Yarmuk and the Jewish "settlement triangle" in the Jordan valley was to be built. The canal would carry 25 million m$^3$ of water in the summer, and in the winter Israel could use all the Yarmuk water that the Jordanian kingdom and Syria would not use. A siphon for transferring the Ghor Canal water to the western Jordan valley would be built.

The second part of the plan was for distribution of Jordan water among the riparians. Lebanon would receive 35 million m$^3$ of water, and Syria would receive 132 million m$^3$ including 90 million m$^3$ from the Yarmuk, 22 million m$^3$ from the Banias to irrigate the Golan Heights, and 20 million m$^3$ from the Kinneret to irrigate the Bataykha valley. Jordan would receive 720 million m$^3$ of water, including 100 million m$^3$ from the Jordan River (from the Kinneret), 377 million m$^3$ from the Yarmuk, and 243 million m$^3$ from the eastern and western Jordan tributaries.

Israel would receive 400 million m$^3$ of water, including 375 million m$^3$ from the Jordan and 25 million m$^3$ from the Yarmuk.

Altogether, 1.287 billion m$^3$ of Jordan and Yarmuk water were to be divided as shown in Table 4.9.

Some specialists dispute the figures in Table 4.9 claiming that Israel was allocated more water, about 466 million m$^3$, which is 37 percent of the total amount of water (Stevens, 1965: 15; Naff and Matson, 1984). There are two versions of the grounds for the disagreement. One blames the plan itself, which provided for Israel to use all the water that remained after Syria, Jordan, and Lebanon (in that order) had used theirs. Because the total discharge of the drainage basin was subject to fluctuations, disagreements arose as the amount of water that Israel would be authorized to use. The second version holds that after Johnston concluded the water distribution, he accepted an argument made by the director of the Israeli Mekorot water company, Simha Blass, at the beginning of 1956. Blass explained to Johnston that the amount of water allocated to Israel should be increased by 60 million m³ of water, which Israel was already using in the Hula valley (Nimrod, 1966; Lowi, 1993: 105–114).

None of the sections requiring cooperation among the states (including cooperation among the Arab states themselves) in the first part of the plan were implemented. Israel accepted the second part of the plan and reiterated that it was committed to the water allocations of the Johnston plan; as long as the Arab riparians also adhered to the amounts allocated to them there was no reason for conflicts to arise. Jordan also accepted this part of the plan, but Syria rejected it, as evidenced by the project that was implemented in the Syrian Yarmuk basin. The Johnston plan, which seemed to be no more than a historical document from the 1950s, is being revived in the peace talks between Israel and Jordan in 1991–1998.

The Johnston plan did not answer several basic problems that had to be solved for the plan to be realized. For example, how would the water be distributed? Who would distribute it? Would the distribution be implemented according to a multiyear average (which has no practical significance)? As the Jordan is capricious, when would the water be distributed: before the beginning of the year? At the end of the year? Each month? Who would decide on the distribution of the water: would it be the United States? Would the distribution be from the Kinneret (thus turning the Kinneret into an international lake)? In the case of the Indus, its water was distributed between India and Pakistan through a division of the water sources, and thus a conflict between the states was prevented. How would this be done in the case of the river Jordan? No answers have ever been given!

The Johnston plan in fact concluded a prolonged period of efforts to create an equitable distribution of the water of the Jordan.

From 1956 the state of Israel acted independently to implement the National Water Carrier project on the basis of the principles and volumes detailed in the Johnston plan. The Jordanian kingdom also acted independently in executing the Ghor Canal project as a solution for its pressing concerns, particularly the need to supply water to the hundreds of thousands of Palestinian refugees who had settled on either side of the Jordan valley. As for Syria and Lebanon, at that time they took no initiative; and the Palestinian entity did not yet exist.

## Plans and Projects in the Jordan Basin from 1955 to 1991 (the Madrid Conference)

In the course of the thirty-six years following Johnston's proposed plan, the Jordan riparian states engaged in implementing earlier plans and producing new ideas for harnessing the Jordan water for their purposes and needs. Almost all the plans were by and for individual states. Exceptions here were two plans that were shared by several states. One was the Arab plan for diverting the Jordan River, the other was the plan to erect the al Wahda Dam on the basis of a Jordanian-Syrian agreement. These two plans were not implemented.

In the period under review "water wars" were fought between Israel and Syria and Lebanon. In the Six Day War Israel captured the Golan Heights, thereby gaining control of all the Jordan sources. In the War of Attrition (1968–1970) Israel struck the Jordanian Ghor canal and the population of the region abandoned it for some time. At the end of the 1980s, when the condition of the Jordanian kingdom's water regime became extremely grave and a serious drought prevailed in the eastern Mediterranean basin, the kingdom threatened to go to war over the issue of water. The Madrid Conference took place in 1991, and it seems to have opened a new era in the Middle East with fresh plans concerning water.

## Water Projects in Israel

### The National Water Carrier

The crowning glory of projects exploiting Jordan water in Israel is the "Jordan-Negev Line" (National Water Carrier, NWC). In 1944 Professor Lowdermilk presented the idea of establishing a multipurpose project on the Jordan. The idea found an engineering solution in the Blass plan, the Hays-Savage plan, the Cotton plan, and others (Kally, 1965:19–26; Blass, 1973; Reguer, 1993; Drezo-Tepler, 1994). Cotton also added the idea of transferring Litani water to Israel, and so bringing succor to the Palestinians. When the state of Israel agreed to implement the Johnston plan, it received financial aid from the United States in order to execute the work speedily despite geological and hydrological problems. The construction of the project continued from 1956 to 1964 (see Figure 4.2). The NWC project was preceded by local irrigation works implemented by Israel in the Jordan basin before and after the establishment of the state: examples are the irrigation works in the Ash-dot Ya'akov area, around the Kinneret, in the northern Hula valley, and in Bet She'an valley; and the Hula drainage project.

The principle of the NWC is to divert water of the upper Jordan from its natural course into the Kinneret through an open canal to the Zalmon region, and from there to carry it via a reservoir in the Bet Netufa valley to the center and south of the country (Figure 4.2). According to the plan, the NWC canal was meant to originate in the south of the Hula valley, but this was not feasible owing to the geopolitical situation that arose following the War of Independence. The alternative location was fixed at the entrance to the Hula valley, but at the time this area was in the demilitarized zone between Israel and Syria, and the latter vehemently opposed the construction of the project in this territory on the grounds that it had military significance. Under American pressure, and after many shooting incidents (which sent Johnston on his trip to the Middle East), Israel agreed to transfer the starting position of the NWC to the Kinneret. This decision had very serious implications for Israel. If the NWC had originated from the Hula valley it would have been able to generate hydroelectric power by cascading water down to the Kinneret, and it would have been possible to move the water from the Korazim region to the Zalmon region by gravity. The actual situation is that the Kinneret water has to be pumped to a height of 697 feet, a highly costly and technically problematic activity (the water is pumped to the open canal that carries the water to the Zalmon). According to the original plan, high-quality water from the upper Jordan intended to be brought south rather than saltier Kinneret water. A further implication of this decision was the greater vulnerability of the water in the NWC to harmful activity. On its way to the Zalmon area the open canal traverses two deep valleys (Amud and Zalmon), which necessitated the construction of siphons. The mountain range between the Zalmon Canal and the Bet Netufa valley, where the reservoir (Eshkol Reservoir) lies, presented a further topographical problem, which was solved by means of a tunnel. Before emerging from the tunnel, the water had to rise to a height of 438 feet, which made it necessary to build another reservoir near the pumping station. An open canal carries the water from Zalmon to the Eshkol Reservoir, where it undergoes purification before entering a 48-mile long pipeline that takes it to Rosh Ha'ayin. From here the water is streamed to the Tel Aviv area and the south of the country through another system of pipes, the Yarkon-Negev line (see Figure 4.2).

At present the NWC serves as the mainstay of Israel's water system, and connects with most of the water systems in the state: the western Galilee-Kishon project, the Eynan-Upper Galilee projects, the Jerusalem water system, the Yarkon-Negev system, and also the systems that mix Kinneret water with the coastal plain water and the plants for pouring water into the coastal plain aquifer.

The NWC project was intended to transfer 320 million $m^3$ of water, a volume not greater than the quota allotted to Israel by the Johnston plan (Garbell, 1965: 31; Naff and Matson, 1984: 213). After the Six Day War Israel's water needs grew owing to the enlargement of its population (including the addition of the population of Judea and Samaria [West Bank] and the Gaza Strip) and the rise in its living standards. Hence, the outflow from the Kinneret was boosted. In the 1970s an average of about 380 million $m^3$ of water was pumped annually, and at the end of the 1980s the figure was about 420 million $m^3$. The Kinneret serves for irrigating lands on the Golan Heights, the eastern Galilee highlands, the central Jordan valley, and the Bet She'an valley. The upper Jordan water is used to irrigate the Hula valley and its surroundings (Figure 4.2).

### Use of the Yarmuk Water by Israel

According to the Johnston plan, in summer Israel may use 25 million $m^3$ of Yarmuk water. In winter it may use all the surplus Yarmuk water not used by Syria and Jordan. Indeed, for many years part of the surplus floodwater has been carried into the Kinneret for storage instead of flowing away into the Dead Sea, as formerly. The storage capacity of the Kinneret is limited, and in rainy years extremely large volumes of water from the Yarmuk reach the Dead Sea without being used on their way. In 1979–1980, a total of 475 million $m^3$ of water passed through the Naharayim Dam, flowing to the Dead Sea (equal to more than half of the Jordanian kingdom's water consumption that year or about 24 percent of Israel's water consumption). The following year a similar amount of water flowed to the Dead Sea. In 1982–1983 a quantity of 383 million $m^3$ of water again reached the Dead Sea, and this distressing wastage occurred time after time. In 1991–1992 a record amount of 647 million $m^3$ water passed through the dam, and in 1992–1993 the figure was 412 million $m^3$ (Kinneret Administration, 1995). Throughout all those years Israel demanded an increase it its summer quota of Yarmuk water, to 40 million $m^3$ of water, but the Jordanian authorities rejected this demand out of hand. After the Six Day War, Israel demanded that the quota from the Yarmuk be increased to 140–150 million $m^3$, for the needs of the residents of Judea and Samaria (West Bank), according to a calculation based on the water allocations in the Johnston plan. Again the request was turned down by the Jordanians. After Syria and Jordan signed the agreement to construct the al Wahda Dam, tension rose in the Yarmuk valley between Israel and Syria and Jordan. Israel informed the

World Bank that it opposed the funding of the dam until such time as the problems of water allocation among the Yarmuk riparians was resolved. In the second half of the 1970s Israel pumped about 100 million m$^3$ of water from the Yarmuk (Naff and Matson, 1984; Naff, 1990). In the 1980s it pumped 70–80 million m$^3$ (*Ha'aretz*, July 26, 1990), of which 25 million m$^3$ were drawn in the summer season and 45 million m$^3$ in the winter (*Ha'aretz*, Sept. 14, 1990). The head of the Water Research Institute at Amman University, Elias Salameh, complained that the shortage of water in the Jordanian kingdom was the result of overuse by Israel and Syria of Yarmuk water: Israel used 100 million m$^3$ and Syria used 170 million m$^3$ (*Yediot Aharonot*, Oct. 2, 1990). However, it is obvious that in the absence of a dam to collect Yarmuk water, large amounts of it were lost to the Dead Sea; clearly, the transfers of water to the Kinneret by Israel did not cause any harm to any riparians in the Jordan-Yarmuk basin, nor were they responsible for the water shortage in the Jordanian kingdom.

Below it will be seen that the Yarmuk water problem has found a partial solution in the framework of the Israel–Jordan peace agreement.

**Water Projects in Jordan**

*The Ghor Canal Project (the Abdullah Canal)*

The Jordanian kingdom's largest and most important water project is the eastern Ghor canal project (Khourie, 1981) (Figure 4.2). These works began in 1957–1958, following the acceptance by the kingdom of the Johnston plan, approximately at the same time as Israel began work on the NWC. The Ghor Canal was part of a larger-scale plan by the kingdom (the Bunger plan, an integrated concept, and additional ideas presented by Baker, Harza, Ionides, and Macdonald). The large-scale plan included the construction of the Maqarin Dam, and subsequently also the Muheiba Dam, and more small dams intended to trap the floodwater of the eastern tributaries of the Jordan River. In addition, there was a plan to build a canal from the eastern Jordan valley to the western Jordan valley, with the aim of irrigating the Jiftlik-Jericho-Dead Sea plain (at the time the West Bank was controlled by Jordan).

Owing to the poor state of relations with Syria, the Jordanian kingdom eventually confined itself only to building the canal. This project was possible in consequence of Syria's agreement to allow the kingdom to use Yarmuk water (Khourie, 1981: 8). The water is carried from the Yarmuk to the canal via a tunnel near the village of Addassiya. Along the entire Jordan valley secondary canals carry water from the Ghor Canal to the fields. The excess water in the fields drains into the Jordan's course. The planners' intention was to use 200 million m³ of water to irrigate an area of 11,700 hectares (*Sawt al Sha'b*, Nov. 1, 1989). However, the canal supplied only 160 million m³. With the addition of water from wells it is possible to irrigate 36,000 hectares with this water (Kally, 1986: 30–31; *Sawt al Sha'ab*, June 6, 1989; Shatanawi and al Jayousi, 1995). The structural design and height of the canal allowed for the possibility of receiving water from the Kinneret should this become feasible owing to a change in geopolitical circumstances. In 1961 stage A was completed, and in 1966 stage B. An extra 50-mile stretch (to Karameh) was added between 1975 and 1978, and in 1991 the canal reached the Dead Sea, its overall length now being 78 miles (Figure 4.2). The canal project also included agrarian reform and the building of a network of roads and villages along the main canal; along the valley center points of agricultural services, clinics, schools, etc., were established. Until the cutting of the canal, the eastern Jordan valley was uninhabited desert terrain. Today vegetables and other crops are grown there, supplying the local Jordanian market as well as being exported to the Persian Gulf countries. With the rise in demand for water in the area, it transpired that an increase in the volume of water in the Ghor Canal necessitated the erection of a storage dam on the Yarmuk. Such a dam would make it possible to double the amount of water in the canal through storage of winter flood water, preventing it from flowing away to the Dead Sea. The construction of such a dam was delayed owing to the failure of the diversion plan, the Six Day War, the War of Attrition, and tension with Syria in the 1970s. Then discussions began on the al Wahda Dam.

In the early 1990s about 160 million m³ of water flowed in the Ghor Canal. This amount is likely to increase on account of Israeli aid as part of the Israel–Jordan peace agreement (1994). In addition to the Ghor Canal, the Jordanian kingdom established a series of dams on the eastern tributaries of the Jordan River (see Table 4.11 and Figure 4.2). These dams increased the storage capacity of the Jordan by an additional 125 million m³ of water, a considerable volume. With certain dams problems of water pollution arose, for example, the Talal Dam, which collects treated sewage from Amman (Table 4.11 and the sources detailed there). The Jordanian kingdom has therefore utilized all the water it could obtain from the Jordan basin; it has even overused its groundwater (some of this is fossil water and cannot be relied on for long). Despite this, in the early 1990s the condition of the kingdom's water regime was extremely serious.

### The Arab Plan to Divert Jordan Water (the Diversion Plan)

The Arab plan to divert half the Jordan sources reflects more than any other scheme the force of the Jewish-Arab conflict in general and its

Table 4.11: Dams in the Kingdom of Jordan

| River | Storage Capacity* | Purpose |
|---|---|---|
| Zarqa | King Talal Dam, 336 feet high; 86 m³; live storage 78 m³ | Irrigation of 4800 hectares, production of 2.1 mgW |
| Ziglab | 4.3 m³ | Irrigation, drinking |
| Arab | 208 feet high; 20 m³ | Irrigation of 1,200 hectares |
| Kafrein | 3.8 m³ | Irrigation of 4,000 hectares |
| Shueib | 2.5 m³ | Irrigation of 2,400 hectares |
| Al Jurum, Rajib | Earthfilled dams, 5 m³ | Irrigation |
| Yabis, Kufrinja | In construction | Irrigation |
| Dead Sea tributaries | Earthfilled dams, 6.5 m³ | Irrigation |

*Sources:* Salik, 1988: 105-106; *al Ba'ath* (Syria) Dec.4,1987; *Sut al Sha'ab* (Jordan) Dec. 4, 1987; June 27, 1989; *al Rai* (Jordan) Feb.11,1990; Nov. 1, 1989.
* in Million Cubic Meters (m³).

concern with water in particular (Kliot, 1994: 204). The Arab world could not view with equanimity Israel's successful realization of its Jordan project; Israel took all the Jordan sources for itself, ignored the water needs of the neighboring states, and in consequence increased its overall power.

In vindication of its unilteral action, Israel argued that it could find no negotiating partners because the Arabs, who did not recognize Israel's right to exist, were unwilling to enter into discussions.

On February 3, 1964, Damascus Radio gave clear expression of Arab fear concerning Israel's Jordan project (Foreign Broadcast Information Service, 1964):

> Undoubtedly the diversion of Jordan river waters to the Negev is the greatest and most important event in the life of the enemy state. It is an action which is no less dangerous than the establishment of Israel in 1948. If Israel could implement its aggressive plan to divert the Jordan river waters to the Negev, it would be able to exploit an area of land which is equivalent to two-thirds of its present area. In addition to the fact that such an exploitation would enable Israel to double its population, it would also enable it to obtain its agricultural requirements from this vast area and turn Israel into an industrial state with considerable potentialities. The new danger we face today is a new challenge to the Arab nation, which is different in nature from the challenge of 1948. It is a challenge to the civilization of our nation and people. It is an attempt to humiliate the masses of our people through the utilization of scientific progress, for imperialist, aggressive purposes. Therefore, we consider this challenge more serious with more far-reaching aims than the challenge of Israel's establishment.

The Arab states were not content with words, but began activity to ensure their rights to half the Jordan water. Thus, the diversion plan came into being (Figure 4.3).

The idea of diverting half of the Jordan's water was first raised by the Lebanese in 1959, when the diversion of the Hasbani and the Banias to the Litani was being considered (Nimrod, 1966: 92; Golan, 1983; Rabinovitz, 1983; Lowi, 1993). This plan, if executed, would have also harmed the Jordanians, and therefore it was abandoned (Khourie, 1981: 74; Naff and Matson, 1984: 44). In the same year, Jordan responded with a counterproposal to the plan of diversion of the Hasbani and the Banias to the Litani, whereby their courses would be diverted south through the Golan Heights to the Ruqqad River (a tributary of the Yarmuk) and thence to the Yarmuk (Figure 4.3). The United States opposed the plan and explained to the plan's initiators that it would assist Israel in preventing the plan's implementation; therefore, the Arab countries

168

*Figure 4.3:* The Arab Diversion Plan

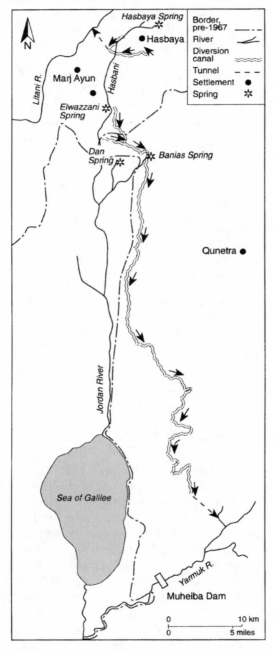

delayed publicizing it and attempting to implement it until 1964 (Nimrod, 1966: 79).

At the Joint Arab Summit held in 1964, immediately after the inauguration of the Israeli NWC, it was decided to adopt the Lebanese plan to divert the Hasbani and Banias to the Litani. If such a plan had been executed it would have harmed Israel, but also the Jordanian kingdom, which would have been left without Jordan water. The opposition of the kingdom to the plan came up against a blank wall of malice. Only after several months had elapsed did the Arab states realize the damage their proposal would cause the Jordanian kingdom. That year a second summit conference convened, at which a Jordanian plan was adopted (Gruen, 1964). Its main features were the following (Figure 4.3). The water of the upper portion of the Hasbani would be transferred to the Litani through a tunnel. The Wazzni springs (the southern source of the Hasbani), located in the lower portion of the river (near Raajar village), would be transferred through a diversion canal by gravity to the Banias Spring within Syrian territory. Some Wazzni water, about 10 million m$^3$, would be used by Syria, and some of it, about 5 million m$^3$, would be used by Lebanon, by diverting the Hasbani and the Banias; about 53 percent of water available to Israel in the upper Jordan would be taken.

From the Banias a diversion canal would direct the Banias and Hasbani water, via the Golan Heights, south to the Yarmuk, to the dam to be built at Muheiba. The dam was planned for a site where it could hold the diverted water, and its volume was planned for this purpose. The Arabs feared that Israel would be able to use the diverted Hasbani and Banias water that would reach Israel via the Yarmuk, and the Muheiba Dam was intended to prevent this from happening. A tunnel would lead from the dam to transfer the water to the Ghor Canal. The length of the diversion canal from the Banias to the Yarmuk was to be about 43 miles, and at some points it would run close to the pre-1967 Israeli border with Syria. Because many streams flow in the Golan Heights, it would be necessary to add bridges or siphons to descend into the deep river courses (Kally, 1965: 137; Inbar and Maoz, 1984; Lowi, 1993; Wolf, 1995a).

The plan had several fundamental problems: without a large dam on the Banias it would be impossible to stop the Banias floodwater from flowing into Israeli territory; there is no suitable place for building such a dam on the stretch between the Banias Spring and the Israeli border (Stevens, 1965: 64). The diversion dam would have to divert 17 million m$^3$ of water per month from the Banias to the Yarmuk or about 200 million m$^3$ per year, necessitating complex engineering solutions. The plan was intended to provide water for irrigation in Lebanon, Syria, and mainly Jordan. In the Arab press three goals were stated: to prevent Israel from having access to Arab water (water that flows in Arab countries); to implement the united water plan of 1953 (Nimrod, 1966: 103); and to propel Israel into a conflict with a united Arab army. Behind the scenes lay an inter-Arab struggle for hegemony and leadership of the Arab world, based on who would lead the activities against Israel: Egypt or Syria (Golan, 1983; Rabinowitz 1983). Work began in 1964, but Israel attacked the earth-moving machinery at the diversion site in Syria, thus preventing implementation. The "water war" led indirectly to the Six Day War. The USSR dispatched a false and malicious message to Egypt that Israel was concentrating forces against Syria in the context of the water war. Consequently, Egypt sent forces into Sinai, which led to the deterioration that was to become the Six Day War.

The Israeli army's victory in that war brought the diversion plan to an end. The Banias Spring came to be located within Israeli territory, which prevents the transfer of Hasbani water to them. The Yarmuk now partially forms the Jordanian–Israeli border, which prevents construction of the Muheiba Dam. Lebanon, of course, abandoned its plan to divert the Hasbani to the Litani. Moreover, with the conquest of the Golan Heights, Israel not only succeeded in halting the plan, but actually enlarged its share of the Yarmuk's drainage basin.

The Israeli position on Arab diversion plan was that the Arab states broke two of the Helsinki Accord rules by embarking on this project: "International river water should not be wasted" (clause 6) and "International river water should not be used in a way which causes serious damage to other riparians" (clause 7) (Kliot, 1994: 204). The Arab stance was stated by the Jordanian geographer Khourie, who said that it was Israel that first broke the Helsinki Accords by constructing the National Water Carrier, thereby transferring Jordan water to another drainage basin. The act infuriated the Arab states, and they therefore decided to frustrate the plan (Khourie, 1981: 73). On this matter, I note that Israel based its actions on the precedent of the transfer of Colorado water from its drainage basin to the Los Angeles region, which was accepted by the Supreme Court of the United States (Reisner, 1993: 124–25).

### The Syrian Irrigation Plan in the Yarmuk Basin

According to the Johnston plan, Syria is entitled to use a total of 132 million $m^3$ of water from the Jordan basin: 90 million $m^3$ from the Yarmuk and 42 million $m^3$ from the Jordan. As noted, Syria has never accepted the plan or acted according to its specifications. Until the 1970s, Syria used 50–60 million $m^3$ of Yarmuk water, mainly for irrigation of the Mazarib lands near Dar'a, near the course of the Yarmuk. Since the 1970s Syria has followed a policy of populating the Syrian Golan, close to the border with Israel. The Syrian population is constantly and rapidly growing in all parts of the country, including the south, Jebel al-Druze and the Hawran, namely, the Yarmuk drainage basin. The Syrian government assists the local population in supplying its own food needs. Since 1975 it has been developing the Syrian Yarmuk basin for the needs of agriculture as well as for political and military purposes. Table 4.12 shows the dams raised by Syria on the tributaries of the river until 1992 and those planned there in the near future. Most of the dams are relatively small, and intended to store floodwater for irrigating sev-

**Table 4.12: Water Projects in the Syrian Yarmuk Basin**

| Tributary | Annual Flow (million m³) | Dam | Storage Capacity (billion m³) | Construction Dates |
|---|---|---|---|---|
| Ruqqad | 84.6 | Rucheina | 1.8 | 1975–1979 |
| | | Barike | 1.08 | 1983–1986 |
| | | Kudna | 30 | in construction |
| | | Adir al Bustan | 10.8 | 1983–1986 |
| | | Gasr al Ruqqad | 9.2 | in construction |
| | | Abdin | 5.5 | in construction |
| | | Al Muntachat | 1.3 | in planning |
| Allan | 30.7 | Al Haga | 0.85 | 1980–1982 |
| | | Tassil | 6.6 | 1980–1982 |
| | | Al Aar | 5.5 | in construction |
| | | Sakam al Gulan | 18 | in planning |
| Aram (Hariri) | 44.4 | Sheikh Maskin | 15.0 | 1980–1982 |
| | | Greater Abta | 3.5 | 1975–1979 |
| | | Lessar Abta | 0.5 | 1975–1979 |
| | | Tafas | 2.1 | 1980–1982 |
| | | Aduan | 5.68 | 1980–1982 |
| Dahab | 14.5 | Al Rom | 6.4 | in construction |
| | | Kanawat | 6 | in construction |
| | | Rasas | 1.15 | 1980 |
| | | Shaba | 1.0 | 1980 |
| | | Al Gharia | 4.5 | 1980 |
| | | Al Tamayya | 2.0 | 1980 |
| Zidi | 21.3 | Sut Hader | 8.75 | 1980 |
| | | Al Ain | 1.5 | in construction |
| | | Habran | 1 | in construction |
| | | Daraa Sharqi | 15.0 | 1975–1979 |
| | | Batam | 2 | in construction |

*Sources: Al Ba'ath* Dec. 4, 1987, Dec. 9, 1987, Mar. 9, 1990, June 24, 1990, Oct. 28, 1991; *Tishrin* April 30, 1988, Nov. 12, 1989, Oct. 15, 1990, Mach 9, 1991; *Achbar al Asbua* Sept. 10, 1987; *Jordan Times* Sept. 5, 1987; Reports: U.S. Army Corps of Engineers, 1991; Canaan, 1990.

eral hundreds or several thousands of hectares close to the river course (Figures 4.2 and 4.4B).

In 1987 a total of 89 million m³ of water that had formerly flowed into the course of the Yarmuk was stored by these dams. To this figure should be added the volume of water used by Syria for irrigating the Mazarib. In 1995 Syria used a total of 200 million m³ of water in the Yarmuk basin. This amount is far higher than what was allocated to it in the Johnston plan. In addition, more dams are at the planning stage in Syria. Together they are intended to store 215 million m³ of water, this being 45 percent of the annual discharge of the Yarmuk (*al Ba'ath*, Dec. 4, 1987). Accounting for evaporation and seepage and the amount of river water used by Israel, the calculation shows that the Jordanian kingdom will be left with only 160 million m³ of Yarmuk water (compared with the 377 million m³ allocated to it by the Johnston plan).

### The Maqarin—Al Wahda Dam: An Unrealized Plan

Construction of a dam features in most of the plans to utilize the Yarmuk water, such as the Bunger plan (1952), the Baker-Harza plan (1955), the Arab plan (1954), and the Johnston plan (1955) (Figure 4.2). The first of these, the Bunger plan, envisaged a dam that would be built on the Jordanian–Syrian border, about 33 miles east of the Yarmuk–Jordan confluence. In the Bunger plan the dam was intended to hold 480 million m³ of water to irrigate 43,500 hectares in the Jordanian kingdom and 8,000 hectares in Syria (Khourie, 1981: 68), and to generate 28 kwh of electricity. In the Baker-Harza plan the dam was meant to hold only 74 million m³ of water, the remainder of the Yarmuk's water intended to be stored in the Kinneret (on the assumption that Israel did not exist).

In the middle of the 1960s, construction of the Maqarin dam was considered once more in the framework of the "Great Yarmuk Plan," which was part of the Arab plan to divert the sources of the Jordan. In the Great Yarmuk Plan it was proposed that a dam be built at Muheiba as well, to contain the diverted Jordan River water. The plan was abandoned after the Six Day War, in which Israeli forces captured the Golan Heights. By then the Jordanians had managed to begin earthworks at the site.

The plan to build a dam at Maqarin surfaced again in 1974, this time with Jordanian financing, based on cooperation between Jordan and Syria. In this version, the proposed dam would be 492 feet high with a carrying capacity of 350 million m³. The Jordanians even received $1 million in American aid to help with their detailed plans (Taubenblatt, 1988: 47). In the end it was proposed to build a storage dam at Maqarin, which would be 557 feet high and with a capacity of 486 million m³, as

*Figure 4.4:* The Water in the Israeli-Syrian Peace Talks

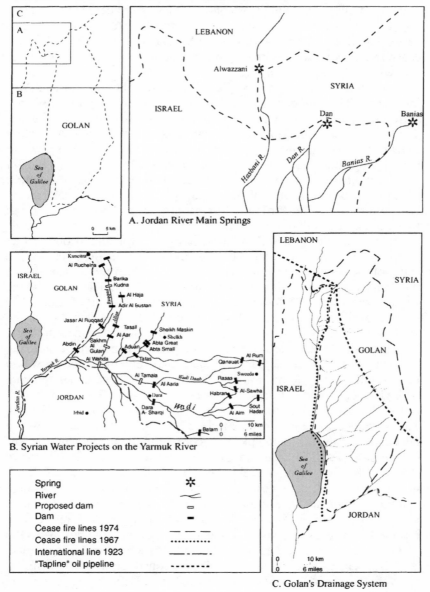

A. Jordan River Main Springs

B. Syrian Water Projects on the Yarmuk River

| Spring | ✳ |
| River | ～ |
| Proposed dam | ▭ |
| Dam | ▬ |
| Cease fire lines 1974 | — — — |
| Cease fire lines 1967 | ·········· |
| International line 1923 | —·—·— |
| "Tapline" oil pipeline | ▪-▪-▪-▪ |

C. Golan's Drainage System

well as a diversion dam in the Addassiya region; there was also a plan to build a power station at the Maqarin Dam to produce 20 kwh of electricity. The construction of the dam was to cost $600–800 million, a very high price for Jordan (Khourie, 1981; Naff and Matson, 1984). Because relations between Jordan and Syria cooled the work of construction was postponed once more.

Meanwhile Syria began to implement its own plan for utilizing Yarmuk water. The Jordanian kingdom feared that if it did not take speedy action it would remain without water from the Yarmuk. It proposed, therefore, to build the Maqarin Dam with its own financing. According to its proposal, it would use most of the water stored, and Syria would benefit from the electricity. On September 3, 1987, a new agreement was signed between Syria and Jordan on the construction of a dam at Maqarin, to be called the alWahda ("unity") Dam. Israel received current reports from the Jordanian kingdom on the agreement and was asked to express an opinion on it.

The new proposal of the Jordanian kingdom was based on the fact that some Yarmuk water would be used by Syria in its own plan for the south of the state, so the Jordanian planners reduced the dimensions of the dam as compared with the original blueprint. Publications gave the height as 380 feet and storage capacity as 220 million $m^3$ of water (150 $m^3$ of it available for use). Eighty percent of the water would go to the Jordanian kingdom to irrigate 25,000 hectares and 20 percent to Syria to irrigate the Mazarib area (Figure 4.4). Some water would evaporate, Syria and Israel would each receive their share, and the kingdom would be left with about 130 million $m^3$. The dam would also generate about 64 kwh of electricity. Of this, 75 percent would go to Syria and 25 percent to Jordan (*Jordan Times*, Sept. 5, 1987; *Achbar al Asbua*, Sept. 10, 1987). The cost of the dam was to be $240–300 million, and it would take about five years to complete. According to the agreement, the Jordanian side would finance construction, and would pay reparations to Syrian villagers obliged to leave the area of the lake. Jordan's willingness to finance the dam, despite its small dimensions and Syria's tough conditions, indicated the seriousness of the water shortage for Jordan at the end of the 1980s. The kingdom applied to the World Bank for aid, but the latter refused assistance because of Israel's objections to the plan as long as its interests in the Yarmuk basin were not safeguarded. As Syria refuses to cooperate with Israel, construction of the dam has not yet started (*Sawt al Sha'b* [Jordan], June 27, 1989; *Ha'aretz*, July 26, 1990).

The peace agreement between Israel and Jordan has made it possible to delay the erection of the dam for several years. Similarly, in the meantime a number of ways have been found for aiding Jordan without the construction of a dam of this kind. If and when there is progress in negotiations between Israel and Syria, the subject of the Maqarin–al Wahda Dam will no doubt be on the table.

## From the Madrid Conference to the Interim Agreement between Israel and the Palestinians (1991–1997)

After 49 years of bloody conflict between Israel and its neighbors it seems that the confrontation is about to end. With the conclusion of hostilities there will undoubtedly be attempts to solve the problems of water in the region.

Below I briefly review the geopolitical background that frames the discussions on water. I analyze what has been concluded between Israel and the Jordanian kingdom and the extent to which signed agreements ensure the distribution of water. Similarly I scrutinize the partial agreements between Israel and the Palestinians and examine which water issues are on the agenda between Israel and Syria and Lebanon.

## Negotiations and Agreements Since the Madrid Conference: Chronology of Events

The collapse of the Soviet Union created a new geopolitical reality in the world, the existence of a single superpower. This was the setting for the opening on October 30, 1991, of the Madrid Conference, where in the presence of representatives of the world powers and other states, delegates of Arab states and of Israel met openly for the first time. In consequence of the Madrid resolutions bilateral talks opened between Israel and each of its neighbors on the subject of arrangements toward peace, and multilateral talks opened also on questions of international and regional interest, including water. This subject was thus discussed in both the bilateral and multilateral frameworks.

The multilateral talks opened in Moscow on January 28, 1992. The subjects discussed were water, refugees, environment, regional economic development, arms control, and regional security. Further multilateral talks were held in Lisbon (May 1992), London (December 1992), Moscow (July 1993), Tokyo (December 1993), and Tabarka (July 1994). Additional talks on water took place between May 1992 and April 1994 in Vienna, Washington, Geneva, Beijing, Muscat, and Athens. Issues discussed were desalination, treatment of recycled water, and training of personnel for water projects. The talks had various goals, including the creation of a positive atmosphere among former enemy states, at least regarding water (Wolf, 1995b).

On April 27–29, 1992, agreement was reached between Israel and the

Palestinians that the question of water rights would be discussed in the bilateral framework. On September 15, 1993, an agreement in principle was reached between Israel and the Palestinians, which among other things included the establishment of a Palestinian water authority. The agreement contained a clause stating that the future control of water sources and administration would be determined in the final stage of discussions because this issue was connected with prior determination of the permanent borders between Israel and the Palestinians. As part of the implementation of stage 1 of the agreement Israel withdrew from the Gaza Strip and the Jericho enclave. In the withdrawal document there is a clause dealing with administration of the water regime in these two places. On October 26, 1994, a peace agreement was signed between Israel and the Jordanian kingdom, and in it a separate clause is devoted to water. The questions of water and the borders were the most difficult problems, and the last to be settled (Uri Shamir, Feb. 15, 1995). On October 30, 1994, four days after the signing of the peace treaty with Jordan, a regional economic conference was held in Casablanca. In preparation for it the participants drew up many development plans, the major ones being water projects. On September 18, 1995, an interim agreement was signed between Israel and the Palestinians on additional withdrawals of Israel army forces from West Bank cities. This agreement refers to the distribution and use of water in the interim stage. The critical question of responsibility for administration of the water regime in Judea and Samaria (West Bank) was postponed by the parties to the final stage of the agreement. This was supposed to begin in mid-1996 but as of mid-1998 it has not yet occurred. From the Madrid Conference to the time of writing there have been secret negotiations (with interruptions) between Israel and Syria and Lebanon. The subject of water heads the agenda.

### Water in the Peace Agreement between Israel and the Jordanian Kingdom: Signed Agreements and Actual Reality

The Jordanian kingdom reached a peace agreement when it was thirsty for water, especially drinking water in the large cities, primarily Amman. The forecast demand for water in the kingdom envisages a difficult situation (Table 4.3). A further concern for the Jordanians arises on account of the use of Yarmuk water by the Syrians in the upper Yarmuk basin and the use of Jordan water by Israel. Even in the absence of drought this combination of circumstances is liable to desiccate the Jordanian kingdom. At present Jordan is trying to overcome the water shortage by pumping fossil groundwater in the eastern desert, an operation that cannot continue for long. In the summer of 1994, in the discussions between Israel and Jordan, Israel took into consideration the gravity of the kingdom's situation and decided to transfer drinking water to Amman for humanitarian reasons.

On the other side of the negotiating table is Israel, which in contrast to the Jordanian kingdom appears like an economic power acting out of a sense that this or that act of generosity will not enhance or diminish its economic strength. Israel has great interest in bringing the ongoing conflict between the two states to a speedy conclusion.

Israel and Jordan have a common border, the longest of the borders between Israel and its neighbors (Figures 4.2, 4.5, 4.6, 4.7). Jordan serves as a buffer zone between Israel and Iraq, a fact that was especially evident during the Gulf War in 1991. The majority of Jordan's population is Palestinian. It is important to bring about the ending of the conflict with this population too. Both states have many mutual matters for consideration, such as the future of Jerusalem, development of the Jordan valley (from the Red Sea in the south to Bet She'an in the north), development of tourism, exploitation of common economic resources such as the Dead Sea, as well as the possibility of large-scale water projects. The geographical location of the Jordanian kingdom, which has no outlet to the Mediterranean, holds out many opportunities for development of Haifa as the exit port of the kingdom. In view of this background, a positive and friendly atmosphere prevails in discussions between Israel and Jordan in any area that does not constitute a security risk. Regarding water, the two states share the course of the Jordan River and its tributaries. Lake Kinneret serves as a reservoir for both. They share the Yarmuk River on its most sensitive sector, its confluence with the Jordan. Both states have a common stretch of the Jordan River from the entry of the Yarmuk at least as far as the Bezek stream, south of Bet She'an. Similarly, they have joint interests in the Dead Sea and the Arava region, which is an important development zone for both states, containing much groundwater.

Both Israel and Jordan are concerned about Syrian coercion in the upper Yarmuk and both have an interest in a political solution for the sector of the border along the river between Bet She'an and the Dead Sea, a question that will be settled in arrangements between Israel and the Palestinians. Israel wishes this sector to be its security border, separate from the fate of the West Bank territory, out of concern for what is termed "Israel's eastern border" (Figures 4.2, 4.5, 4.6, 4.7).

Both countries are also associated with the Johnston plan. This plan, described earlier in this chapter, was accepted by Israel and the Jordanian kingdom in 1955 through a verbal and written statement. The agreement of the two states gave the United States a reason to finance the water projects of both. Although those conducting negotiations deny

178

*Figure 4.5:* Israel-Jordan Peace Agreement

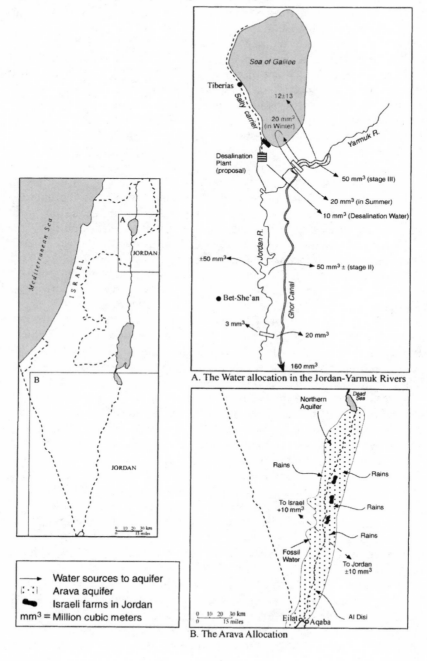

A. The Water allocation in the Jordan-Yarmuk Rivers

B. The Arava Allocation

*Figure 4.6:* Water Peace Projects in Palestine (Proposals)

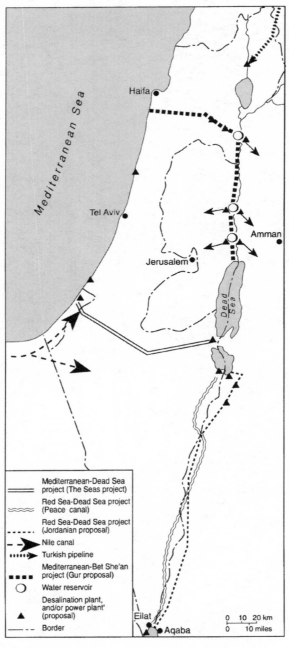

180

*Figure 4.7:* Geopolitical Circles in the Jordan River Basin

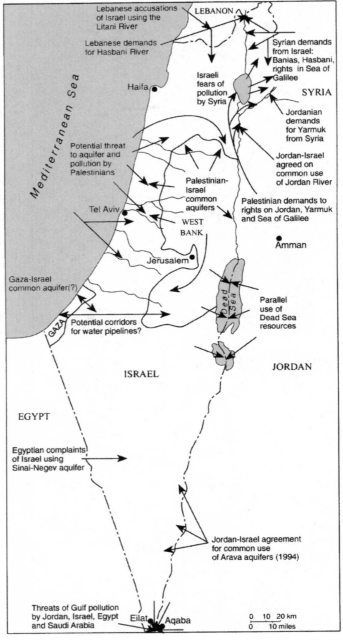

any connection between the present talks and the 1955 Johnston plan, the fact is that certain clauses in the new agreement between Israel and the Jordanian kingdom are reminiscent of parallel clauses in the Johnston plan.

## The Israeli-Jordanian Agreements: Water Clauses (Clause 6 and Appendix II)

Clause 6 in the peace agreement is declarative. Regarding practical details it directs the reader to Appendix II. Several important opening positions appear in the declarations: recognition of the rights of both sides (at a certain stage in the talks the Jordanians claimed unilateral rights to the water; Israel made it clear that in such a case there will be a paper with rights but there will be no water); agreement that neither state will harm the resources of the neighboring state; recognition by both sides that the water sources are inadequate for all the needs of the two states. It is clear from this that additional water must be created for both sides. Appendix II covers the following subjects: allocations of water and their times, with precise details of the volumes of water allocated to Israel and the Jordanian kingdom from the Yarmuk and Jordan Rivers and the times of their use by each of the partners (Figure 4.5A); capability of storing water, with recognition of the very limited storage capacity of the Kinneret (not exceeding 650–680 million $m^3$ annually). The Kinneret's limited capacity is distressing because it prevents the storage of water from rainy seasons for dry seasons and of good years for poor years; it also prevents the realization of opportunities for planning, saving, and optimal operation of the water regimes in the region. Other matters covered by Appendix II are the quality of water and its preservation; groundwater in the Arava (section 4); details of water allocations to Israel and the Jordanian kingdom in the Arava region (Figure 4.5B); the siting of water transfers; and the siting of dams planned for the future in the agreement (Figure 4.5A).

### Interpretation of the Agreement

The agreement contains several clauses that have been deliberately left vague. Regarding them, each party publishes different data. The Jordanians maintain before the Arab world that they will receive 215 million $m^3$ of water according to the agreement.

By contrast, the agreement states that Israel will in fact give Jordan only 100 million $m^3$, and regarding 50 million $m^3$ more, the agreement states: "Israel and Jordan shall cooperate in finding sources for the supply to Jordan of an additional quantity of (50)m $m^3$/year" (see section 3 in Appendix II; Gur, Jan. 3, 1994; *Ha'aretz*, May 2, 1995; May 25, 1997; June 13, 1997; June 15, 1997).

What is the water that is to be given by Israel to Jordan, and where is it to be found?

Twenty million m³ will be from the Kinneret in winter; in winter, Israel will take 20 million m³ from the Yarmuk water, and these will be returned to Jordan in summer, when the demand for water grows in the region!

Ten million m³ from the salt water carrier: this refers to water from the salt water carrier skirting the Kinneret shore that is to be desalinated at Israel's expense, thus reducing the salinity of the Kinneret water (20 million m³ flow in this carrier).

The rest of the water earmarked for Jordan is more problematic. The agreement states that "Jordan is entitled to store for its use 20 million m³ of the flood in the Jordan river south of its confluence with the Yarmouk." This refers to the stretch of the river up to Nahal Bezek. Here the Jordan river begins to flow along the border between the West Bank and the kingdom of Jordan. From the above sentence is sounds as if it may be possible to build a dam in this area, but it is not clear who will build it, nor is it certain that there will be water to store behind it.

A more complicated clause concerns the transfer of water to the kingdom of Jordan equal in volume to that which Israel uses in the section of the Jordan from the Yarmuk–Jordan confluence to the point of the River Jordan's entry into the area between the West Bank and the Jordanian kingdom. As Israel uses about 80 million m³ water in this section (some of it brackish), the kingdom is assured that it will receive 50 million m³ (*Ha'aretz*, June 13, 1997). The wording of this clause (section 3 in Appendix II) is also problematic: "Israel is entitled to maintain its current uses of the Jordan River Waters," namely, new sources have to be found for the Jordanian kingdom without harming Israel. At the same time, it is not stated who will develop these new sources. This clause became a matter of dispute between Israel and Jordan in May 1997 when Jordan required Israel to implement the second part of the water agreement. Jordan demanded that in addition to the 30 million m³ water that was already being transferred to the kingdom (20 million m³ from the Kinneret and 10 million m³ from the salt water carrier, which also originates in the Kinneret) Israel transfer a further 50 million m³ in accordance with section 3 of Appendix II of the agreement (*Ha'aretz*, May 25, 1997; June 13, 15, 1997).

After a harsh exchange and a break in contact between the two governments for several days, Israel agreed to transfer this water at its own expense!

Where can this water be acquired? There is a plan to intensify water use for fishing in the Bet She'an valley, with the consequent release of water for the Jordanian kingdom. The practical significance of this will be the elimination of the pools in the Bet She'an valley and the transfer of the fishery branch to enclosed ponds applying growing methods that still have to be learned. This water is brackish and will have to undergo desalination for drinking and agricultural use in the Jordanian kingdom. Furthermore, according to the agreement, Israel will have the task of maintaining the quality of the Jordan water. It may become polluted as a result of the desalination and as a result of other uses (including sewage), and to prevent pollution Israel will be forced to invest in the construction of special installations.

The cost of this dramatic change in the Bet She'an valley is about $150 million, and according to the Water Commissioner (in a conversation on June 17, 1977) these funds have not yet been found. Nor is it clear whether the agreement of the farmers in the area has been obtained. Until these problems are solved, Israel has begun to transfer Kinneret water to the kingdom. At stage A (summer 1997) 25 million m$^3$ were transferred, and steps were taken to transfer a further 25 million m$^3$ in the future. By the end of stage B Jordan will have received about 80 million m$^3$ water from Israel. The Kinneret water is transported to Jordan by a pipeline to the large storage pool near the Yarmuk (near Kibbutz Ashdot Ya'akov), from where it is pumped to the Abdullah Canal.

Stage C will necessitate the building of a dam on the southern Jordan River to retain a further 20 million m$^3$ water, and it will be time to begin implementation of the last clause of the agreement on "Additional Water" (section 3 in Appendix II). The intention is to construct a dam near Addassiya in Jordan where the Yarmuk leaves the gorge and enters the Jordan plain. According to the plan, 50 million m$^3$ of Yarmuk water is supposed to be stored behind this dam for the Jordanian kingdom. Below the reservoir there is an opening for the transfer of Yarmuk water to the Abdullah Canal; and thus, at last, the flow of water to the canal will be regular, and not subject to the river's caprices as it has been since the 1950s.

But this project too touches on sensitive geopolitical questions. On the Israeli side the dam and the lake are to be located in the demilitarized zone between Israel and Syria, the terrain known as the al Hama enclave.

This part, which was in the territory of Palestine, was defined as demilitarized in the Syrian–Israeli armistice agreements of 1949. It was captured by Syria in 1951, and retaken from the Syrians by Israel in the war of June 1967. Will Jordan agree to build this dam there, thus legitimizing Israel's remaining in the area? On the other hand, if the dam is not built, Jordan will not be able to obtain the additional water of which it is assured in the agreement. Syria, for its part, may impose sanctions on Jordan, and indirectly on Israel too, if Syria increases its use of upper Yarmuk water at the expense of the downstream states. As for the funding of this dam, the agreement states that Israel and Jordan will do all in their power to seek sources for financing the project among the wealthy states. If such sources are not found, Israel, by the precedent of stage B, will presumably acquiesce in Jordan's demands and will also assist in finding the additional water sources; then those 50 million m³, like the water of stage B, will be taken from the Kinneret.

Table 4.13 displays an attempt to calculate the total flow of water in

**Table 4.13: Estimated Annual Flow of Southern Jordan River and Yarmuk Water (million m³)**

| | |
|---|---|
| Average discharge from the Yarmuk | 475 |
| To Syria | 200 |
| Remainder | 275 |
| To the Jordanian Ghor (Abdullah) Canal | 160 |
| Remainder | 115 |
| Many-year average outflow from Kinneret to Jordan River | 69 |
| Remainder | 184 |
| Transfer of Yarmuk water to Israel by agreement | 25 |
| Remainder | 159 |
| Israeli use along the lower Jordan River | 50 (approx.) |
| Remainder | 109 |
| Transfer to Jordanian kingdom, by agreement, parallel to use in Israel | 50 (approx.) |
| Remainder | 59 |
| Additional transfer to Jordanian kingdom, by agreement | 20 |
| Remainder | 39 |
| Additional transfer to Israel, by agreement | 3 |
| Remainder allocated to flushing Jordan River into Dead Sea | 36 |

*Note:* In addition to the quantities listed above, Israel undertook to transfer an additional 20 million m³ of water to the Jordanian kingdom every summer. This amount will be returned to Israel in the winter. Israel will also transfer to the kingdom a further 10 million m³ potable water produced by desalination of water from the saltwater carrier (Kinneret bypass) and carried directly to the kingdom from the Kinneret. However, on either side of the Jordan valley there is also water that flows back into the river, and presumably this water will cancel out these additions.

In recent years data has appeared estimating the Yarmuk discharge at 447–456 million m³. If these figures are correct it is obvious from the above calculation that no water will be left for flushing the Jordan.

the sector south of the Kinneret that is intended to serve the Syrians, Israel, and the Jordanian kingdom. These calculations do not include the Palestinians, who are also legitimate partners in the Jordan basin. The figures show that despite the limited storage capacity of the Kinneret, no problems are expected in the realization of the agreement in wet years. If the agreed plans to build dams in the Yarmuk gorge and the southern Bet She'an valley are implemented, it is expected that the storage capacity will even increase. (This future increment is not reflected in the figures in the table.)

The water problem will arise in all its severity in years of drought or near drought. Then there will be no surplus of water from the Kinneret (about 69 million $m^3$ on average), and the level of the lake will drop, approaching the lower red line. At such times the Yarmuk discharge will also be limited. Some may argue that owing to the great importance it attaches to the peace agreement with Jordan, Israel, out of humanitarian considerations elicited by the thirst for water in the Jordanian kingdom, will continue to release a volume of 150 million $m^3$ of water at times of drought also, thus running great risks of its own. It must not be forgotten that a volume of 150 million $m^3$ equals 25 percent of Israel's total operative water reserve in the Kinneret (which, it is recalled, stands at 640–680 million $m^3$). Release of the promised quantity to Jordan in a dry year means lowering the red line 3 feet (1 meter), a fact that exacts a heavy ecological price.

If indeed this critical situation is reached (it occurs in cycles of three to seven years), Israel will be faced with difficulties at home, and presumably pressure will mount to make desalination possible sooner in Israel. The significance of this is that more and more natural water will be transferred to the Jordanian kingdom, and thence to the Palestinians and possibly the Syrians too; in all cases it will be pumped from the Kinneret and Israel will pay for the desalination. As of Summer 1998, the kingdom of Jordan has faced another water crisis and the Minister of Water has resigned, and Israel has been asked to help again (*Ha'aretz*, Aug. 21, 1998).

In the Arava region, the direction of water transfer will be the reverse: from the Jordanian kingdom to Israel. Following the agreement, Israel continues to cultivate Arava land that has been worked for several decades and that, according to the border demarcation between Israel and Jordan, was located within the Jordanian kingdom (Figure 4.5B). According to the agreement Israel is authorized to continue to irrigate this land with groundwater originating in Jordanian territory and in quantities estimated at 25–35 million $m^3$. Israel is likewise entitled to increase its pumping by up to an additional 10 million $m^3$ to enlarge its agricultural areas. The remaining groundwater in the Arava may be used by the

Jordanians as they see fit. The agreement and its accompanying proto-
cols detail the procedures of entry into Jordanian territory and operation
of the wells in coordination with the Jordanian police and military.

This agreement is fixed for twenty-five years, with the option of extension for a further period. The settlement in the Arava is most important for Israel, and it is difficult to envisage the existence of this settlement without the use of this international groundwater. The Jordanian
kingdom has thus made concessions in the south of the country, in return for compensation in the north.

The Israeli–Jordanian agreement constitutes a historical international
precedent on several matters: Both states are signatories to an agreement determining the use of international groundwater. One state (the
Jordanian kingdom) has handed over its land and water (in the Arava)
to be worked and used by another state (Israel). One state (Israel) do-
nates its water (in the north of the country) for the needs of another state
(Jordan). One state (Jordan) operates a water pipeline within another
state (Israel).

It is noteworthy that from Israel's viewpoint the agreement contains
an extremely sensitive point concerning ownership of the Kinneret and
evoking controversy within Israel (*Ha'aretz*, May 2, 1995). Israel has
always made certain that it will maintain sovereignty over the Kinneret.
This issue was settled after tough negotiations with Johnston (Rabinowitz, 1983). To prevent the impression that there is some kind of interna-
tionality regarding the Kinneret, Israel insisted that the new agreement
with the Jordanian kingdom would not mention the name "Kinneret" in
any clause. This in fact is the case, but the agreement does state that the
kingdom will receive water from "upstream from the Deganya gates."
Any aware person realizes that this means that water will be from the
Kinneret (and see Figure 4.5A).

This issue is of great importance, beyond semantics. If the Kinneret
is recognized as a water reserve common to Israel and the Jordanian
kingdom, this will constitute a precedent that the Syrians and Palestinians are liable to take as their grounds for demanding a hold on the Kinneret also (and on this matter see also below, the section on negotiations
between Israel and Syria and between Israel and the Palestinians).

The ghost of the Johnston plan hovered over the negotiating table, regardless of denials by Israel's official delegates to the talks. This is
plain from the following facts: It was agreed that Israel would transfer
a net volume of 100 million $m^3$ to the Jordanian kingdom (after subtracting the amount that Israel would receive in the Arava), exactly as
recommended in the Johnston plan. It was agreed that Israel would
pump 25 million $m^3$ from the Yarmuk exactly as recommended by the
Johnston plan. The surplus Yarmuk water would be meant for the Jorda-

nian kingdom, this too matching the Johnston plan (and disregarding Syrian activity).

In consequence of the water agreements between Israel and Jordan we are left with this central question: Can this agreement solve the problems of water shortage of the Jordanian kingdom in the foreseeable future? A further question is: To what extent can Israel show generosity toward the Jordanian kingdom in allocating water without harming its own vital interests? As stated, Israel is committed to the transfer of about 150 million m³ of water annually to Jordan in the north of the country, and in return to receive about 50 million m³ in the Arava (the Jordanians will pump an additional 10 million m³ of water in the region, thus exhausting the potential of the water there).

In 1995 Jordan was short by 200 million m³ of water. This lack was made up by pumping fossil water and by Israeli assistance (Rozental at a conference in Beer Sheba, Feb. 15, 1995). In 2005 Jordan's water shortfall (mainly in the north) will reach 700 million m³. Israel will transfer 150 million m³ (not subtracting the water in the Arava), and this volume will equal only 21 percent of the Jordanian kingdom's missing water. In 2020 Israeli assistance will amount to only 8.5 percent of the missing volume (Tables 4.2 and 4.3). Israel will be unable to make up the Jordanian kingdom's water shortage. It will be able to perform a limited humanitarian gesture and provide Jordan at most with 50 million m³ (on condition that there will be no need for a similar gesture toward the Palestinians and the Syrians), but nothing more.

In sum, the peace agreement and Israeli assistance postpone the water crisis in the Jordanian kingdom for just a few years. Members of the Israeli delegation to the talks expressed their fear that the problems will appear in the future; the Jordanians will have disappointments and the Israelies will have problems.

### Plans to Transfer Water to the Dead Sea

Israel is interested in the stability of the Jordanian regime, as are the world's economic powers. Therefore, great efforts are being made to speedily assist Jordan. At the Casablanca Conference (1994) different international factors presented plans for the generation of cheap electricity that would make it possible to desalinate seawater from the Mediterranean or the Red Sea for the Jordanian kingdom. The underlying idea of the plan is to stream water down from the Mediterranean or the Red Sea to the Dead Sea, exploiting the difference in levels between the seas (1,312 ft) to create hydroelectric power (Figure 4.6).

In recent years various plans have been put forward, further motivated by the drop in the water level of the Dead Sea by almost 66 feet, causing severe environmental damage. The drop is the result of use of Jordan River water: between the 1930s and the 1950s the level fell by 16.5–26 feet; between 1950 and 1992 it fell a further 46 feet (according to Ze'ev Shalev, April 26, 1994).

If water from the Mediterranean or the Red Sea is not transferred to the Dead Sea, its level is liable to drop 33 feet more within a decade, going down to −1361 feet. The plans for transferring water to the Dead Sea are intended to raise the water level and to repair the environmental damage.

As early as 1890 the Swiss engineer Max Bourcart proposed streaming seawater from the Mediterranean to the Dead Sea. His detailed proposal was for the transfer of water from Haifa Bay to the Bet She'an valley, and thence to the Dead Sea. The idea recurred in the plans of Ruthenberg, Lowdermilk, Hays, Shlomo Gur, the Seas Project (in the 1980s), and in a more detailed form in the plans of several politicians and economists in the 1990s (Figure 4.6) (Israel, *Development Options*, 1994; 1996).

The plans of the 1990s envisage the desalination of 800–900 million m$^3$ of water. The operation, according to the plans, will be implemented by means of cheap electricity produced by the descent of water from the Mediterranean or the Red Sea to the Dead Sea (after the water has first been elevated to a certain height). Two of the plans concern the transfer of Mediterranean seawater to the Dead Sea: one is a repetition of the Seas Project and envisages taking water from the Mediterranean at the Gaza Strip and carrying it over the cliffs at Ein Boqeq on the Dead Sea. According to this plan, the transfer of the water will be accomplished by pumping it to a height of 328 feet above sea level, moving it through a tunnel under the Judean mountains, and subsequently cascading it from a height of 1,433 feet, passing through a power station. The length of the water carrier will be 69 miles and the cost of the plan about $2 billion (Israel, *Development Options,* 1994; 1996; Murakami, 1995: 216–226).

The second plan is called the Northern Plan (of Shlomo Gur) and it adopts the earlier concepts with several amendments. According to it, the project will begin at Atlit and the water will pass along a tunnel under Mount Carmel, being raised to a level of 197 feet above sea level. The water will flow from there through the Jezreel valley to the Bet She'an valley, and thence to the Dead Sea. The carrier will be 106 miles long and its cost about $3 billion (Israel, *Development Options*, 1994).

Two other plans are for the transfer of water from the Red Sea to the Dead Sea. One is Jordanian, and envisages a canal through Jordanian territory only. The other plan is Israeli, and calls for a joint Jordanian–Israeli enterprise in which the Red Sea water will be raised to a height of 656 feet above sea level at the Arava watershed (between the Red Sea and the Dead Sea), from where it will run down to the Dead Sea. The length of the carrier will be 131 miles and its estimated cost is about $4 billion. (Israel, *Development Options*, 1994; Jordan, *Tomorrow Has Arrived*, 1994; Murakami 1995: 167–212).

The World Bank has prepared plans that encompass all the Jordan valley. These are less grandiose and may be accomplished more rapidly than the previous ones outlined. Among other things they include recycling of water, turning the lower Jordan River into an international park, retention of floodwater, and more (World Bank, 1994).

To sum up, the Israeli and Jordanian plans are grandiose and each requires an investment on the order of $2–4 billion. Their implementation would cause very serious environmental damage to the Arava or the Jordan valley north of the Dead Sea, and also serious harm to the Dead Sea itself, which at present is an important source of income for the two states. A further problem is the timetable. Even if any of the projects were to begin at once, it would take at least a decade to complete (Kally, 1996).

### Water in the Peace Talks between Israel and Palestinians

The Jordan River is international. Whoever controls the eastern part of the West Bank of the Jordan is a full partner in the river. Control of the Jordan River leads to a claim to the Yarmuk, or at least to al Hama, which is a disputed area. The Palestinians demand it as an additional enclave of theirs. From here also stems the claim for control, in some manner, over the Kinneret. From this reasoning, the Palestinians demand participation in the Johnston plan.

Figure 4.1 shows the body of water common to Israel and the Palestinians: the central highland aquifer. This is the most important water source for both sides, and hence it is the main area of disagreement over water.

In the agreement signed on September 15, 1993 (the Declaration of Principles), it was agreed that Israel would transfer responsibility for water and sewage issues to the Palestinians in Gaza and Jericho, and in the remainder of the territories in the future. In this agreement it was also resolved that the final agreement would be reached in the last stage of the talks, when the permanent borders would be decided.

### The Agreement on Gaza and the Jericho Enclave

On May 4, 1994, a document was signed on Israeli withdrawal from Gaza and the Jericho enclave. A few days later Israeli troops evacuated these areas, except for the Jewish settlement in parts of the Gaza Strip (as agreed). The document has a special clause dealing with water. The geological structure of these zones and their water potential facilitated withdrawal from them (Figure 4.1): geologists estimate that the Gaza coast aquifer is a closed system with no connection to the northern aquifers. They likewise believe that there is no groundwater flow from east to west, that is, from Israel to the Gaza Strip territory (Gvirtzman, 1993). Other researchers hold that there is a connection between the Gaza aquifer and the Israeli aquifers in the north and east, but it is minor (Zohar and Schwartz, 1991). If the latter assessment is correct, then the Gaza aquifer is an international body, but even so this has no implications for the agreement as Israel agreed that the Gaza aquifer would be Palestinian property. Israel's sole demand in this matter was the right to pump water from this aquifer (under Palestinian inspection) for military facilities and the Jewish settlements remaining in the Strip (until the permanent accord).

The first clause of the document states that all the water systems, from water pumping to sewage water, will be administered and developed by the Palestinian authority.

From the start it was clear that the volume of water of the Gaza Strip is small and it would not supply the needs of the population, and that ultimately Israel would be obliged to transfer water to the Strip. Therefore, it is stated in the document that the Mekorot Company, the Israeli water supplier, will transfer water to the strip for payment.

Regarding the Jericho enclave, it was determined that Mekorot would be responsible for the network of water pipes passing through the territory of the enclave to other parts of the West Bank. Other clauses in the document deal with ecology and protection of the quality of the water in the Gaza Strip and in the Mediterranean (Gaza-Jericho agreement, May 4, 1994: 31)

### Water in the West Bank

At the time of writing (mid-1998) there is still no agreement on control and administration of the water sources on the West Bank. It is true that an interim agreement was signed on September 28, 1995, but no compromise was found regarding water, and the matter was postponed until the final stage of the negotiations.

The major questions on the agenda are: (a) Who will control the highland aquifer? (b) What are the rights of the Palestinians over the River Jordan? (From the latter question derives that of the rights of the Palestinians to the Yarmuk and the Kinneret.)

As stated, the issue concerns three main aquifers, all of which traverse the Green Line (Figures 4.1, 4.7): the eastern, the northern, and the western. Even though the Green Line is a cease-fire line and not an international boundary, the aquifers are international. The northern and eastern aquifers drain into the Jordan River and, therefore, whoever controls them will naturally be a partner in the Jordan basin. Even if Israel remains in the Jordan valley and the river itself remains Israel's security border, the West Bank inhabitants have rights to the Jordan River.

### The Claims of the Parties

The Palestinians claim almost all the water in the territory of Judea and Samaria (West Bank) on the basis of the principle of full sovereignty over what they possess on the ground or under the ground. They claim 500–560 million m³ of water on the West Bank and the Gaza Strip, and in addition they claim rights to the Jordan River amounting to 150–200 million m³. In their view, this volume is theirs by virtue of the Johnston plan. It is recalled that the Johnston plan was published in 1955, when all Palestinians, on both sides of the Jordan River, were under the rule of the Jordanian kingdom (El-Hindi, 1990; Zarour and Isaac, 1991; Assaf et al., 1993).

In contrast to the extreme Palestinian position, Israeli experts argue that Israel has historical rights to the water of the West Bank (see also the above section on the aquifers): formerly the water of these aquifers surfaced as springs in Israeli territory, and Israel was the first to develop and use them (before 1967); these are the most important water sources for Israeli cities on the coast, and they supply two million citizens in the Tel Aviv metropolitan area, Jerusalem, and elsewhere. The Israeli specialists also argue that if Israel does not control these sources of water they are liable to be polluted, and eventually all the rivers entering Israel will be polluted (Zohar and Schwartz, 1990; Gvirtzman, 1994, 1995). There are also compromise approaches: one of these starts from the assumption that it is impossible to administer a joint water regime, and an aquifer cannot be divided between authorities. On the basis of this assumption two alternatives are offered.

The first is Israeli control over all three aquifers. This has a clear advantage for the Israeli water regime, but with a heavy demographic and political price.

The second alternative is to concede the Nablus-Jenin aquifer, above which lives a large Palestinian population, and keep the western and eastern aquifers in Israeli hands. The advantage to Israel is obvious: water for the inhabitants of the coastal plain would remain under Israeli control, as would water for the Jewish settlements in the Jordan valley.

The demographic price would be tolerable. With this alternative the Palestinians would retain control over the water at their disposal as in 1996, and a further 120 million m³ from the Nablus-Jenin aquifer, a total of 250 million m³ of water, which would suffice for them as drinking water for a long period.

A third alternative is to leave the western aquifer (Yarkon-Taninim) in Israeli hands and to transfer the two other aquifers to Palestinians. Israel would thus forgo 360 million m³ of water out of the 670 million m³ existing in the Judean mountains. The Palestinians would receive 300 million m³ (Gvirtzman, 1995).

A different approach, which has adherents among Israelis and Palestinians, envisages the possibility of joint administration of the water regime on the West Bank. Joint administration requires prior agreement on the method of water division between the two populations. A proposal exists for allocating water only for domestic use with a little farming around the house. This method of allocation is called minimum water requirement (MWR) (Assaf et al., 1993). It is based on the assumption that the amount of water available will in any case not be sufficient for all needs, so all the water of Palestine would rightly be used for domestic purposes. By this approach every inhabitant would receive 125 m³ of water yearly, and each population would receive a quota according to it size. In 2008 the Jewish population would get 963 million m³ of water and the Palestinians 475 million m³, a total of 1.438 billion m³. In 2023 total domestic consumption would be 1.875 billion m³, namely, the full water potential of Palestine (excluding recycled water). In each of these years the Jewish population would receive about 66 percent of the potential and the Palestinian population about 34 percent. For the sake of comparison, in 1995 the Jews received 90 percent of the volume of water that was exploited, and the Arabs of Gaza and the West Bank received 10 percent (Assaf et al., 1993: 47). The adoption of this approach would oblige the government of Israel to embark on the drastic curtailment of Israeli agriculture. This would sound the death knell for the sector, apart from some crops irrigated with recycled water. In this context several grave problems arise: the state of Israel would be obliged to transfer to the Palestinians good quality water in increasing quantities and to pay for this with radical changes in its economy; furthermore, there is no answer about what would take place if the Palestinians realized their "right of return" and absorbed half a million to a million refugees. In such a case Israel would have to transfer most of its good water gradually to the Palestinians. When the potential of natural water was exhausted it would be necessary to move to the stage of desalination; the question remains as to who would fund the desalination—both populations or the Jewish population alone.

It is difficult to believe that Israel will adopt this approach, which calls for one-sided generosity on Israel's part. The agricultural lobby in Israel would be unlikely to support it. The environmentalists too would oppose the desiccation of the country, as would important political elements. It is hard to believe that Israel will be willing to hand over its water resources to the Palestinians as full partners. On the other hand, it is equally hard to assume that the Palestinians will agree to Jewish control over the water of the West Bank. Likewise, a joint administration of the water resources would probably not function properly for long.

In recent years more ideas have been put forward for the division of the aquifers, particularly by Western scholars who advise Israel to allocate more water to the Palestinians, without dealing with the internal problems in Israel; and the implications of these concessions for Israel directly and indirectly.

Libiszewski (1995) proposed carrying water from the National Water Carrier to Gaza and allocating more water to the West Bank. Lonergan and Brooks (1995) made a similar suggestion, as did Allan (1996b) and others.

In 1997 Libiszewski reintroduced a proposal that had already been discussed previously by Wolf and others. It held that the solution to the water problem was to be seen as part of an overall solution to the conflict, and the quest for it should follow several parallel tracks.

The "twin track" would mean bottom-up action for ad hoc solutions and top-down solutions on the national level, not necessarily connected with water. A second course is "track two diplomacy," which is similar to the first but with the emphasis on removal of psychological and other barriers, and not only in bargaining over water (Libiszewski, 1997). The "third track" relates to informal, quasi-academic meetings, with the elaboration of models for a solution to the water problem. Of this sort are the three documents published by Feitelson and Haddad, titled *Joint Management of Shared Aquifers* (1994; 1996). Libiszewski's solution seems right, but much time is required to bridge the gaps. The Oslo Accords, by contrast, squeezed the entire negotiation schedule into a short time span.

Another approach to the water problem, which is usually raised in academic circles, tends to see water as a tradable good in all respects. By such an approach, so the researchers believe, water will be traded like any other product that has a price, and its use will be rational (Beecher, 1997; Brown, 1997).

According to Arlosoroff, it is still possible to save a great amount of water in Palestine, up to 10–15 percent, or immediately in Israel up to

80–120 million m$^3$, and thus to put off crises and desalination (Arlosoroff, 1996).

Al Kloub and Al Shemmer (1996) also attempted to propose a model for distribution of Jordan water according to the Helsinki Accords and the ILC, and they tested various alternatives. They concluded that first priority was to be given to the Jordanian kingdom, then to the Palestinians, then to Syria, and last to Israel and Lebanon.

Johnston, as is known, granted Jordan first priority (together with the Palestinians) and then Israel, and only lastly Syria and Lebanon.

The most acceptable solution seems to be territorial compromise inside the area of the West Bank. In such a compromise framework the most logical and fair alternative appears to be the transfer to Palestinian hands of the northern (Nablus-Jenin) and eastern aquifers. Israel would then remain with 350 million m$^3$ of good quality water, sufficient as drinking water for all the Israeli coastal plain, and the Palestinians would receive 300 million m$^3$ from the other two aquifers. With such an arrangement, Israel would concede 100–150 million m$^3$ of water annually. A simple calculation shows that the volume of water that the West Bank received would supply drinking water to a population of four million, even if the living standard rose and the annual water requirements per person at stage 1 reached 50 m$^3$ or more. The allocation of water for the West Bank would steadily increase until it was fully exhausted. The significance of this is that in the first stage the administration of the water regime would remain in Israel's hands, and only after 2010 would the administration of the eastern and northern aquifers pass to the Palestinians. An evident political conclusion arises from this: Israel's boundary with the Palestinian entity must run east of the Green Line, so that the entire western highland aquifer, or at least its drilling zone, remains in Israeli hands.

Regardless of the approach selected, it is clear that natural water is running out quickly, and alternative sources of water have to be sought for both the Palestinian and the Jewish populations. If the Northern Plan is adopted, the residents of the West Bank will be able to desalinate water for themselves along this carrier. Alternatively, they will desalinate water on the Gaza coast and transfer it to the West Bank.

To sum up, the highland aquifers on the West Bank give rise to a complex situation unprecedented in international law and international relations. There can be no doubt that any agreement between the partners to the aquifers will have to provide answers to issues of control of the water, supervision of its quality, and the method of its distribution. Israel at this stage has agreed to recognize only "rights to quantities of water," but not Palestinian control of it. Territorial compromise respecting aquifers will be of great importance in determining the border between Israel and the Palestinian people. It is not by chance that the location of most of the Jewish settlements on the West Bank is on land over the western aquifer. It was clear to the Jews from the outset that a problem would arise regarding the aquifer. The Jewish demographic array serves to reinforce the Israeli claims that will be made: claims for water and claims to thicken Israel's "narrow waist" in the Kalkiliya-Tulkarm area.

What about Palestinian demands regarding the Jordan River, Lake Kinneret, and al Hama? It is inconceivable that Israel will treat Palestinian claims to the Kinneret and al Hama seriously. Since Jordan water is completely used, no water remains to be given. A solution to the Palestinians' water problem in the coming years will emerge from the territories of the West Bank themselves, and in the more distant future through desalination. In the Oslo 2 agreement statements may be found on this subject. The agreement affirms that the Arabs have "rights to water on the West Bank" but there are no statements regarding rights in the Jordan basin (Israel–Palestinian Interim Agreement, Sept. 28, 1995).

My assertions in connection with the Israeli–Jordanian agreement should be reemphasized here. It is a mistake to think that the peace agreements have solved all the problems between the two states (and in the present instance between the state of Israel and the Palestinian people). The peace agreements settle relationships and transform the atmosphere, but they are incapable of providing water that does not exist. The Palestinians who are at this moment fighting for an entity, a state, and their agriculture, will in the future be obliged to come to terms with reality and move on from a mythical posture to a pragmatic posture.

## Water in Negotiations between Israel and Syria (and Lebanon)

Syria and Israel come into contact at four points regarding water issues (see Figure 4.4): Syria has direct and indirect control of the northern sources of the Jordan River, including the Dan springs fed by the Mount Hermon, the section of the Banias in Syrian territory (since before 1967), and the springs of the Hasbani located in Syrian and Lebanese territory. Before 1967, Syria controlled the Golan Heights. It thereby in fact controlled the quality of Kinneret water (among other things, because the Saudi oil pipeline crosses the Golan Heights on its way to Sidon). After 1967 Israel constructed large reservoirs on the Golan Heights. In the event of Israeli withdrawal from the Golan these will pass into Syrian hands. Syria controls the upper and major part of the Yarmuk basin, and therefore it is able to determine the fate of lower Jordan water, and to a small extent to influence Israel's water. If Israel withdraws to the pre-1967 borders Syria will control a very significant part of the Kinneret.

Between Israel and Lebanon the following points of contact exist regarding water. Lebanon controls the Hasbani River and its water, and also the Ayun River, which drains into the Jordan (Figures 4.2, 4.4). The Ayun discharge is small and insignificant. It should be made clear that, de facto, Lebanon is annexed to and governed by Syria in every respect and, therefore, the two countries should be seen as a single body.

Before reviewing each point of contact listed above, note that on the Israeli side there is official willingness for withdrawal (partial or full) from the Golan Heights in return for full peace between Israel and Syria. Yet even in the event of a decision on total withdrawal by Israel from the Golan, a debate will arise as to the line to which Israel should retreat. In the peace agreements with Egypt and with Jordan the international boundary was the frontier agreed on by the two parties in each case. Regarding the Israeli–Syrian border there are various demarcations of the international boundary as a result of the bloodstained history of the relations between the two states. The international boundary was fixed in 1923 between the French-controlled zone in Syria and the British-controlled zone in Palestine (Figure 4.4C); the cease-fire lines were drawn in 1949 between Israel and Syria, with demilitarized zones determined within Israel (Figure 4.4C); the boundary that existed on June 5, 1967, at the outbreak of the Six Day War in which the Golan was captured by Israel, was demarcated de facto by an endless chain of armed border incidents in which the Syrians took advantage of their topographic superiority and bit into the frontier. This line has great implications for water issues (Figure 4.4C). Rumors abound that Syria is demanding that Israel return to the boundary that existed on the eve of the Six Day War. Israel cannot agree to this.

Below I review the bodies of water common to Israel and Syria and Lebanon (see Figure 4.4). Then we shall consider alternatives for a fair distribution of water.

### The Northern Jordan Springs

The Dan Spring, the chief of the Jordan springs, is in Israeli territory, 33–48 feet from the international Israeli–Syrian boundary. Its water sources are on Mount Hermon. Syria can pump water before it reaches the spring, or can harm the quality of the water (intentionally or by error).

The Banias Spring is inside Syrian territory, about 0.6 miles from the international boundary. Syria claims full use of it.

The Hasbani River marks the border between Lebanon and Syria, and at a certain point between Syria, Lebanon, and Israel. It creates a Syrian enclave that penetrates westward from the Golan Heights to the Hasbani (see Figure 4.4A). Hence, Syria is a full partner in this river and in some of its springs (the al Wazzani Springs). If Israel withdraws to the international boundary, Syria will have full control of the Banias and the Hasbani and indirect control of the Dan. Such a situation existed until the Six Day War. Since then the demands for Jordan water have greatly increased, as have the risks of pollution of the water sources.

### The Golan Heights

Israeli withdrawal to the international boundary will restore Syrian control over all the Jordan tributaries that empty into the Kinneret. Water pollution in this area will harm Israel's most important water source. In consequence of an Israeli–Syrian peace agreement the flow of oil in the Saudi pipeline would undoubtedly be renewed. Any damage to this pipeline would be catastrophic for the Kinneret. According to frontier maps of 1921–1922, the course of the Jordan itself (between the Golan Heights and Israel) is located in Israel. According to the frontier lines of 1967, the Syrians will become full partners in this stretch of the Jordan River.

### Lake Kinneret

Syria will return to the shores of the Kinneret according to any of the three versions of the international boundary. That of 1921–1922 is 32 feet away from the shoreline; according to the two other versions Syria will be a full partner in the Kinneret water and will demand territorial rights over it, as it did in the 1960s. In either case it will not be possible to inspect Syrian activities in the Kinneret, and the significance of that is that the Kinneret will become an international lake with all that this implies.

### The Yarmuk Basin (Figure 4.4B)

Syria holds the key to the Jordanian water regime. This fact has serious geopolitical implications from the Israeli viewpoint, as the Jordanian kingdom is highly sensitive to coercion on the part of Syria.

**Alternatives for a Fair Distribution of Water between Israel and Syria/ Lebanon**

### The Johnston Plan

The Johnston plan recommends that Syria use 20 million m³ of Banias water and a further approximate 22 million m³ for irrigating the Bataykha valley to the northeast of the Kinneret. This amounts to rights over 42 million m³ of water. The Johnston plan allocates 35 million m³ of Hasbani water to Lebanon. The volumes given to Syria and Lebanon total 77 million m³ of water, or 10 percent of the water potential of the upper Jordan River. The plan apportions 90 million m³ of Yarmuk water to the Syrians. In fact, today the Syrians use at least 200 million m³ of this water. If the principles of the Johnston plan are accepted, Syria will be obliged to give up Yarmuk water to receive more water in the upper Jordan.

Syria is not committed to the Johnston plan, and it may claim that it has rights to Jordan water in proportion to the amount it contributes to this water (about 50 percent of the upper Jordan). It will invoke the Helsinki principles, arguing that the land of the Golan Heights requires irrigation and that Syria's south suffers a dearth of water. It will also claim that in return for this water it is paying the price of full peace with Israel. Agreement by Israel to such a model as this means agreement that Syria will use 77–100 million m³ of water of the upper Jordan River and 200 million m³ more in the Yarmuk basin, a total of 277–300 million m³. Such a deal would require the Syrians to be certain to keep away from Lake Kinneret and the Dan Spring, and to prevent harm to the quality of the water in the Kinneret. It would be impossible to impose these demands on them, but only to rely on their goodwill and reasonableness.

I cite here the words of General Uri Sagi, chief of Israeli military intelligence until October 1995: "As far as I am concerned, the matter of water is more vital than other matters that we are arguing about. If the political process leads to the loss of our control over our important water sources we are liable to find ourselves forced to alter this situation, and then Israel will be perceived as the aggressor. Wrong handling of this problem is liable to accelerate friction, prevent economic development, and in the worst case lead to violent confrontation" (Sagi interview, Sept. 9, 1995). On this question too some will argue that Israel can desalinate seawater instead of transferring Kinneret water to the Tel Aviv metropolitan area and the Negev, and that therefore there is nothing to prevent Israel from handing the Kinneret over to the control of the Syrians, the Jordanians, and the Palestinians. According to this logic, doing so would result in considerable financial saving. The question of the exact border between Israel and Syria would then become irrelevant.

Another proposal put forward to overcome the water shortage in southern Syria envisages a large pipeline being laid from the Euphrates to the Damascus region and southward, thus freeing the Jordan River entirely, and possibly the Yarmuk also, for Israel, the Palestinians, and the Jordanian kingdom.

## Conclusion

Between the Madrid Conference and September 28, 1995, the date of the signing of the interim stage of the Declaration of Principles between Israel and the Palestinians, relations between Israel and its neighbors underwent a revolutionary change. In consequence, there were great hopes for cooperation between states that were hostile and there was talk of a common market on the European model.

In the second half of the 1990s there is some flexibility, and practical solutions are being sought with less talk of macro solutions. Similarly, the human aspect is being stressed among the negotiators, along the lines of the multilateral talks.

At the time of writing, the Gaza and Jericho agreements have been signed between Israel and the Palestinians, and Israeli withdrawal from the large towns on the West Bank has been implemented, but the road to the final conclusion of the negotiations on water is still long. This subject is inextricably bound up with questions of security, refugees, corridors, the future of the Jewish settlements on the West Bank, and the future of Jerusalem.

Meanwhile, various teams from both sides are going ahead with solving urgent problems such as a common sewage system for Israeli and Palestinian cities, running water supply to the growing population, and the like.

A comprehensive peace agreement has been signed between Israel and the Jordanian kingdom. As already noted, this agreement does not in fact solve the water problems of the region but merely postpones the crisis as in the past. Negotiations with Syria and Lebanon have not yet been concluded. At this point it is worth being aware of several issues: Israel is the only developed state in the Jordan basin. Consequently, demands are being made on Israel to be the first to enter the age of desalination and to revolutionize its economy.

Indeed, on May 30, 1997, the Israeli water commissioner stated that preparations were under way for desalination of seawater as early as 2005. According to the plan, by 2040 the supply of desalinated water would stand at 800 million m³, at a cost of $0.65–1.00 a cubic meter (*Ha'aretz*, 30 May, 1997). Natural water, therefore, will be shared increasingly with the Jordanian kingdom, as already noted, and with the Palestinians, as we saw in the list of various alternatives (Fig. 4.7).

In consequence of the water agreements between Israel and the Jordanian kingdom, the Palestinians and the Syrians will almost certainly de-

mand that Israel sign similar agreements with them. At the end of such
a process Israel is liable to find itself in the following situation: giving
150 million m³ of water to the Jordanian kingdom; giving 250 million
m³ of water at least (140 million m³ more than in 1995) to the Palestinians on the West Bank; giving 10–50 million m³ to Gaza to overcome
urgent human distress; in the near future giving at least, 77–100 million
m³ to Syria and Lebanon following the Johnston plan. In sum, this
means that Israel will give away 500–550 million m³ of good quality
water, which is 25 percent of all Israel's water sources.

This conclusion has implications for Israeli domestic politics. In Israel voices are heard claiming that there is no precedent in the world
for such openhandedness with national resources. The argument (which
today is supported by a majority in Israeli society) is that it is not worth
gaining peace in return for which Israel gives the other party such a
wealth of land and water resources.

If Israel agrees to this arrangement in return for full peace, already in
the present decade 1995–2005 it will have to acquire this amount of
water by desalination in order to satisfy the water requirements of its
population. There will be a heavy cost for desalination in the economic
and the ecological spheres.

## The Legal and Geopolitical Situation in the Jordan-Yarmuk Basin

Among the riparian states there is no agreement on the joint use of the
entire Jordan-Yarmuk basin, but there are full or partial agreements
among several of the states on utilizing parts of it. The first agreement
is the treaty signed by Britain and France in 1920, which determined
that a joint committee should be established to study the agricultural
and electricity needs in the basin of the Jordan and its tributaries, and
to decide the water distribution to the satisfaction of the residents of the
countries under the rule of these two powers (Saliba, 1968: 60).

In 1922, Britain and France signed an additional agreement, in which
the rights of Lebanese and Syrian residents to sail and fish on the Hula
Lake, Lake Kinneret, and the Jordan River were made no less important
than the rights of the residents of Palestine (Saliba, 1968: 60).

In 1953, Syria and Jordan signed an agreement concerning the joint
use of Yarmuk water according to the Bunger plan, which was based on
the construction of a dam at the Maqarin site. According to the agreement, Syria would receive 75 percent of the electricity to be generated
by the dams to be built on the Yarmuk, and Jordan would receive all the
water except that required by Syria (Stevens, 1965: 37; Nimrod, 1966:
35; Saliba, 1968: 37). This agreement was not implemented, and each

state built its own development projects. In September 1987 the two states signed further agreements for constructing a dam at the Maqarin site, the al Wahda Dam. This agreement also determined that Jordan would use most of the water, except for certain specific needs of Syria for irrigation, and Syria would receive 75 percent of the electricity. Despite this agreement, Syria and Jordan are divided over Syria's water development projects in the upper Yarmuk.

From 1955 to 1994 there existed between Israel and Jordan (through the agency of the United States) a de facto agreement on the adoption of the Johnston plan. There were several disagreements between the two states over the interpretation of the plan, for example, regarding the volumes of water that were to be transferred to the Palestinians on the West Bank at the expense of the Jordanian kingdom, and also regarding the amount of Yarmuk water Israel was authorized to use. Still, Israel and Jordan managed to find the "golden path" between these interpretations.

In 1994 Israel and Jordan signed a full peace agreement of which clause 6 and Appendix II deal with questions of water of the Jordan and Yarmuk Rivers. Meanwhile, the birth of the Palestinian entity has taken place, which did not exist at the time of the Johnston plan, and it too claims rights to the water in the Jordan basin. At the time of writing, interim agreements have been signed between the Palestinian entity and Israel, and the final agreement will apparently be signed not before May 1999.

Syria and Lebanon are not committed to the Johnston plan. Syria is adamant in its demand for the return of all the Golan Heights and control of its water sources. Lebanon, which is controlled by Syria, insists on its right to Hasbani water, which since the 1970s has been inside the Israeli security zone.

Throughout this chapter we have seen the close connection between the subject of water and the Israel–Arab conflict: Arab pressure resulted in a change in Israeli water planning and the diversion of the National Water Carrier from the Hula to the Kinneret. Israel's achievements in realizing the NWC were the stimulus for the Arab diversion plan. This, in turn, was the cause for the deterioration of the situation on the eve of the Six Day War. It is possible that the water shortage of the Jordanian kingdom was a major catalyst in its alacrity in signing the peace treaty with Israel. Water issues continue to be a serious obstacle to the attainment of full peace between Israel and Syria and the Palestinians.

## Distribution of Jordan River Water

The principles recommended in the distribution of Jordan water were in fact laid down in the Johnston plan. In 1966 these principles served as the basis for the Helsinki Accords principles on international rivers. Professionals in all states connected to the basin accepted them (Table 4.14). However, the plan was not implemented and meanwhile the situation in the region has changed markedly, so there is room for consideration of new principles of distribution. Meanwhile, also, the Palestinian entity has come into being. In every state of the region except Lebanon water projects have been implemented that have completely changed the water balance of the river and its tributaries. Is there any water left to distribute? Should an attempt perhaps be made to modify existing projects and existing plans? I have recounted the actions taken in the field and have presented various models of solutions to the water shortage of every state in the basin. I concluded that in truth there is nothing left to distribute and there is nowhere else from which to take water. The transfer of water from one state to another is a highly temporary solution. A long-term solution is linked to desalination, in addition to efforts at saving water and recycling sewage water.

The case of the River Jordan is unique in world hydropolitics and geopolitics owing to the combination of a small quantity of water and a large number of partners, among whom there exists a prolonged and very serious conflict. The principles of water distribution to be fixed in the future peace agreements with the Palestinians and the Syrians (and Lebanese) will serve as a model for all countries of the world.

Table 4.14 shows the criteria that should be taken into account if Jordan River water is to be redistributed. All the partners in the basin are located in arid zones, all contribute water to the basin to some degree or other, and all use the water to the maximal extent. Israel's incomes are far larger than those of the other states, therefore it is Israel that is called on to concede water in favor of the other partners in the basin, and this, indeed, is what Israel is doing, in keeping with the peace agreements.

It should be recalled that apart from the existing tensions between Israel and its neighbors over water, there are also tensions between Syria and Jordan on the question of the Yarmuk, between Syria and Lebanon on the use of Lebanon's water, and there is a potential for tension between the Palestinians and the Jordanian kingdom.

Table 4.14: Criteria for Water Allocation in the Jordan Basin

| Country | Share in Area of Basin (%) | Water Contribution to the River (%) | Present Use (million m$^3$) | GNP 1995 | Treatises and Legal Agreements in the Jordan Basin |
|---|---|---|---|---|---|
| Lebanon | - | - | 5 | 2660 | |
| Northern basin | 24 | 16 | - | - | |
| Southern basin | - | - | - | - | |
| Syria | - | - | 200 | 1180 | Franco-British agreements 1920, 1922 with Jordan 1923, 1987 |
| Northern basin | 38 | 21 | - | - | |
| Southern basin | 41 | 50 | - | - | Peace Agreement with Jordan - 1994 |
| Israel | 38 | 63 | 650 | 15920 | Declaration of Principles with Palestinians, 1993, 1995 |
| Northern basin | | | | | |
| Southern basin | 6 | 2.5 | - | - | |
| Jordan | | | 270-400 | 1510 | Peace Agreement with Israel - 1994 |
| Northern basin | - | - | - | - | |
| Southern basin | 45 | 43 | 100 | 1511 | Declaration of principles Sept. 13, 1993 with Israel, including some items on water allocation sharing |
| Palestinians' | | | | | |
| Northern basin | - | - | - | - | |
| Southern basin | 8.0 | 4.5 | | | |

# Chapter 5

# The Orontes River as a
# Geopolitical Problem

## Drainage Basin and Flow Regime

The sources of the Orontes (the Asi) lie in Lebanon, a few miles north-west of the Litani's sources, near the town of Baalbek in the Beqa valley. Since the 1970s this region has been completely under Syrian control. The Orontes flows in Lebanon for about 22 miles. At its entry point to Syria it crosses the Homs plain, part of which is covered with basalt, traverses the cities of Homs and Hama, then turns west to the Ghab valley. There it flows north for about 39 miles, and enters Turkey. The Ghab valley, 39 miles long and 7.5 miles wide, was for centuries flooded by the waters of the Orontes, which transformed it into a foul swamp until the French, and later the Syrians, drained it. For a distance of about 25 miles the Orontes serves as a border determined in 1939 between Turkey and Syria. In Turkey the river turns sharply southwest and empties into the Mediterranean not far from the city of Antakya (ancient Antioch). The length of the river within Turkey is about 31 miles.

The flow regime of the river varies according to its location. In the Lebanon region is receives melted snow water from Mount Lebanon and the Anti-Lebanon Mountains, and its discharge upon leaving Lebanon is about 380 million m³. In its continuation in Syria the river enters a Mediterranean region and receives 16–20 inches of rain annually. In this region, between the Syrian-Lebanese border and Hama, an additional 80 million m³ are added to the river. Close to the Ghab region, in the Ansarian Mountains, the amount of rain reaches 60 inches annually. In this region the river receives stream and spring water from the west (the Ansarian Mountains) and from the eastern hills, and when it enters the Ghab valley, it receives an addition 700 million m³ of water.

In Turkey the river receives 260 million m³ from the tributaries entering from the north: the Afrin, which rises in Turkey, flows mostly through Syria and ends in Turkey; and the Kara Su and the Ofor, which drain the northern extremity of the Syrian–African rift, and whose general direction is north to south. The average annual discharge of the Orontes is 1.47 billion m³ (US Army Corps of Engineers, 1991).

## Use of the Orontes Water

The river Orontes was already used for irrigation in antiquity, as attested by the ancient wooden water wheels on the river at Homs and Hama. Near Homs, there is also a Roman dam. The system of aqueducts and irrigation canals around these two ancient cities likewise indicates the use of the water in early times. It appears that in the Ghab valley, too, irrigation networks were established, but in Ottoman times they fell into decay through neglect and the river flooded the valley, creating the swamps.

As noted, work on draining the Ghab swamps began during French rule in Syria and a new dam, the Qatina, was built near Homs (Figure 5.1). It was completed at the end of the 1930s, being 3,675 feet long, 40 feet high, and with a storage capacity of 200 million m³ water able to irrigate 20,000 hectares (50,000 acres) between Homs and Hama by means of a modern irrigation canal (Soffer, 1992).

Syria began systematic draining of the Ghab swamps in 1954 and completed the work in 1968. The riverbed was deepened and widened, and a dam, the Asharna, was built at the entrance to the valley, supplying water to all its regions by canals running along its entire length. Miles of drainage channels were likewise dug in the valley. As a result, the valley changed its appearance; the swamps that had covered an area of 43,200 hectares (108,000 acres) were gone, replaced by farmland: 68,000 hectares (170,000 acres) of fertile land, some formerly swamps, were prepared for irrigation, and they yielded a variety of crops, mostly cotton. Several more thousand hectares of land were prepared in the vicinity of the Asharna Dam for irrigation by water from that dam as well as from another built nearby on the Maharde River and storing 60 million m³ of water (Figure 5.1).

Between Homs and the Maharde lies more land with high agricultural potential. Some of it, between Homs and the Rastan Dam, which was built on the Orontes, has already been reclaimed for agriculture. The Rastan Dam is 12.5 miles north of Homs, and it stores 250 million m³ of water that irrigate the land on the riverbanks approaching Homs.

Additional smaller water projects were built on the riverbanks, such

*Figure 5.1:* Water Projects in the Orontes Basin

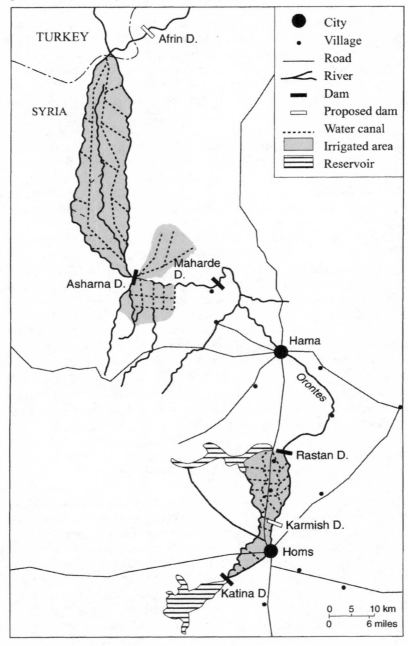

as the Yafiya Dam, about 12.5 miles north of Hama, which stores 65 million m³; the Tanuna Dam, with 2.6 million m³; the Tel Dan Dam, with 15.6 million m³; and a dam on the Hama, for irrigating 100 hectares (250 acres). Similarly, it is planned to build two more dams: the Karmish, to be constructed north of Hama with a capacity to store 275 million m³ for irrigating 25,000 hectares (62,500 acres), and the Afrin dam in the north, with 230 million m³ for irrigating 20,000 hectares (50,000 acres) in the river valley between Aleppo and the Turkish–Syrian border. There is also a plan to drain a swamp area of 15,000 hectares (37,500 acres) that has not yet been treated (Manner and Sagafi-Nejad, 1985: 262). In all, the dams on the Orontes and its tributaries store about 600 million m³ of water, which irrigate about 68,000 hectares (170,000 acres).

Two of the dams also generate electricity: the Rastan Dam produces about 100 million kwh a year, and the Maharde Dam 6 million kwh a year.

Owing to the large-scale use of the Orontes water and its pollution with effluents, it is not used for drinking. Epidemics of typhus, dysentery, and even cholera are frequent in the lower Orontes because people drink the water (Naff and Matson, 1984: 118). Another problem linked to the Orontes is overpumping of the groundwater in its basin (Beaumont et al., 1988). The Ghab project seems to have reached maximum capacity. In 1991 about 1.5 million people lived in the Ghab valley, being 12.5 percent of the total Syrian population, and it is densely inhabited. Land reform laws instituted in this crowded region allocated about 11,000 hectares (25,250 acres) of land to landless farmers, a measure that improved their economic circumstances. The importance of the valley to Syria is very great, as attested by the development projects and the population centers along its length.

## Geopolitics and Use of Orontes Water

The Orontes is an international river that rises in Lebanon, flows mostly through Syria, and ends in Turkey. However, its use, for the present, does not arouse open conflict among its basin states. Lebanon is not at odds with Syria over use of Orontes water because there is no government in Lebanon that will fight for its rights, and the part of Lebanon through which the Orontes flows is under Syrian control (Figure 5.2). The importance of the Orontes to Turkey is not great, either for irrigation or for drinking (for the residents of Antakya), owing to the pollution in its water. One estimate puts the amount of water entering Turkey at about 120 million m³ . As Syria is about to build two new dams, the

*Figure 5.2:* Geopolitical Circles in the Orontes Basin

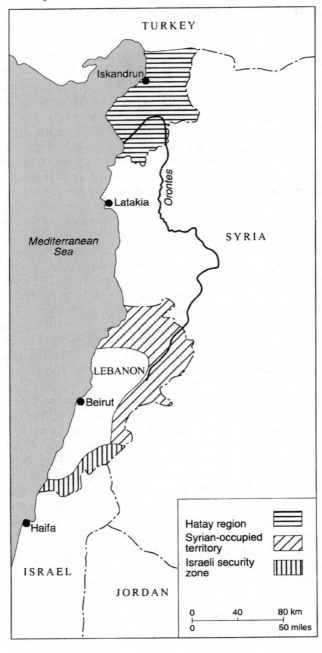

Zeizoun and Kastoun, the quantity entering Turkey will drop to about 25 million m³ (Turkey, 1995).

Although the use of the river does not appear to cause problems, the true situation is different. In 1972 Syria and Lebanon announced that they had signed an agreement whereby Lebanon would use about 80 million m³ and Syria would use the rest. On September, 20, 1994, both states again announced the signing of a new agreement and again gave a figure of 80 million m³ used by the Lebanese in normal years, while in drought years the quantity would be reduced by 20 percent (*al Ba'ath* Jan. 18, 1995; announcement by Syrian irrigation minister). However, the agreement is not enforced and Syria uses most of the river's water. The fact that the Orontes's sources are located within Lebanese jurisdiction disturbs Syria greatly. Syria has informed Lebanon that due to the lack of security that prevails in the northern Lebanese Beqa valley, the defense treaty that is to be signed between the two countries will include a section ensuring Syrian control of the Orontes headwaters even if Syria withdraws from all Lebanese territory (Cooley, 1983: 11). Syria insists on its need to control the Orontes headwater also owing to the perceived threat posed by Israel. The Syrians argue that the Israeli army advanced very close to the Orontes headwaters (Ein Zarka, the source of the Orontes, is "only" 47 miles distant from the point to which the Israeli army penetrated on the Beirut-Damascus axis in 1982), and that this vulnerability poses a threat to the Orontes. Meanwhile Syria has annexed Lebanon (with the silent assent of Israel and the United States), so the Lebanese Beqa valley may be regarded as a Syrian geopolitical unit in every respect. Syria will continue to do as it pleases with the river.

Turkey does not need Orontes water and is willing to sign an agreement with Syria that will allow the latter to exploit all the river water. However, in return Turkey demands that Syria give up on its demands regarding the Hatay region (Syria claims ownership of this region, which in 1939 was transferred from it to Turkey) (Figure 5.2). Syria needs a comprehensive agreement with Turkey concerning use of the Euphrates, and therefore it will have no choice but to agree to this (Naff and Matson, 1984: 122). As long as Turkey continues to use increasingly more Euphrates water at Syria's and Iraq's expense, Syria's need to reach an inclusive agreement with Turkey on water use, including that of the Orontes, grows greater. Syria will be forced soon to yield to Turkey and to recognize the annexation of the Hatay region; in return Turkey will allow Syria to use most of the Orontes water.

## Factors in the Division of the River Water

Apart from the Syrian–Lebanese agreement of 1972 there are no international agreements concerning use of the Orontes, and Syria has been the primary beneficiary of the river. As to whether conflicts are likely to arise concerning use of the river water, some factors that determine its fair division should be examined.

### River Basin Area and Length of the River within Riparian Countries

The Orontes rises in Lebanon, but this country's share of the river basin is only about 12 percent. Turkey, the downstream state, contains about 25 percent of the basin, and the remainder is in Syrian territory. As for the length of the river, about 23 miles, or 5.5 percent, is in Lebanon; 309 miles, or 81 percent, is in Syria; and 31 miles, or 8 percent, is in Turkey. For a stretch of 25 miles (5.5 percent) the Orontes serves as the border between Turkey and Syria. According to the factors of river basin area and length of the river, Turkey is entitled to use Orontes water. Lebanon, on the other hand, has a very small portion of the river basin and only a short section of the river's length.

### Contribution of the Riparians to the River's Flow

The upstream discharge of the Orontes, within Lebanese territory, is about 380 million m$^3$ annually. The discharge in Syria contributes 830 million m$^3$ annually. I have no data on the Orontes's discharge in Turkey, but it is known that the Afrin tributary contributes 260 million m$^3$ to the Orontes. From this fact it can be calculated that the three states are entitled to use the water: Lebanon is entitled to 27 percent, Syria to 60 percent, and Turkey to the remaining 13 percent. In fact, Turkey actually deserves less than this, because the Afrin flows mostly through Syria; moreover, the tributaries that join the Orontes within Turkish territory have not been taken into account here.

### The Climate

Syria's climate is more arid than that of the other two states. Lebanon and Turkey have plentiful rainfall and water sources for irrigation.

### Past and Present Use of River Water

Syria has historical rights over use of Orontes water and is also its primary user today. As stated, an agreement exists between Syria and Lebanon granting Lebanon the right to use 80 million m$^3$ of water annually, but it is unknown whether Lebanon in fact uses this water. Turkey utilizes the Orontes, if at all, only locally; there are no large water projects on the Orontes within Turkish territory. It is known that Turkey uses the northern tributaries of the Orontes for agricultural purposes.

*Economic and Social Needs*

Syria is locked in a difficult economic situation and is battling constantly to increase its food production and to curb the growth rate of its population. The economic and social needs of Turkey in the Orontes basin area are less that Syria's. Lebanon requires rebuilding throughout its territory, including the Orontes basin area.

Considering all these factors, it seems that Syria is entitled to use most of the Orontes water.

The Orontes's supply is too meager to be a cause of real riparian conflict. However, the river will certainly come up for discussion in any agreement to be signed in the future between Syria and Turkey.

Will enough water be left in the river to satisfy Syrian as well Lebanese needs? It seems that today Syria has already exhausted its possibilities of using the river water, and will therefore need other sources for the growing population in this already heavily populated region of the country. Since, in the foreseeable future, Syria will have no other available water resources, it will have to become sparing in its use of the river water, taking less for agriculture, particularly for cotton and other crops, and allocating more to domestic and industrial needs. In such a situation Syria seems unlikely to allow the development of water projects on the Orontes in the Lebanese Beqa valley for the use of local Lebanese inhabitants. The problem is that in the Beqa the mostly Shi'ite population has increased at very high rates and its requirements have grown accordingly. The water problem of this population will be solved by bringing water from the western part of the state or from the Litani. Another emergency solution is also possible: if the water situation in the Damascus basin becomes worse, Syria will divert part of the Orontes to the Zbadani River, which flows into the Damascus basin. To compensate for the water diverted eastward, Syria would expedite the transfer of water from western Lebanon in the Beqa or the transfer of Litani water northward and then eastward. Lebanon's current and apparently future chronic weakness and its de facto occupation by Syria will make it easier for Syria to do as it pleases.

*Chapter 6*

# "Internationalized" Water Sources: The Litani River

The previous chapters have dealt with rivers whose exploitation sparks conflict because they are international. This chapter addresses water sources that are not international, but for historical and geographical reasons they have led to verbal conflicts between Middle Eastern states and so have become "international."

The case in point is the Litani River, which runs entirely within Lebanon.

The Litani rises in the Beqa valley, close to Baalbek. From there it flows southwest and approaches the Israeli border about four miles north of the Hula Valley. At this point the river turns almost at right angles westward and empties into the sea (Figure 6.1). It is about 106 miles long, and its drainage basin is about 884 square miles. The sources of the Litani are karstic springs that flow into it from both sides of the Beqa and springs fed by the snows of Mount Lebanon and the Anti-Lebanon Mountains. Most of the river's water is from winter rains and melting snow in the spring.

The upper section of the river flows through the Beqa plain, and therefore it is quite easily utilized here for irrigation. Its middle section flows through a gorge in a hilly region. The lower section of the river is also stepped, and it becomes level only on entering the coastal plain.

### Flow Regime and Discharge of the Litani

Because the river's sources are primarily karstic springs, it flows all year round, although like every Mediterranean river its main flow period is during the rainy winter months and the spring when the snow melts. Sixty percent of its water flows from January to April (see Figure

213

*Figure 6.1:* The Litani River and Environment

6.2; Naff and Matson, 1984: 13–64). The discharge of the Litani changes from year to year owing to variation in the amount of precipitation in the region. The annual discharge graph from 1947–1971 shows a four to five year cycle, with extreme differences between the high and the low periods (Figure 6.3). In 1954 the discharge was about 1 billion m³, and in 1970 it was only 184 million m³. The multiyear average is about 580 million m³ annually. About 45 percent of the discharge is from the upper section of the river, about 45 percent from the middle section, and only about 10 percent from the lower section (Ron, 1982: 93; Naff and Matson, 1984: 67). These data conflict with other figures published in the past. Rutenberg estimated the Litani's flow at about 2 billion m³ per year; Blass's estimate was 1 billion m³; and De Vaumas estimated the flow at 610 million m³ (Rutenberg, 1920, 29; De Vaumas, 1954; Nimrod, 1966).

## Exploitation of the Litani Waters

During the period of the French mandate there was a plan to utilize the upper section of the river by building a series of diversion dams. An-

*Figure 6.2:* The Litani Monthly Flow (1954, 1963, 1970)

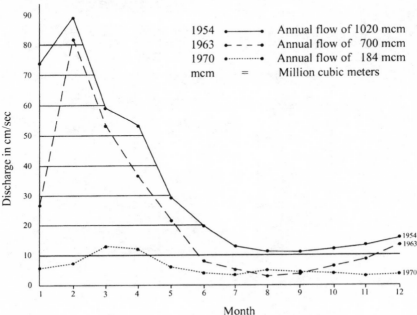

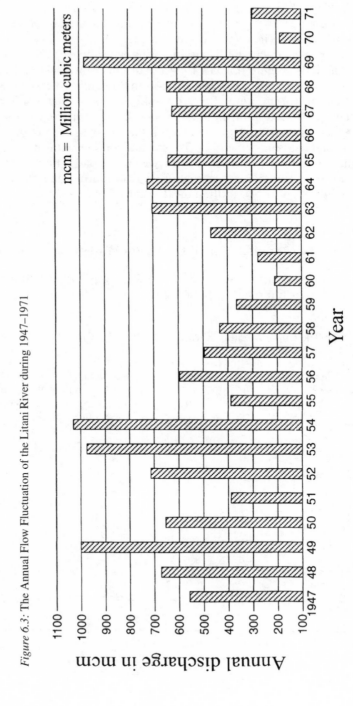

*Figure 6.3:* The Annual Flow Fluctuation of the Litani River during 1947–1971

other plan proposed to use the river water in the Anjar region of the Lebanon valley. In 1944 Lowdermilk proposed diverting the Litani into the Jordan. In 1954 the authority for developing the Litani was established, and serious planning of water use began. In 1966 Kuwait offered to build a dam on the Litani close to Nabatiyeh (the Moifadon Dam) to irrigate the Nabatiyan heights (Naff and Matson, 1984: 64, 65, 73–81).

The 1954 plan was to build three dams on the Litani: one at Qarun on its upper section to divert the Litani to the Awali to generate electricity; one at Khardala to store 120 million $m^3$ for electricity and irrigation; and one in its lower section. In 1956 the foundations of the Qarun Dam and two power stations were laid (Figure 6.4A). For political and ethnic reasons the building of the dams was delayed for years, until finally only the Qarun Dam was built, its construction lasting from 1961 to 1966. It is 197 feet wide, 3,608 feet long, and its capacity is 220 million $m^3$ (of which 4 percent is lost to seepage and an additional small quantity is lost to evaporation). The dam allows water to be stored seasonally and annually and thereby ensures a fixed flow of water to the power station downstream.

**Electricity Production**

For electricity production, most of the Litani's water is diverted through a channel and tunnels to the Awali River. The hydroelectric project consists of four power plants (Figure 6.4A, B). The first station, at the Qarun Dam, has not yet been completed. The second station is located close to Marqaba and can produce 34 megawatts of electricity. A four-mile tunnel brings the water from Qarun Dam to the plant, and the electricity is produced by the force of the water falling about 460 feet. Third is the Awali plant, which produces 108 megawatts. The water reaches the station from below the Jebel Niha ridge in an eleven-mile tunnel. The height difference between the two stations is about 1,378 feet. The fourth and last is the Jun plant, whose capacity is 48 megawatts. The water reaches the station through a 4.1-mile tunnel and falls a total of 492 feet. The amount of water planned to flow in the tunnel system is about 520 million $m^3$ (495 million $m^3$ from the Litani, and about 30 million $m^3$ from subterranean springs). There are different data concerning the actual amount of water flowing in the system. The generating capacity of the three operating plants is 190 megawatts. They provide electricity for Beirut, Sidon, Tyre, and all the southern Lebanon villages.

**Irrigation**

The original plan was to irrigate 25,000 hectares (62,500 acres) in southern Lebanon, including the Nabatiyan plateau, with water intended

*Figure 6.4:* The Litani-Awali Hydroelectric Project

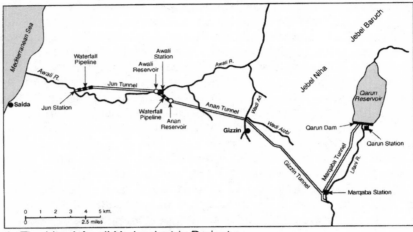

A. The Litani-Awali Hydroelectric Project

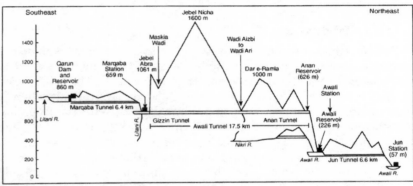

B. Cross-Section of the Project                    According to Z. Ron 1982

to flow from one of the power plant tunnels in northern Lebanon, but this has not yet been accomplished. In fact, water flows directly from the river in canals and aqueducts on the coastal plain (about 100 million m³). Large quantities of water are utilized (according to estimates, about 100 million m³) from Lake Qarun for irrigation in the Beqa (Naff and Matson, 1984: 71–72).

According to a US Army document (US Army Corps of Engineers, 1991), the Awali receives only about 236 million m³ and the supply in the lower portion of the Litani is 500 million m³. From personal observation by the author of the water flowing in the lower channel (1982–1985), it seems that this document is completely groundless; at its mouth, the Litani's flow is as small as that of the small Israeli coastal rivers.

According to estimates, about 80 million m³ of water are used in this region for irrigation. It follows that about 20–70 million m³ are not used at all. According to another estimate, about 120 million m³ are not utilized (Ron, 1982). On January 8, 1995, the chairman of the Litani Project executive council stated that work had begun on the building of the dam at Khardala to store 120 million m³ for irrigation, and in addition to irrigate 20,000 hectares in the Beqa (*al Ba'ath*, Syria, Jan. 8, 1995).

## The Geopolitical Aspects of the Litani

Although the Litani is not an international river, its links with the Zionist enterprise made it into one, so to speak. Three historical proposals connected the Litani to the Zionist endeavor. One was that made by the World Zionist Organization to the League of Nations in 1919 concerning the borders of the Jewish entity to be founded in Palestine (*Hebrew Encyclopedia*, vol. 6, pp. 524–28). This proposal included the Litani basin within the borders of the entity. The League of Nations rejected the proposal out of hand. Some Zionist leaders claimed that the Litani basin was the natural northern border of Eretz Israel, and some spoke of the potential of the wasted water in the Litani.

The second proposal came in the 1940s in the Lowdermilk plan. This was widely publicized: it called for overall utilization of the Jordan and its tributaries (Lowdermilk, 1945). Subsequent to the Lowdermilk plan, Blass and Hays produced a new idea. The intention was to divert the Litani to the Hula valley and to produce electricity for Lebanon through the waterfall to be obtained from this diversion (Kally, 1965; Blass, 1973). The idea was then first mooted to irrigate parts of the western basin of Palestine and also both sides of the Jordan valley with surplus water from the Jordan, Yarmuk, and Litani Rivers. The Kinneret would then be the main reservoir. This plan could have been realized only with the agreement of the Arab states, but they refused to cooperate with Israel, and each state went its own separate way in developing the Litani and the Jordan water sources.

The third proposal was by Blass during Johnston's mission in the region (1953–1955). Blass, a member of the Israeli delegation, insisted that the Litani River be included in the potential water for reallocation of the Jordan basin. His proposal was rejected by Johnston and was removed from the Israeli demands (Blass, 1973).

In the 1960s an Arab diversion plan spoke of diverting water from the Hasbani springs, one of the main sources of the Jordan, to the Litani to prevent Israel from using Arab water. As is recalled, Israel prevented execution of this plan, and the Israel–Litani connection once more was removed from the international agenda. On September 8, 1967, Israeli Prime Minister Levi Eshkol declared that wasted water from the Litani amounting to half a billion cubic meters could be used to aid the residents of the region (Naff and Matson, 1984). However, this connection continues to exist through repeated rumors that Israel uses Litani water or plans to use it.

The Arab accusations are expressed in various publications, for example: "The general opinion is that Israel diverted the Litani water to the Hasbani by a tunnel, and through it 500 million m³ annually reach Israeli territory. In this way Israel hurts Lebanese farmers who used the water" (Musallam, 1989: 6).

Another publication says that "Israel has a plan to divert 400 million m³ annually of Litani water from the Khardala Dam (close to the Khardala Bridge, where the river once turned westward), which is planned to be built. This quantity is about 60 percent of the total Litani discharge. With this deed Israel is returning to execute its plans of 1919" (Halawani, 1985: 52). Halawani added that in order to divert the Litani's water, the Khardala Dam, which still does not exist, must be built, and a five-mile tunnel must be dug.

In 1990 Musallam wrote: "It is widely believed that Israel has diverted water from the Litani river through a tunnel, thereby delivering to Israel an additional 500 MCM annually" (Musallam, 1990). Al Akram stated that the transfer of Litani water to Israel would allow an enlargement of irrigated area in Israel by 25 percent (Al Akram, 1992: 93–94).

Many such claims were heard in the non-Arab world also, one even coming from a Russian source, head of the Institute for Middle East Research in the former USSR, Eugeni Primakov, and Russian foreign minister in 1997, wrote: "Israel has already begun diverting the waters of the Litani" (*Monday Morning*, Dec. 26, 1982).

A western publication stated: "Lebanon is afraid that Israel has already begun diverting the Litani and there are recurring, although unproven, rumors that Israel has already begun to transfer water to the Galilee settlements in an underground siphon" (*Mideast Market*, July 22, 1983: 10).

About one month later, journalist John Cooley wrote: "I would not be surprised if it turns out that Israel's first diversionary project of the Litani water has already been born" (*Middle East*, July 22, 1983, p. 10).

On January 29, 1991, *MEED* reported: "Fresh rumors say that Tel Aviv is in the final stages of transferring water from the Litani to the northern Galilee" (*MEED*, Jan. 25, 1991).

In 1990, in testimony before the US House of Representatives on water problems in the Middle East, Professor Naff stated definitively: "In fact, owing to serious shortages Israel is presently conducting a large-scale operation of trucking water to Israel from the Litani river" (Naff, 1990).

To carry water from the Litani to the Jordan in a truck (for example, a milk tanker, enlarged, say to hold 50 $m^3$ of water), the vehicle would have to descend to the bottom of the river course close to Khardala, and then ascend, filled with water, about six to nine miles up a difficult, twisting road to the course of the Jordan or one of its tributaries. A cautious estimate is that the truck could manage this trip between four and six times a day, and so transfer between 200 and 300 $m^3$ of water. The cost of running a truck is about $1,000 a day. This would mean that each cubic meter of water would cost $3.5–5, almost double or four times the price of desalinated water.

Where did this notion come from? It is possible that its source is the trucks that bring water from the Litani for domestic use in the villages near the river, such as Marj Ayun and Kliya—a method also commonly used by the Bedouins in Upper and Lower Galilee in Israel whose homes are far from the local pipe network. It is also possible that the soldiers of the South Lebanon Army use the Litani water in their camps for drinking.

In addition, Western and Arab specialists on the Middle East maintain that Israel embarked on the military "Litani Operation" (1978) as well as the Lebanon War (1982), and that Israel today occupies the southern Lebanon security zone, not for security reasons but in order to draw water from the Litani (*Mideast Market*, 1983; Naff and Matson, 1984: 75; Halawani, 1985; Amery, 1993; Schofield, 1993).

Professor Naff, who has published much about the water sources in the area, wrote on this issue in his 1984 book, and again in 1993 he mentioned "recurring and repeated rumors that Israel is in Lebanon because of her water needs" (Naff and Matson, 1984; Naff, 1993: 13).

As for Israeli denials, one person to respond to the charges of Israeli exploitation of Litani water was the author of this book (Soffer, 1994). The rejection of the claims is based on some central factors.

First, let us scrutinize the argument as to the possibility of moving water to Israel secretly. Efficient pumping from the Litani riverbed to the Marj Ayun heights would require the building of a dam to trap the water and the installation of pumps to raise the water several hundred feet. Another alternative would be to dig a tunnel under the gorge up to the Hula valley in Israel, a distance of 2.5–3 miles. Either alternative would be very expensive (Figure 6.1).

Second, regarding the claim of the transfer of water through the Tapline to the Golan Heights, made as early as 1994 (Gabar, 1994:43): while it is possible to run the water into the Tapline, which crosses the river, even then a storage dam and an installation for pumping the water would have to be constructed. Could all this be done in secret? Obviously not.

Third, it would be quite easy to interview hundreds of UN soldiers from the Netherlands, Ireland, Finland, and Norway, who spent years in the region between 1978 and 1997, for information on the removal of water from the Litani by Israel.

Fourth, could a dam being built or a tunnel being dug be hidden from the American spy satellites over the region? Of course not. In the Litani gorge are concentrated hundreds of thousands of Lebanese (in and beyond the security zone). Could such activity be concealed from their eyes and their cameras? Naturally not.

Fifth, it may be asked whether the amount of water that could be diverted from the Litani would justify the economic effort required for the operation and the grave international censure that such an operation would incur.

As I have shown above, diversion of the Litani within Lebanon to the Awali River for electricity production takes much water from the Litani, leaving only a relatively small quantity in the lower reaches of the river. In this area there is much irrigation, and little excess water remains. In the summer there is hardly any flow from the river to the sea, and the water at the coastline is stagnant.

Furthermore, I personally hosted Professor Kolars and Professor Allan separately on tours along Israel's border with Lebanon in quest of a pipeline, a canal, or any installation at all that could possibly serve for carrying water from Lebanon to Israel. The search was in vain (Soffer, 1994: 971).

On October 4, 1991, Professor Naff lectured at a conference in London, and the article he published later stated: "The rumors about transfer of water from the Litani River by Israel are apparently untrue" (Naff, 1993).

But the best proof for dismissing these accusation comes from Lebanon itself.

The Lebanese minister for water resources and electricity, Mohammad Yusuf Bizun, requested that the development council provide him with $2.4 million to complete a research project on how to use the Litani-Awali project more efficiently. Moreover, the director of the national water company of the Litani, Nasr Nasrallah, stated that "we are currently progressing in the Al Kasmiyah-Litani river project, which irrigates 5,000 hectares (12,500 acres) in southern Lebanon, and we are also considering the possibility of improvements by erecting a new pumping station, a dam on the Al Kasmiyah river, and offices for those working on the project" (Soffer, 1994).

On January 8, 1996, Radio Beirut announced that the above projects had gone into operation.

In other words, two officials in the Lebanese government who deal with the issue of the Litani and know what is going on in southern Lebanon are not complaining that Israel robs the Litani of water; rather, they are concerned to continue to develop the Litani region. If Israel were to touch this water they would raise the alarm and would find it difficult to proceed with the development.

## Conclusion

We have seen how experts and journalists have tried to transform the Litani into an international river and to implicate it in the Arab–Israeli conflict. The Litani is not an international river and the laws relating to international rivers do not apply to it. The "internationalization" of the Litani in the past arose only from regional water plans, which regarded the river as part of an international system for allocating water to the countries in the region. But the Litani is not one of the Jordan's sources, and it is entirely located within Lebanon and is for its sovereign use. Only if we perceive the state of Lebanon as some kind of federation of communities does the Litani become international. The river provides drinking water, irrigation, and electricity to the Shi'ites in the south, to the population in the Israeli security zone, to the Palestinians in the camps, to Christians in Jezzin, and to Christians, Sunnis, and Druze in the north and in the cities of the coastal plain. The river is also apparently the reason why the power plants, the electricity lines, and the water pipes in southern Lebanon have not been damaged, despite the many wars there. This water system serves all the players involved, and they have made sure that the installations have not been harmed.

The river flows very close to Israel; it is located in a war-torn but water-blessed country; the Israeli army controls the bend of the river near Nabatiyeh; and in the past Israel wanted to use its water. The combination of these facts sparks rumors and creates tension. But the rumors and tension are baseless.

The quantities of water that flow in the Litani today are too small to be an object for theft by Israel. On the contrary, Israel sends water without charge from the Galilee (inside Israel) into the Lebanese villages in the security zone that suffer from water shortages. Moreover, the small Litani discharge is inadequate for the construction even of a regional water project, if and when regional peace is attained, as several Israeli experts have proposed (Ben Shachar et al., 1989). These experts suggest that Israel use the Litani's water in its downstream section for electricity generation. The Lebanese, on the other hand, plan to increase the river's use for irrigation purposes. If this happens, the water in the river's downstream portion will be reduced and will not be available for hydro-electric production.

## Chapter 7

# International Groundwater Conflicts in the Making

### Introduction

The groundwater flowing from the territory of one state into that of another raises the question of ownership of the water.

Until recent generations this question was not asked because the demand for groundwater was not so great as to endanger the aquifer, and before the introduction of the mechanical electric pump relatively tiny quantities of water were drawn. Moreover, the extent of the aquifer was not known, so the problem of ownership did not arise.

In recent years, with increasing use of groundwater worldwide, particularly in arid and semiarid zones, issues concerning the use of groundwater are appearing on the international juridical and political agenda. Among the many questions now arising are, how can it be determined that one state is harming the groundwater of its neighbor? How is nonrenewable fossil water to be treated?

In contrast to flowing surface water, it is often difficult to estimate the amount of groundwater present in the subterranean depths, and therefore it is difficult to assess the amounts of water that may be drawn. The boundaries of the subterranean drainage basin are not always known, so it is also not clear whether the basin is international. It is equally hard to know the directions of flow of the groundwater, and hence whether a state above it is upstream or downstream. In this book I will not address all the geographical distinctions among types of groundwater. However, experience has taught that overpumping of groundwater has the potential for catastrophic results that are almost irreparable, either through seepage of seawater into the aquifer or pollution of the groundwater, and much labor is required to restore the water to its pristine quality.

225

## Groundwater in International Law

Groundwater has been used since ancient times, and over the centuries procedures evolved in various regions and countries regarding its use, priority over it, ownership, and forfeiture of rights. There are various approaches to this subject: some regard the users of groundwater as its absolute proprietors (e.g., the states of Indiana and Texas in the United States), some consider groundwater a public resource, some adopt a compromise position of "reasonable and rational use" of groundwater, and some deem all participants in its use as owners of full rights to this water. In recent years an approach has developed that considers joint administration of groundwater essential. This outlook has mainly developed in the western United States (Caponera, 1993; Rhodes, 1993).

The Helsinki Accords of 1966 refer to groundwater, and define an aquifer as international when it crosses the border between states, when there is any kind of connection between one aquifer and another, or when the aquifer is connected to a surface river. In every case it crosses an international border. The Helsinki document lays emphasis on cases where the groundwater contributes to a lake or a surface river.

Since the formulation of the Helsinki Accords, rights over groundwater have been discussed in several international forums and conferences, including UN agencies. In 1977 a conference took place at Mar de la Plata where the discussion concerned the equitable use of resources (Barberis, 1991; Caponera, 1993). At a conference held the same year at Nairobi, the subject was the efficient and rational use of common water resources (Caponera, 1993). In 1980, at the 35th UN General Assembly, consideration was given to the question of water rights and international systems of international water courses (surface and subterranean) where use at one place might cause injury at another (Hayton, 1981). In 1986, at a conference at Seoul called on behalf of the International Law Association (ILA), it was stated: "An aquifer that receives surface water in an international drainage basin or contributes water to a drainage basin is considered part of an international drainage basin." At the same conference discussions were held on common administration of water systems, meaning surface and underground water (Kliot, 1994). In 1987 the Bellagio draft was drawn up, dealing with "common responsibility for reasonable and equitable development of groundwater in the region, for the benefit of the nations involved." Ways were suggested for the implementation of this principle: in straightforward cases by the states themselves, and in unusual and awkward cases by international intervention (Hayton and Utton, 1989).

To summarize, despite great progress in respect of groundwater, the international legal community has not yet found a formula or formulas that solve the problems affecting this resource. However, in this regard the 1994 agreement between Israel and Jordan is in fact a breakthrough and an important precedent.

At the time of writing, the international agenda includes the arrangement of the use of groundwater in the western highlands of Palestine by Israel on the one hand and by the Palestinians on the other. Such an arrangement will likewise promote international procedures regarding the use of common groundwater.

## The Map of the Groundwater in the Middle East

The map of groundwater in the Middle East indicates the wide dispersal of groundwater collections in the region extending from North Africa in the west to the Persian Gulf in the east, from the Turkish–Syrian border in the north to Sudan and Egypt, Saudi Arabia, Oman, and Yemen in the south. Some is fossil water, some is renewable, and there are estimates of extremely large quantities (Figure 7.1).

Without detailing all the aquifers and their content, I note that they include international aquifers between Turkey and Syria, which are little used at present; aquifers between Israel and all its neighbors (Lebanon, Syria, Jordan, Egypt, and the Palestinians), which are much used (see Chapter 4); aquifers between Syria and Jordan; and aquifers between Saudi Arabia and Jordan and Jordan's other neighbors to the south and east. All these aquifers are international, some in present use and some not used as yet. There are also aquifers of groundwater between Egypt and Libya, and between Libya and its other neighbors.

According to Shahin (1989: 216), the total groundwater potential of all the Arab states is 18.1 billion $m^3$ (without the states of West Africa and without data on Iraq). If this estimate is augmented by figures of Israel's groundwater and a conservative estimate of the Syrian–Turkish aquifer and the Iraqi aquifer, we arrive at 25 billion $m^3$, most of which is international groundwater (Figure 7.1). Of this amount, 10 billion $m^3$ are used at present (Gross and Soffer, 1996). The chief consumers of this quantity are Saudi Arabia and its neighbors, which use about 200 million $m^3$. Libya plans to use about 2 billion $m^3$, a figure that represents the potential of Mu'ammar Qaddafi's great water project. At present only part of it is used. Israel and its neighbors use all their potential groundwater (about 700 million $m^3$).

In sum, the entire region uses about 40 percent of the entire existing groundwater potential (according to Shahin, 1989: 216, with verification by the author). This contrasts with 85 percent use of surface water

228

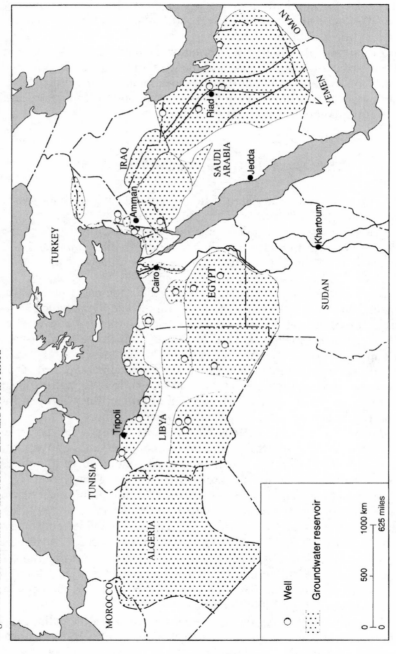

*Figure 7.1*: Groundwater in the Middle East and North Africa

in the Middle East (excluding Turkey): out of 156 billion m³ of surface water, 134 billion m³ are used.

Is the use of groundwater heavy or light?

As stated, Israel and its neighbors fully exploit their groundwater. In the Arabian Peninsula use exceeds potential, which is possible by the use of fossil water, causing cumulative damage to the aquifers. Only in North Africa is there little use of groundwater.

Is it possible to indicate areas of tension or conflict over groundwater already existing, and areas where such tension and conflict are likely in the future? Tension on this matter arose between Israel and its neighbors: between Israel and Jordan, and between Israel and the Palestinians. The tension with Jordan was defused in 1994 with a detailed agreement on the permissible amounts to be drawn by each side. An agreement of this kind was also signed with the Gaza Strip, but an agreement on the use of groundwater in the western highlands of Palestine has not yet been concluded, and the matter is creating great tension.

There is concealed tension between Jordan and Syria regarding the future use of groundwater in the Yarmuk basin (Israel is also a minor partner in this basin). There is tension between Jordan and Saudi Arabia regarding the large subterranean basin, Disi, in southeastern Jordan (Murakami, 1995). Tension exists, mainly psychological, between Egypt and Libya, and between Egypt and Israel on the Israel–Sinai border.

As the needs of the region increase and the amount of surface water is depleted, the use of groundwater, including international groundwater, rises. Heightened tension over this issue may be expected between Turkey and Syria and perhaps between Turkey and Iraq. With the development of oases in western Egypt, tension is liable to arise between Egypt and Libya. No tension is likely in the foreseeable future between Saudi Arabia and its neighbors to the south, or between Libya and its neighbors to the west.

For more than 20 years, on both sides of the Egyptian–Libyan border, drilling activities have taken place for the purposes of agricultural development and groundwater pumping. The extent of development programs and the degree of their implementation differs in Egypt and in Libya owing to differences in the physical structure of the region and in the culture of its residents. Naturally, in both countries there is some sensitivity to these development plans, and each country fears that its neighbor's plans will inflict damage on its own groundwater supplies.

From the geological point of view, generally speaking, wide exploitation of groundwater resources should influence mainly the hydrological conditions of the immediately adjoining environments. However, a different situation is likely to develop in basins with a simple and uniform

geological structure and of considerable expanse; here effects are possible extending for tens of miles and more (Arad, 1988: 1). In the following, we will test whether Arad's conclusions also apply to the case of the groundwater in Egypt and Libya.

**Pumping Groundwater in Egypt**

Egypt pumps groundwater at the Siwah oasis, 31 miles from the Libyan border, and small amounts along the coast close to the border. Groundwater pumping at Siwah oasis is intensive, but the quantities of water pumped are small relative to the total amount of water that Egypt uses, and the effect of the pumping on the groundwater level is not felt outside the area of the oasis (Arad, 1988: 24).

Heavier pumping, albeit still fairly modest, takes place away from the border, at oases located in the series of morphological depressions such as Kharijah, Farafirah, Dakhilah, and Bahriyah. At these oases all water pumping is based on local groundwater, whose origins are apparently aquifers fed from southern regions (equatorial and savanna areas). When the Aswan High Dam was near completion, Egypt planned to develop the oases by using water from Lake Nasser to cultivate about 1 million hectares (2,500,000 acres) of land and to settle several million people in this area. The plan was called the New Valley Project or Development of the Western Desert. But in the end the plan was not executed (Murray, 1952; El Baz, 1979; Fisher, 1979; Blake et al, 1987). It seems that the chief economic activity in this region will be based in the future only on groundwater. Moreover, water pumping at the oases showed that the groundwater level drops quickly, which implies that there is a danger in using this water.

**Groundwater Pumping in Libya**

The first to develop agriculture in Libya were the Italians; from the beginning of the century until the 1940s they developed the coastal plain in the Banghazi region, Tripoli, and Gefara. After the Second World War, development in these areas continued through cooperation between foreign companies and local farmers. Groundwater pumping became more considerable and the water level dropped by 23–32 feet. In consequence, salt water penetrated into some wells, which had to be closed. After the 1970 revolution the new government pressed on with the pumping and sought to increase agricultural self-sufficiency. This, of course, adversely affected the water balance in the country. In 1976, when the seriousness of the situation became clear to the Libyan authorities, a cutback in agriculture was implemented.

In the 1950s and 1960s, following oil explorations in Libya generally and in the south of the country specifically, many data were collected indicating that enormous subterranean water reservoirs existed under the Sahara Desert (Figure 7.1). The principal reservoir is located in an aquifer located in layers of Nubian sandstone 328 feet and more below the surface (in some places it attains a depth of about 9,840 feet), and sloping from south to north (Pallas, 1980).

Experts are divided about the amount of water in this reservoir. Some say it is in the region of hundreds of billions of m³, and believe that it is possible to utilize 3–4 billion m³ annually for about 100 years (McLachlan, 1987), while others gauge the usable annual potential at only 2.5–3.5 billion m³, for an unknown period of time (Allan, 1988: 145).

When the seriousness of the groundwater situation in the north of the country became clear, Libya began to pump water from the southern groundwater reservoir, and to develop the desert regions in which water is located: Sarir, Kufra (about 94 miles from the Egyptian border), and Tazerbo (Figure 7.2). Libya began a land amelioration operation and pumped about half a billion cubic meters of water from hundreds of wells (Allan, 1988: 141), but it quickly became clear that there was no economic sense in developing areas so remote from the north (281–500 miles from Benghazi). The project would involve the transport of fresh agricultural products a great distance to the cities in the north (Benghazi, Tripoli, etc.). Moreover, the Libyan farmers did not incline to settle in the distant desert oases, preferring to continue living in the coastal area. In 1979 a bold decision was made. It was decided to transfer the water from the desert aquifer at Tazerbo and from the other aquifers to the north, in what became known as the Great Man-Made River Project, or GMMR.

The decision was made at a time when revenues were skyrocketing; a single year's income from oil was enough to finance the massive project, whose price was estimated that year at $25 billion (Allan, 1988: 142; 1989; 1994). The project had five stages (Figure 7.2).

*Stage One*

In Tazerbo 120 wells were to be dug and the water was to be transported northward to Sarir. There an additional 120 wells would be dug and their water would be carried together with the well water from Tazerbo to the eastern coastal cities (Benghazi and Surt). The amount was to be 0.75 billion m³ of water annually. This was intended for irrigating 50,000 hectares (125,000 acres) of land and for domestic use in the eastern cities (Allan, 1988: 143).

*Figure 7.2:* Libya—The Great Man-Made River

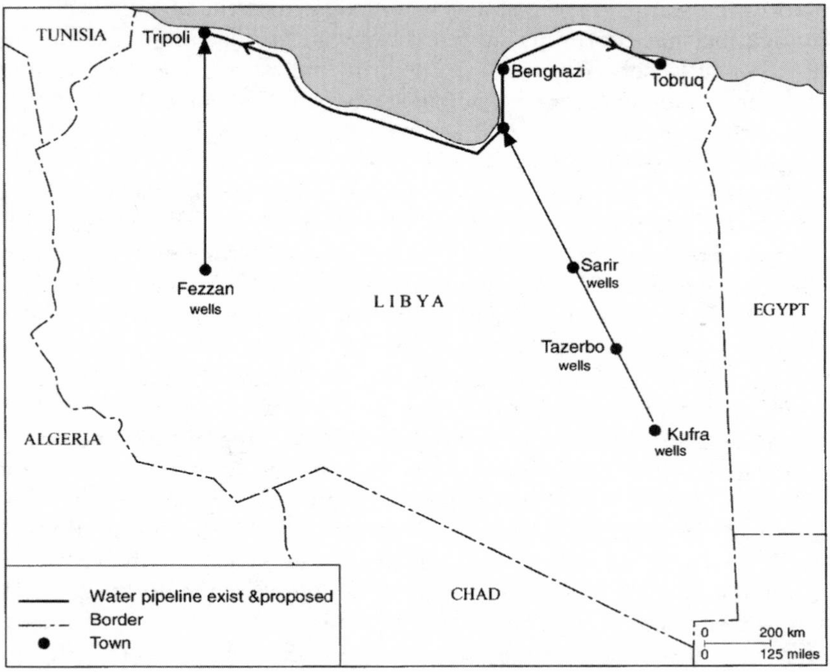

### Stage Two

From the desert aquifer in the western part of the state 0.6–0.7 billion m³ of water was to be transported north to the western coastal cities, just as water was transported in the east of Libya.

### Stage Three

The eastern carrier's supply would be increased to 2.2 billion m³ by the addition of water from the Kufra wells (Murakami, 1995: 123–124).

### Stage Four

Water would be transported from the eastern to the west coastal region (toward Tripoli).

### Stage Five

Water would be transported from the Benghazi region eastwards to Tobruq and the Libyan–Egyptian border.

In 1990 the laying of the stage 1 pipe was only partially completed, with 269 miles laid, and in 1995 the work continued, the intermediate cost (1993) being estimated at $18 billion. However, in the period following the start of the project, oil prices dropped, financial reserves dwindled, and doubts began to arise as to whether the enterprise was worthwhile, with its $27 billion price tag (*Middle East and North Africa Yearbook*, 1996).

The inefficiency of the project also became clear from a different perspective. Even if 2.5 to 3.6 billion m³ of water annually were diverted northward, Libya would still be unable to supply all its food needs and would still be dependent on the international market. Considering this, perhaps the project is not necessary at all, and available water should be for domestic and industrial use only.

### The Geopolitical Aspects of Groundwater Pumping

Does intensive pumping of groundwater in Libya affect the state of the groundwater in Egypt? The slope of the aquifer, as stated, is from south to north, and therefore it seems that this water, wholly or in part, originates in the sandstone in the rainy region south of the Sahara, in northern Chad and Sudan. Moreover, from the enormous quantity located in the deep aquifers of the Sahara Desert we know that this water includes not only renewable water but also fossil water (some estimate the renewable water to be about 2.6 billion m³ a year and the fossil water at about 1.1 billion m³). It seems that pumping groundwater, where this is conducted at present (Sarir, Kufra, and elsewhere), cannot influence the condition of the aquifer across the border. Even supposing that there is only fossil water, the great volume held in the aquifer would satisfy Libyan needs for over fifty years (economic considerations are not relevant for this discussion) with no adverse effect on the groundwater on the Egyptian side, which is fed also by renewable water from Sudan (the Darfur area) or from direct infiltration from the Nile or from the Chad. If the Egyptian water is fossilized as well, it is not certain that this aquifer is in fact shared with Libya at all.

Moreover, according to hydrological projections made 7.5–16 miles distant from the center of water pumping in Libya, it seems that the influence of the pumping is decreasing, and the groundwater level has dropped about 1.6 feet over a 7.5-mile radius from the drilling site (Arad, 1988: 24). Arad therefore concludes, on the basis of computerized models and additional sources, that after fifty years of pumping at the current levels, the radius of the effect will extend to about twenty-four miles from the pumping stations, so pumping at these levels will not be enough to affect groundwater in Egypt (Ahmed, 1983; Arad, 1988).

Despite all this, tension and suspicions abound between the two nations, and each suspects the other of harming groundwater. Here too, as in the Litani cases, psychological factors rather than objective reality give rise to tension.

Could the groundwater pumping cause a crisis between the two countries? If the Nile's discharge falls and Egypt's needs grow (as was concluded in Chapter 2), it is possible that Egypt will take the same path that Libya has followed, and will pump intensively from groundwater in the Sahara. This will certainly lead to additional tension between the two countries, perhaps to a crisis in their relations. Such an occurrence is likely to take place only after the year 2000.

*Chapter 8*

# Nonconventional Solutions to the Problem of Water Shortages in the Middle East

## Introduction

In the foregoing chapters we have seen that all the international rivers in the Middle East are being intensively exploited by the residents of the region. The Jordan and the Yarmuk are used mostly by Jordan, Israel, and Syria; the Nile is reaching the maximum in terms of its use, and it is most likely that all of the plans to increase the flow of the river by development projects will not be executed in the near future for social, political, and geopolitical reasons. As for the Tigris and Euphrates, their discharge has until recently satisfied their riparian countries' needs, but owing to intensive development in Turkey and Syria it seems that within ten to fifteen years a regional water shortage will arise. Such is the case with the Orontes basin too, and essentially with all the water sources in the region, including internal rivers and groundwater. The conclusion is clear: the Middle East, whose population is increasing at rates higher than the global average (3 percent natural increase annually as compared with the rest of the Third World, which is 2.5 percent, or doubling in 23 years), will encounter a water shortage if the irrigation methods and the present plantations continue to be employed. However, because the states of the region seem unable to accomplish this within the next two decades, they will have to search for new sources of water.

The danger facing the peoples of the region is that if additional water is not found their fate is liable to be famine, drought, disease, and even migration (out migration, assuming there is somewhere to migrate to, or to their own cities). This was the fate of Ethiopia, Somalia, Sudan, and the Sahal states (south of the Sahara) in the 1980s.

235

At the end of the twentieth century human society has various means of tackling the water problem. Some of these are traditional and others are innovational. Among the former are trapping of flood water, economical irrigation methods, and saving water through choice of crops. This group may also include war and the destruction of water-holding devices in neighboring countries as a way of acquiring sources of water. The innovative methods are cloud seeding, desalination, transfer of water to remote places (even hundreds of miles distant), and transportation of water in large containers, as is done with oil. Recycling of sewage water for irrigation of crops is also a new way of obtaining water, as well as preventing pollution of groundwater.

The problem of water shortage may be approached by way of economics, which regards water as a product for which a real price must be paid. Such an approach will lead to a reduction in water use for agriculture and the transition of inhabitants from agriculture to other sectors, such as tourism, industry, and services.

A further option much discussed in international forums should be studied: cooperation among the countries of the region. Could such cooperation lead to a solution to the water problem?

Some of the above methods increase the supply of water (for example, trapping of flood water, cloud seeding, desalination, import of water, recycling of sewage water, war—or its alternative, international cooperation), while some reduce demand (saving in water use, substitution of economic sectors).

In this chapter I consider these ideas, the likelihood of their implementation, and their geopolitical significance. We do not deal with the technologies involved.

## Importing Water

Water may be imported in pipes from a place where it is plentiful to a place where it is lacking. In the United States, for example, the water of the Colorado River is carried by the Colorado River Aqueduct to the Los Angeles area and by the Coachella and the All-American Canal to the Imperial Valley and Los Angeles area.

Water may also be imported by sea in containers, like oil. In the following we shall examine the possibilities of implementing these methods in the Middle East.

### Importing Water in Pipes

The idea of transferring water from one country to another in the Middle East has been posited on several occasions, chiefly in the 1980s and 1990s. There were proposals to carry Nile water to the Sinai Desert, and thence to the Gaza Strip and Israel. Following the signing of the peace agreement between Egypt and Israel in 1979, leaders of the two states considered the notion. Subsequently, several specialists tried to translate it into an economic plan (Kally, 1986; Ben Shachar et al., 1989). Hardly was the ink dry on the peace documents than opposition to the idea was voiced by Ethiopia, arguing that before Nile water was removed to a different drainage basin its rights had to be considered. In Egypt, too, objections were raised to the transfer of Nile water to the Jews. In Israel there were some who argued that Israel must not be dependent on Egypt in respect of such an important resource, while others gave the pollution of Nile water as a reason not to bring it to Israel.

Transport of Euphrates water to Amman (Kally, 1986; *al Maged*, Feb. 23, 1995) and of Litani water to Israel also were considered. The latter idea was rejected several times by the Lebanese government (see Chapter 6).

### The Turkish "Peace Pipeline" Plan

The idea that won the most headlines was that of the Turkish Peace Pipeline (Figure 8.1). In 1986 Turkey announced its Peace Pipeline proposal, which was based on carrying about 6 million m³ of water per day (about 2.2 billion m³ annually) from Turkey to the arid states of the Middle East (Irbec, 1993). According to initial estimates, the project would cost about $21 billion. Already budgeted is $2.1 million for an initial survey (Duna, 1988).

The project was conceived by the Center for International and Strategic Studies in Washington, D.C. (*MEED*, Mar. 26, 1988: 30). The Center asserts that the water shortage problem will be the most serious in the region by the end of the twentieth century and will lead to international conflicts.

The American company that will undertake the project claims that the price of water brought by the Peace Pipeline will be cheaper than the price of desalinated water in the Persian Gulf; the cost of 1 m³ of desalinated water in the Persian Gulf is about $5, whereas the price of a cubic meter of water brought by the Peace Pipeline will be only about $1.07.

The pipeline will carry the surplus water from the Seyan and Ceyan Rivers, and others in the same area, that empty into the delta at whose center lies the city of Adana (Figure 8.1). At present there is a large dam on the Seyan on the northern outskirts of Adana, and the water of its vast reservoir irrigates the lands of the Ceyan valley north of the town of Ceyan and east of the Adana delta. The discharge of the two rivers,

*Figure 8.1:* The Peace Pipeline

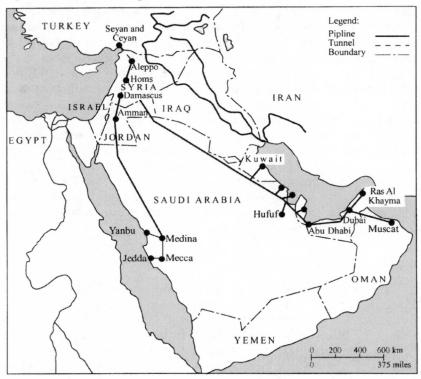

which flow down from the Taurus Mountains, is 39.17 million m³ daily, of which about 23 million m³ are used. The remainder, about 16 million m³, is being offered by Turkey to Middle Eastern states.

According to the plan, the water will be carried to the Aleppo plateau in a 9.5–12.5-mile tunnel under the Nur Mountains (Nur Dogloru) that rise between the Adana plain and the valley of the Orontes. From the Aleppo plateau (1312–1640 feet above sea level) the pipeline will run to the town of Homs, where it will divide into two branches. One will continue to Damascus and Amman. Both these cities are 2,296 feet above sea level, but between them the pipeline must traverse the Irbid heights, which are lower. From Amman, the line will proceed to Madina and Mecca, and thence to the coastal towns of Jedda and Yanbu (Figure 8.1 and Table 8.1). This branch will be 1,656 miles long, and will carry 3.5 million m³ water per day (about 1.3 billion m³ annually). Eleven huge pumps, requiring 500 megawatts of electricity, will propel the water.

**Table 8.1: Participants and Amounts Piped in the Turkish Peace Pipeline (thousands m³ per day)**

| Eastern Pipe | Amount[a] | Recipient |
|---|---|---|
| Kuwait | 600 | Kuwait |
| Saudi Arabia | 800 | (Jubail 200; Damam 200; al Kubar 200; Hufuf 200) |
| Bahrain | 200 | (Manama) |
| Qatar | 100 | (Doha) |
| United Arab Emirates | 600 | (Abu Dhabi 280; Dubai 160; Sharja 120; other cities 40) |
| Oman | 200 | |
| Total Eastern Pipe | 2500 | |

| Western Pipe | | |
|---|---|---|
| Turkey | 300 | |
| Syria | 1100 | (Aleppo 300; Hama 100; Homs 100; Damascus 600) |
| Jordan | 600 | |
| Saudi Arabia | 1500 | (Tabuk 1001; Medina 300; Yanbu 100; Jedda 500; Mecca 500) |
| Total Western Pipe | 3500 | |

Sources: *MEED* 18.3.1988; Frankel 1992

[a] Amount of water piped in thousand cubic meters per day.

The other branch will run from Hama southeast, cross the Syrian desert highlands in Syria and Jordan (2,952 feet above sea level), and continue parallel to the Tapline oil pipeline, passing through Saudi Arabia, Abu Dhabi, Dubai, and Ras al Khayma, ending in Muscat in Oman (Figure 8.1). Along the way secondary arms will fork off: one to Kuwait City, one to the Saudi oil cities (Jubail, Damam, al Kubar and Hufuf), another to the town of Manama in Bahrain, and a third to the town of Doha in Qatar. This branch will be 2,438 miles long, and will transport 2.5 million m³ of water daily (about 0.9 billion m³ annually). Five massive pumps, consuming 600 megawatts of electricity, will move the water.

The original plan envisaged that the first branch line would cross from Syria to Israel and the West Bank, and thence to Jordan and Saudi Arabia. But a revised plan by the eight states due to participate in the enterprise excluded Israel on the grounds that the Palestinian–Israeli conflict was not yet settled, nor was there peace between Israel and its neighbors. (An official statement of the Turkish Foreign Ministry of March 16, 1988, said that the issue was raised at a meeting with the Turkish foreign minister during a visit to the oil states that month.)

Owing to the dispute with regard to Israel, the Turkish government decided that when it embarked on the construction of the pipeline it would begin with the eastern branch running to the Persian Gulf. This work would take about ten years. Turkey's profits, if the price of a cubic meter of water is $1, would be about $2 billion a year.

### Geopolitical Assessment of the Plan

The assessment will be made from several viewpoints: the technical aspect asks whether the project is practicable. Next, Turkey's motives and the advantages and disadvantages of the project for the participating states are examined.

### *The Technical Aspect*

According to the above data, the Peace Pipeline would be one of the largest water projects in the world. The total length of the pipeline, including both branches, would be about 4,094 miles. The project includes tunnels (for example, a tunnel through the Oman hills) and in some places pumping water to great heights (2,296 feet in branch A and 2,952 feet in branch B). The Peace Pipeline would be very long, the topography along the length is rough, and the climatic conditions are most severe. All this would certainly make its construction and maintenance difficult. To complicate matters further, there are eight countries participating in its construction besides Turkey. On the other hand, over similar distances the Hejaz railroad was laid, as were thousands of miles of oil pipelines and roads and highways. Despite the large scale of the pipeline in terms of length and capacity, it is feasible from a technical perspective.

### *Turkey's Motives*

The primary motive is financial. After the construction costs (which will possibly be financed from the start by the consumers) have been recovered Turkey will earn about $2 billion annually from water that is currently emptying into the sea.

The second motive is geopolitical. The project will give Turkey control over the "elixir of life" of the entire Middle East and consequently, Turkey will resume its position as a very important geopolitical player in the area. Syria will become its vassal, because even without the pipeline Syria is fully dependent on Turkey regarding the use of the Euphrates River. The Peace Pipeline concept is, among other things, a Turkish experiment to assess how Syria will react to the establishment of a water project in the Hatay region, which Turkey is pressuring Syria to recognize as Turkish sovereign territory (see Chapter 5).

Proof that the geopolitical motive is significant in establishing the Peace Pipeline is that Turkey on the one hand robs Syria and Iraq of Euphrates water and on the other offers Syria water from the Ceyan and the Seyan. Again, Turkey may claim that it must reduce the Euphrates water flowing into Syria and Iraq because of its own needs in the east, and that it must build dams on the river to divert the water to the Jezira plains in Turkey; yet Turkey offers to sell Syria about 2 billion m³ of water a year. This makes one wonder, because Turkey could have diverted the excess water from the Seyan and Ceyan in its planned tunnel (under the Nur Mountains) to the Gaziantep and Urfa regions in its own territory, and develop a Euphrates–Seyan–Ceyan project that would send excess water to Syria and Iraq. Since Turkey is not doing this, one must conclude that the principal reason for the plan is geopolitical. Turkey is looking beyond the year 2000 and seeks to control the Middle East by means of water, whose lack will be felt everywhere south of Turkey and whose price will be higher than, or at least equal to, that of oil.

The third motive is the wish for positive image building. Alone, Turkey cannot and has no desire to construct this expensive and elaborate project. Since it is clear that the other countries will not agree to finance it, the entire idea should be seen as a successful advertising campaign, a gesture of good will, in the context of the tough criticism Turkey suffered because of its water projects on the Tigris and Euphrates.

## Advantages and Disadvantages of the Project for the Arab States

The biggest advantage of the project is obvious: states of the region will receive large quantities of high quality water at a relatively cheap price. The principal disadvantage from any Arab state's point of view is the power the pipeline will give to Turkey. Moreover, Saudi Arabia would be dependent not just on Turkey, but also on Syria and Jordan, through which the two branches of the pipeline would pass. Jordan would also be dependent on Syria; and the Gulf states would be dependent on Syria, Jordan, and chiefly Saudi Arabia.

An additional disadvantage is that the water needs of half the Arabian Peninsula are already great and the project, if executed, will take at least ten years. In the meantime desalination plants must be built.

Because of the fear of dependency and because of the length of time needed to complete the project, the Arab states would probably prefer desalinated water over pipeline water, even if the cost is five times higher. This is the price they will pay for their independence.

The idea, which originated in the United States, suits the modern western attitude toward international cooperation in terms of advantages of scale and building mutual confidence. Inasmuch as regional cooperation and confidence are not among the most outstanding traits of this region, the chances that the project will be realized are slight, unless the water shortage forces the states of the region to change their attitudes and world outlook.

The sobering experience of Syria and Iraq with regard to Turkey and the use of Euphrates water will certainly not contribute to the realization of the idea. Meanwhile, the Turks too have cooled to the concept, and Turkish president Demirel has described it as merely a dream.

In the 1990s a number of Israelis presented the idea of a "small" Turkish pipeline. This would carry water to Israel, Jordan, and the Palestinians on the West Bank (but not the Arabian Peninsula), (Ben Shachar et al., 1989; Wachtel, 1994: 363–374).

Middle Eastern realities, however, will require many years of warm peace and absolute trust between Israel and Syria for Israel to be able to accept the thought of water reaching Israel via Syria. Assuming that this idea is indeed workable, about twenty years would still be needed for its realization. What is going to happen in the next two decades?

**Importing Water by Sea**

Another way to solve the water shortage in the region is to import water from water-rich countries nearby, just as countries import wheat or oil.

The idea is not new, and in the 1970s agreements were signed among the Gulf states, for example, and the Philippines, on transporting oil from the Gulf to the Philippines and transporting water from the Philippines to the Gulf in tankers on the way back. (This does not refer to filling empty tankers with water to stabilize them, a method in use for many years.)

The idea arose in Israel in the 1980s, when importing water from southern Turkey was the main focus. Dozens of rivers flow from the Taurus Mountains and empty into the sea, and Turkey does not utilize their water owing to topographical factors. Former Yugoslavia, Italy, and France also have abundant water close to their coastlines, but they are further from Israel. The idea is to transport water from a river in Turkey with a large discharge—the Manavgat River opposite Cyprus—to an Israeli port in special containers built for this purpose. These containers, known as "jellyfish," are 1,968 feet long and made out of a plastic material with double walls. Each container can carry about 2 million m³ of water when it is sunk in the sea and is towed by a tugboat (Pope, 1990; Libiszewski, 1995: 56–57; Schiller, 1996). Another idea is a floating "water snake," which its inventors believe is less costly than the "jellyfish" (*Ha'ir*, Feb. 11, 1994).

Importing water raises several difficulties, economic and geopolitical. To reduce the cost of the water and its transportation, a suitable terminal must be built at the port of exit, which will include water containers and pumps to transfer the water from the river to the containers or directly into the jellyfish. In addition, a special port or installation for docking the tugboat and its containers must be built in both the exporting and importing countries, and in the latter a system to direct the water from the containers to the national water system. A fleet of tugboats and jellyfish will be necessary for transporting the water. According to an initial estimate (interview with Israeli Water Commissioner Dan Zaslavsky, July 6, 1990), an investment of about $200 million will be necessary: about $50 million for a terminal in the exporting country, about $100 million for a terminal in the importing country, and about $50 million for the fleet. The hypothetical cost per cubic meter for imported water is $0.22–0.25—about the cost of nonimported water. Others believe that the price will be about $0.75 (Pope, 1990; Zaslavsky, July 6, 1990; Allan 1994: 77).

The geopolitical difficulty is that when a state compensates for its water shortage by importing water, it becomes dependent on the exporting country. Such a dependency does not exist with oil imports, because many countries export oil. Because importing water is a new idea that requires special facilities, and because no other states will be exporting water, the geopolitical dependency of the importer on the exporter will be great. The situation is particularly sensitive when the states in question are Israel and Turkey, states with different religions. Therefore, it is worthwhile for Israel to wait until other states start to export water, and when its bargaining power will increase.

Middle Eastern states are approaching the point when they will have to consider the possibility of importing water, as they import oil and wheat. From a strategic perspective, just as states that need energy must diversify their energy resources (coal, gas, hydroelectric power, nuclear power, and imported electricity), the states of the region will have to diversify their water resources—desalinated water, fossil and renewable groundwater, river water, imported water, and water from neighboring countries.

In sum, the idea of importing water is not feasible at present, either because there are more accessible alternatives in most states of the region or because of real and imaginary geopolitical fears.

## Desalination

Desalination of seawater may answer the water shortage in arid and semiarid regions in the world generally and in the Middle East specifically. This is an unlimited source: the oceans or abundant brackish water in arid regions. The know-how for desalination also exists, and today it is already possible to desalinate all kinds of existing water, albeit at a relatively high price.

In 1991, on average, about 13.3 million $m^3$ of water was desalinated daily, or about 5 billion $m^3$ per year, throughout the world. Twenty-seven percent of it was brackish water (with salinity lower than seawater); 8 percent was recycled and purified sewage water, domestic drainage water, and polluted groundwater; and 65 percent was seawater (Gleick, 1993).

Of all the desalinated water in the world, about 54 percent was treated in the Middle East: about 26.8 percent in Saudi Arabia, about 10.5 percent in Kuwait, and about 10 percent in the United Arab Emirates (Water International Symposium, 1990; Glick, 1993). In the oil states of the Middle East, water has been desalinated for several decades and used for domestic purposes by many inhabitants of the Persian Gulf, who mostly live in a few cities—those of the Persian Gulf, and by residents of the new cities of Saudi Arabia, those on the Red Sea coast—and as additional water for old cities. Most desalination plants in the Middle East treat seawater (on the coasts of the Persian Gulf and Red Sea), and only few treat brackish water, and even fewer recycled water. Desalination in these states does not solve the shortage of an entire state but of trouble spots. The Gulf states did not have to choose among alternatives to desalination: having no water at all, desalinated water is their only water source. In addition, oil for powering the plants there is cheaper than water.

In the remaining states of the region there are hardly any desalination plants except at Eilat and Aqaba, where water is desalinated for tourists and the urban population's needs. Israel also has experimental desalination plants in the Negev, altogether about 40 plants; the capacity of the desalination plants in Israel is about 18.2 million $m^3$ per year, or 1 percent of the country's total supply. Egypt has desalination plants in small oases and tourist sites in Sinai, for example, at Sharm al Sheikh, Dhahab, and Nuweiba. What can these states learn from the accumulated knowledge in the region in this field, from the economic, technical, political, and even strategic points of view? Can the experience of the Gulf states be projected to the other states of the region, such as Egypt, Syria, Jordan, and Israel, or Gaza and the West Bank?

Should the pollution of the Persian Gulf in the Gulf War have been a warning sign? One cannot compare the situation in the Persian Gulf with the situation in the Mediterranean (Earle, 1992). In the Persian Gulf there is a unique combination of many desalination plants and many oil wells and terminals; in the Mediterranean no such combination exists. Moreover, prior to the ecological catastrophe in the Persian Gulf area in 1990–1991, water had been desalinated there for years without difficulty, even though seven years of cruel war between Iran and Iraq (1980–1987) had ravaged the region. The danger of polluting the water in the Mediterranean and the Red Sea is therefore smaller, unless terrorist activities increase in the coming years: and such a security risk exists not only for desalination plants, but also for power plants, water pumps, and dams.

In the Gulf states the cost of desalinated water is worthwhile economically. But in the other states, Syria, Jordan, Egypt, and the Palestinian entity, oil is not so cheap and the cost of water will be very expensive.

According to Israeli Water Commissioner Zaslavsky (press conference, July 6, 1990), an initial investment of $600–700 million will be necessary to desalinate 250 million $m^3$ per year for a period of about fifteen years. In addition, an investment of about $250 million will be required as operating expenses for the same period. Over fifteen years, therefore, about $1 billion will be necessary. For two installations, which will desalinate 500 million $m^3$ of water for Jordanian, Israeli, West Bank, and Gaza needs, about $2 billion will be necessary, including $1.2–$1.4 billion of initial investment. (Compared with expenditure on armaments, this is a relatively modest amount that could solve many problems.)

From the start of the 1990s many fresh calculations have been made, and the estimated cost of establishing a desalination plant with a capacity of 500–550 million $m^3$ fluctuates between $1 billion (Glickstern, 1996: 2) and $1.4 billion (Braverman et al., 1994); the Israeli government, in a publication in preparation for the Cairo Conference, spoke of $3.2 billion (Israel, *Development Options*, 1996).

Hence, we also obtain figures for the price of desalinating a cubic meter of water: they generally vary in the range of $0.75–1.00 (Eckstein et al., 1994: 333; Glickstern, 1996: 5; Glickstern and Priel, 1996). (Because we are dealing with the subject in principle we will not extend the discussion here to the types of desalination plants. For information on this matter, see Brosh, 1980; Fisher, 1993, 32–37; Glick, 1993; Dabbagh et al., 1994; Murakami, 1995).

The questions arising are how the nonoil states in the Middle East will obtain funds for such projects, and what purposes they will serve. Will they be to irrigate cotton, bananas, and other tropical crops, as in the past?

Yet the principal problem is not the know-how for desalination, but the ability of desalination to solve the water shortage in the region. In the Gulf states, water is only for the domestic use of the urban residents, and the total amount of desalinated water in the Persian Gulf in 1990 (2–2.4 billion m$^3$ annually) is enough to satisfy Egypt's needs for two weeks only. In Syria, Jordan, Egypt, and Israel, the water is used principally for agriculture, and for this need desalinated water is not enough. Syria needs another 2 billion m$^3$ of water to satisfy its requirements for one year and Egypt must have another 5–10 billion m$^3$ of water to satisfy its yearly needs in this decade. No desalination plants can satisfy such great needs. In Egypt and Syria such plants will not solve the chief problem. At most, local plants can answer local needs such as domestic supply for the city of Damascus.

The requirements of Israel, Jordan, the West Bank, and the Gaza Strip are smaller. Jordan lacks 100–200 million m$^3$ annually, and it is possible that by 2000 this figure will rise to about 300 million m$^3$. In the West Bank and Gaza Strip there will be an annual shortfall of 200–400 million m$^3$. A similar quantity is lacking in Israel, not including the deficit from the groundwater aquifer. The total shortage is about 1 billion m$^3$ of water annually, and this can possibly be supplied by desalination.

Several points arise regarding desalination unconnected with its high price or its economic and technical side, but having to do with geopolitical and psychological considerations.

It is possible that Israel will be requested to concede an aquifer to the benefit of the Palestinians on the grounds that it possesses the technology, know-how, and money to desalinate water for its domestic needs. The next step would be that in view of the enormous needs of the kingdom of Jordan, Israel must yield Lake Kinneret also. Syria would likewise have demands regarding the Kinneret. In that case, the probable argument then to be raised would be that there was no reason for Israel to continue to operate the National Water Carrier, which elevates the water to a height of 1,230 feet above sea level and then carries it 62 miles south. Instead of elevating the water so high and carrying it so far, the argument might run, it may be given to the Jordanians and Palestinians for irrigation in the Jordan valley and the Jericho region. The water may also be presented to the Syrians to supply their needs in the Damascus basin and the southwest. This logic will contend that Israel can desalinate Mediterranean seawater near the Tel Aviv metropolitan area where there is the greatest demand for drinking water. At the same time, the neighboring states will continue to use water with the present wasteful methods, including development of agriculture. This is evident in the plans of Egypt, Syria, and Jordan, and in the programs of the Palestinians (Rogers, 1994: 306–307).

The issues, then, are geopolitical and psychological, not necessarily economic. Obviously, the international demand that the use of "natural water" be replaced by the use of desalinated water will be addressed to Israel and not to its neighbors, as Israel is the most advanced state in the region. Intimations of this have already been heard. In this context it is possible to return to the idea of cutting a canal from the Mediterranean to the Dead Sea, or from the Red Sea to the Dead Sea, with the goal of creating cheap electricity for desalination (see Chapter 4 and Figure 4.6). To create waterfalls and cheap hydroelectricity, immense investments will be needed, on the order of $3–6 billion; this is apart from the heavy ecological cost that these canals will exact along their courses. We may say that this idea too, which has fired the imagination of many, is not at all cheap and not at all simple.

Desalination has a further aspect: to desalinate water, power stations and much energy are required, with the use of coal, gas, oil, or other sources. The desalination plants will have to be established along the Israeli coast, which is extremely crowded as it is. The desalination enterprise would thus carry a painful, double ecological price: diminution of open coastal land and exacerbation of pollution, which is bad enough already (Hopner and Windelberg, 1996; Morton et al., 1996).

An empirical study conducted on desalination plants on the shores of the Arabian Peninsula found that a plant with a capacity of up to 5 million $m^3$ water annually occupied a length of coastline of about 1,700 feet and covered an overall area of 60 acres.

A plant that desalinates up to 100 million $m^3$ requires 3,000 feet of coastline and an area of about 250 acres; and a large plant, producing up to 200 million $m^3$ of water a year, requires 4,500–6,000 feet of coastline and an area of 500 acres.

Still, the Israeli water commissioner estimates that with more economical methods a very large desalination plant (producing far more than 200 million $m^3$ of water a year) would require an area of 100 acres only, and a very short stretch of coastline (conversation, June 17, 1997). This matter is of the highest significance for the state of Israel, which is densely populated and has a short coastline with many demands made upon it.

Despite the concerns raised here, and despite the skeptics, it is entirely clear that the states in the region are approaching the point where desalination will be inescapable. This point will be reached when all other ways of saving water, trapping flood water, recycling sewage water, and modifying states' economies have been exhausted. Desalination will begin on a small scale. Over time, with the improvement of the economic condition of the countries, the scope of desalination will steadily expand. Without economic progress, states will not be capable of accomplishing desalination projects.

Regarding Egypt and Syria, in the foreseeable future these states will be able to desalinate water only on a small scale. Therefore, they will be obliged to solve their expected water shortages in ways that today are unacceptable to them: saving on water for agriculture and recycling of sewage water for use in agriculture.

In conclusion, desalination is a reasonable way to solve the water shortage especially in Israel, the West Bank and Gaza, and Jordan. Desalination can neutralize the water time bomb that is ticking in the Jordan valley and the Gaza Strip. Jordan can first desalinate brackish water and recycled water, but then it will have to treat seawater.

# War

If a state finds all peaceable means of solving its water problems unworkable, and remains thirsty even after economizing maximally on water, it may decide to use force to obtain what cannot be obtained otherwise, namely to take control of the sources of an international river (Homer-Dixon et al., 1993; Glick, 1994).

Upstream states have no need to go to war because they control the sources and can do with them as they wish. In the Middle East the upstream states are Turkey, in the Tigris and Euphrates basin; Israel on the Jordan River (1996); Syria on the Yarmuk; and Ethiopia and the equatorial states on the Nile.

The states that might turn to a military solution are the downstream states: Iraq and Syria in the Tigris and Euphrates basin; Jordan and Israel in the Yarmuk basin; Jordan in the Jordan basin (against Israel, the upstream state); Israel, the downstream state (until 1967) in the Jordan basin (against Syria and Lebanon, the upstream states); and Egypt and Sudan, the downstream states in the Nile, against Ethiopia and the equatorial states.

To solve their water shortage, Iraq and Syria would have to go to war (together or separately) against Turkey, to destroy all the dams it has built on the Euphrates, and those that will be built on the Tigris. Consequently, the rivers would flow along their courses as in the past. They may also leave the dams intact and capture only the drainage basins, which will give them control over the drainage in the rivers. Another possibility is to occupy other parts of Turkey to win bargaining power— but this is not a valid option since negotiations may last years, and meantime Turkey will retain full control over the water supplies of the two downstream states. Therefore, to achieve their goals, the two states would have to conquer significant portions of Turkish territory in the GAP region. According to rumor, a Syrian commando unit has been training to conduct raids against the GAP Projects, but no raid has actually been carried out, nor does one seem possible.

Jordan must conquer the entire Yarmuk basin from Syria to gain control of the Yarmuk's sources, and to take from Israel at least the entire area of the Kinneret and the Jordan Valley to win control of the course of the Jordan (in the case of deterioration of relations with Israel in spite of a peace agreement between the two countries).

Israel's objectives in a war against Syria over water would be to conquer the sources of the Yarmuk. Egypt's objectives would be to prevent the upstream states from building development projects on its water sources.

Wherever power between the downstream and upstream state in the region is balanced, or almost balanced, the downstream state will not start a water war; obviously it will not do so when the upstream state is manifestly stronger than itself. Syria and Iraq cannot go to war with Turkey, separately or together, with other enemies to their rear (Israel and Jordan behind Syria, and Iran behind Iraq) and when they face such intractable military targets.

Jordan is weaker than Syria and Israel, and therefore it will not launch a water war; if it does so, a general war will break out, and it is unlikely that it will be capable of winning it. The conclusion is clear: all of Jordan's threats of war in recent years have not been serious. Israel will not launch a water war, even though it could win it, because it is not worthwhile and because of the internal and international political cost. Egypt, the downstream state on the Nile, is the strongest in that area, and therefore it can threaten the weak upstream states with violence if they use the river's water. This is enough to restrain Ethiopia. Nonetheless, it is possible that Ethiopia's water shortage will cause that country to decide that confrontation is preferable to delaying development of its water sources. Should this happen Egypt will presumably embark on a limited military action.

Any water war could spark a general war, with a heavy price in blood, as well as billions of dollars of expense—which might have been used to construct desalination plants. The cost of constructing a desalination plant to handle about a quarter of a billion cubic meters of water in fifteen years is equal to the cost of about one day of modern warfare—$1 billion. The conclusion is clear: For economic, social, and political reasons, it is not worthwhile launching such a water war.

A country will engage in a limited military action with the goal of attracting international attention to its problems and to pressure its co-riparians to consider its needs. This has already occurred in the past between Israel and its neighbors, and between Iraq and Syria in 1975 (when Iraq mobilized military forces to threaten Syria), and one must suppose that it will happen in the future too.

Still, perhaps unconnected to the gravity of the country's circumstances, an ambitious and ruthless leader may arise, on the model of Iraq's Saddam Hussein, who will decide to embark on war and a campaign of conquests for the purpose of bettering his economic situation—national or personal. Another way is possible also: to destroy the water installations of a neighboring upstream state, thus releasing a great amount of water for the downstream state suffering from water shortage. A threat to destroy installations planned or under construction may be made.

What lessons can be learned from the past? Before the present century, wars over water were conducted in places where there were few sources: such is the case in the Middle East and in the western United States. In the twentieth century there have been but few instances of states going to war over water or using water installations as a weapon. There was a war for Jordan water when Syria, Lebanon, and the Jordanian kingdom fought Israel; in the War of Attrition in 1968–1970 a number of water installations in the Jordan valley and in Fresh Water Canal near the Suez Canal were damaged; there have been attempts by Arab saboteurs to strike at Israeli water installations and even to poison water sources. Yet there have been no large-scale acts of destruction against water installations.

In World War II an important dam on the Ruhr in Germany was blown up, causing massive inundation that drowned thousands of people, including prisoners of war, as well as thousands of animals, and it destroyed over a hundred factories. The results of this action did not justify it. Again, at the time of the partition of India and its war with Pakistan there was anxiety that India would use the Indus River as a weapon. This did not happen. The international community hurried to assist in determining the division of water between the two states, with the aim of preventing a dispute in the future. Another case is the war of the Serbs in Bosnia in 1992–1993, which included an attempt to destroy one of the major dams in the country. Had this attempt succeeded it would have caused untold devastation. To take other examples: if in the Vietnam War the United States had struck the dams surrounding Hanoi; if Israel in the 1967–1970 war, or in the 1973 war, had hit Egypt's water installations; if in 1991 the Allies had damaged the dam system in Iraq; or if in 1980–1985 the Iranians had done so—in all these cases the results would have been as catastrophic as those caused by a nuclear bomb.

In fact, there was no such destruction. There seems to exist an unwritten moral code, whereby water is not touched even in the course of a bloody war. Such at least is the situation at the time of writing; but we cannot foretell the future. International terror is spreading ever farther afield, seeking new ways of striking at international civilized society, and it is liable to think and act differently from what was acceptable in the past (Homer-Dixon et al., 1993).

## Trapping Flood Water

This method was applied in the past and is in use at present in all the states of the Middle East. Historical examples of this method are the Nabatean water installations near Shivta, Avedat, Nitzana, and Mamshit, and the Roman water works at Tadmor (in Syria), in the Arava, the Jerusalem Hills and many other places. Among contemporary examples, in Israel for decades trapping flood water has been applied in the Judean Mountains (the Bet Zayit and Sha'alavim Dams) and in the northern and central Negev (the Nahal Shikma and Yeruham Dams, and many other small dams throughout the Negev). In Jordan attempts to trap flood water have been made in the Wadi Rum area and on the Jordan tributaries. The Syrians trap flood water all along the Yarmuk basin (see Chapter 4). Trapping flood water in arid zones is problematic as it is impossible to forecast the times or quantities of the floods. Similarly, a large part of the water seeps into the earth and some of it evaporates. Therefore, the amount of water that will be available to potential settlers in the area cannot be determined with certainty.

## Cloud Seeding

The cloud seeding method was devised after World War II when it was realized that certain chemical substances such as silver iodide could act as catalysts for cloud accumulation. The invention seemed to herald a solution to the water shortage in arid zones. However, during the decades since then it has become clear that this method has not brought about such salvation. In northern Israel improvements of 10–15 percent in mean yearly precipitation have been measured, but in the southern parts of the country the methods have not shown evident gains. It is also clear that cloud seeding cannot cause rainfall when there are no clouds (Glick, 1993: 414; Ohlsson, 1995: 64).

Seeding has created international tensions with the claim that improvements in the amount of precipitation in one area are at the expense of the amount of precipitation in the neighboring area. According to this argument it is possible, for example, that seeding clouds on the Israeli coast harms the amount of rainfall in southern Syria or northern Jordan. However, this claim has not been proven.

In sum, the Middle East cannot rely on this method as a solution to its water problems.

## Recycled Water

As the urban population grows larger, so does the quantity of water used for domestic purposes. In 1995 about half the population of the Middle East, 100 million people, lived in cities or their environs. Average annual per capita water consumption was about 50 m³ (this figure will rise with the rise in living standards). A simple calculation shows that the urban population of the Middle East produces about 5 billion m³ of sewage water. This is a considerable amount of water, and it is likely to double in about ten years on account of expected population increase (the total Middle Eastern population doubles every 23 years) and the never ending migration to the towns.

In the Middle East, sewage water can solve the water shortage for agriculture. Purification is in any case necessary to prevent pollution of groundwater and of rivers. The only problem here is the social, religious, and psychological barrier. The solution will be the gradual introduction of the use of recycled water: first for watering lawns and ornamental plants, and ultimately for agriculture. Water used for urban and industrial purposes may be retaken almost entirely and with the correct treatment may be brought up to a purity level close to that of drinking water. Recycled water may be used in agriculture for irrigating industrial crops (e.g., sugar beet, cotton). High-quality recycled water may also serve for irrigating citrus groves and other orchards.

The pioneer in this respect in the Middle East is the state of Israel. In the Tel Aviv metropolitan area in 1996 facilities recycled about 130 million m³ of sewage water (Mekorot, 1991; 1996). The Haifa and Jerusalem metropolitan areas have large purification plants, and such installations are due to be added throughout the country. An important subject that will arise in the peace talks between Israel and the Palestinian entity will be water arrangements. In this framework Israel will require cycling of water on the West Bank as an essential condition for concessions on its part. Such recycling is vital because the West Bank residents live in an area that is topographically higher than areas of the state of Israel, and their sewage drains into the streams that flow down into Israel, or seeps into the groundwater that serves both authorities. In the Gaza Strip the groundwater is already brackish and polluted, so there is urgent need to recycle sewage water to prevent further deterioration of the groundwater. In the kingdom of Jordan too the condition of groundwater and river water is extremely poor. Steps must be taken without delay to recycle sewage water, to prevent pollution of the Jordan River and of the Dead Sea.

The big crowded cities of the Middle East (e.g., Cairo, Baghdad, Damascus) and the settlements on the banks of rivers (the place of most dwellings in Egypt and Iraq) must also engage urgently in treatment of sewage water. Failure to do so will result in continued penetration of sewage into rivers, polluting them and endangering all inhabitants lower down the river.

In 1997 the situation of recycling sewage water was not good, but was about to change. The subject came up on the agenda of the states involved, and all have programs on this issue. In Israel, in 1990 about 270 million $m^3$ of sewage water were recycled, of which about 190 million $m^3$ were used. The forecast for the year 2020 is for reuse of half a billion cubic meters of sewage water (Water Commissioner, 1995). In Jordan, in 1991 about 45 million $m^3$ were recycled. The outlook for 2000 envisages recycling 86 million $m^3$ (Shatanwi and al Jayousi, 1995: 92). In Egypt, in 1995 about 3 billion $m^3$ were recycled. The government's plan hopes to achieve recycling of 7–8 billion $m^3$ of sewage water by 2020.

From the discussion of recycled water it may be concluded that the quality of the water has greater importance than the quantity. Only the highest quality water will be allocated for drinking. Agriculture will receive water surpluses as noted above, and also recycled water. With population increase the amount of water allocated for consumption will rise and this amount will be taken from the quantities of high-quality water previously assigned to agriculture. The subject has implications for the agricultural potential of states such as Israel and Jordan and for the Palestinian entity, since most of their good water will no longer be allocated to agriculture but to drinking.

## Saving Water

Many ways exist for saving water, and this issue has great importance throughout the world, and in the Middle East particularly. One of these ways is to reduce agriculture and to import food. For example, bananas may be imported from South America. Rice, wheat, and other cereals may be imported from other places, and thus water presently used to irrigate crops in the arid Middle East would be saved and put to the direct use of the population.

Obviously, it is possible to introduce efficient and economical irrigation methods. In the large river valleys and many places in the Middle East, irrigation by flooding the fields is still practiced. This method is wasteful in the extreme, and also contributed to the considerable salinization of the land, which in turn harms the crops. This irrigation method should be stopped and replaced by more effective methods such as bubble, drip, or microspray irrigation, controlled showering, and underground watering. Growing plants in greenhouses also cuts down water loss by evaporation. Billions of cubic meters of water may be saved by these systems. The old irrigation methods have been passed on from father to son down the generations. To change them much capital is needed for the acquisition and placement of new equipment, but mainly for the reeducation of millions of farmers, most of whom lack minimal schooling. It is a long, complex process, but there is no alternative to it. Correct transportation too can save large amounts of water. Today in many places water is moved to open earth canals. This method results in a large loss of water by evaporation, seepage, and the growth of wild plants that use up water. The transition should be made to transportation of water in concrete canals or pipes. This step too, like the previous one noted, requires an investment of billions of dollars. But it can be carried out rapidly as it does not depend on the farmers themselves.

A further mode of saving is avoidance of growing water-excessive crops, such as cotton, bananas, sugar beet, rice, and citrus, and concentration on water-saving crops. The former type of crops may continue to be grown only if recycled water is available for their irrigation.

If the Middle East states (especially Sudan, Egypt, Syria, Iraq, and Turkey) make an effort to save water in the ways outlined above it should be possible to save a total of 50–60 billion m³. Egypt will save one-third of the amount of water it uses, namely, about 20 billion m³; a similar quantity will be saved in Iraq. In Turkey, following completion of the GAP Project, it will be possible to save about 10 billion m³, in Syria 2–3 billion m³, in Sudan 4–10 billion m³, and in Jordan smaller amounts. By these methods it will be possible to solve the problem of water throughout the Middle East, at least for another two or three decades.

Some experts suggest encouraging such saving as this through turning water into a commodity with a financial value, like oil, wheat, or steel. They argue that the need to pay for use of water will necessarily bring about more effective use and saving in the water regime (Allan, 1994: 88–89; Eckestein, 1995: 400–467).

Commercialization of the use of water will also gradually result in essential structural changes in the economies of the Middle East. This means the steady reduction of agriculture and the number of those engaged in it, reduction of agriculture on marginal land unsuitable for irrigation, and a shift to the industry and service branches. Such a transformation is likely to lead to a significant drop in the amount of water used in the Middle East, principally water for irrigation.

But in the meantime the populations of the states of the region are expanding and the governments continue to build dams, enlarge agricultural areas in marginal zones, and promote irrigation by traditional methods and growing of traditional crops (on the dependence of the states of the region on agriculture, see the chapters on the Nile, the Euphrates and the Tigris, and the Jordan).

Of the ways of saving water listed above, only technological means that do not depend on retraining the farmers and whose implementation will be internationally supported may be introduced relatively soon. The other transformation will necessarily be slow and will produce results only in several decades.

Not only may irrigation water be saved, but also domestic water. This is possible, among other things, by the repair of urban water supply systems that are corroded and leaking. But it must be borne in mind that the quantities saved in this way are dwarfed by those saved from irrigation.

## International Cooperation in Water Issues in the Middle East

The idea of cooperation among the states of the Middle East is not new. Decades ago the British proposed the Century Storage plan (see Chapter 2). Some of the development projects of the Jordan basin were based on the idea of international cooperation: the Lowdermilk plan and the later ones of Hayes and of Johnston (see Chapter 4).

The Turkish Peace Pipeline plan is also based on international cooperation. Since the meeting of Israelis and Arabs at the Madrid Conference on October 30, 1991, and particularly since the signing of the Declaration of Principles between Israel and the Palestinians on September 13, 1993, and the peace accord between Israel and Jordan on October 26, 1994, many cooperative projects between Israel and its neighbors have been published.

Additional projects were mooted following the economic conference at Casablanca in October 1994. These spoke of a "new Middle East," and a "Common Market for the Middle East," along the lines of the European Common Market. In all, about 100 different projects have been put forward, aimed at altering the map of the Middle East entirely, and within it the water map. The estimated overall cost of implementing these programs is in the region of $15–27 billion (Peres, 1993; Israel, *Development Options*, 1994, 1996).

To assess the chances of international cooperation on water issues in the Middle East we should first clarify certain matters, namely, whether such international cooperation exists anywhere else in the world; whether cooperation on the subject of water in the Middle East provides a solution to the water problems of the region; and how far cooperation is possible on water issues in the special circumstances of the Middle East.

Cooperation can take place on many matters without jeopardizing the sovereignty of any of the partners: together they may build dams; transport water; prevent flooding; prevent water pollution; use a common river for trade and transport, fishing, and joint tourism; and carry out joint activities to improve efficiency of agriculture in the river valley.

Full cooperation is extremely uncommon in the world and often comes only of necessity. Even in the United States, it required deep economic hardship in the 1920s to force the states of the Tennessee basin, the Colorado basin, and the Columbia basin, to cooperate; the result was the establishment of large common water installations. The Nile valley seems to present a case of ideal cooperation, in that the upstream states, Sudan and Uganda, retain reserves of water for the downstream state, Egypt. Agreements also exist on the distribution of water between Egypt and Sudan. But the expression "seems to present" is used because these agreements were imposed on the participating states by Britain, which ruled the three states involved.

Voluntary and far-reaching cooperation has existed in recent years in the La Plata basin in South America. Here, Uruguay, Argentina, Brazil, Bolivia, and Paraguay participate. Since 1910 these states have exchanged information, ideas, and plans intended to exploit the enormous potential of the river. To this end they also established an international committee that included representatives of the United Nations. The aim was to use the river for drinking, shipping, agriculture, and generation of much electricity, and also to prevent flooding. In 1972 the preparations and plans were completed, and in 1973 work on implementing the enterprise began. In 1982 the first project of the series was ready, and in 1991 the construction of the largest power station on earth, at Itapo, was finished. Four years have passed since this project was completed, and only now are data relating to its huge ecological cost beginning to accumulate, including damage in the city of Buenos Aires. The partnership may now be on the point of breaking up.

The fact that full cooperation among the riparian states of a river basin is so rare indicates the existence of a fundamental problem: cooperation involves some yielding of sovereignty, and states try to avoid this concession. The infrequent examples of full cooperation concern states with abundant rivers and vast territories, and among which peaceful relations have prevailed for decades. Such states are able to absorb a slight territorial disadvantage here and there or some minor error. In most cases existing international cooperation is limited, and covers only exchange of information, shipping on the river, fishing, flood prevention, and dealing with ecological problems.

The question before us now is whether international cooperation can solve the water distress of the Middle East. Cooperation may enlarge the potential of the water through construction of reservoirs at optimal sites, with full coordination among all the states of the basin. In this way the opportunity will arise for enormous saving and use of better systems.

Cooperation in agriculture in growing and marketing may achieve optimal exploitation of water. This may be illustrated by considering the three drainage basins covered in this book.

### The Nile Basin

The construction of dams on the Ethiopian highlands and a reduction of Lake Nasser Reservoir may save tens of billions of cubic meters of water that at present are lost from the reservoir. Cooperation among the basin states may lead to the optimal ecological and economic solution for the Sudd swamps. The Century Storage plan is a further example showing that cooperation can bring about a solution to the water shortage in the entire Nile basin.

### The Euphrates and Tigris Basins

For the first time ever, the Turkish dams built on the Euphrates and the Tigris adjust the capricious flow regimes of these rivers for the benefit of the riparian states. The problem is that among these three countries—Turkey, Syria, and Iraq—relations are devoid of trust and replete with suspicion, while the two Arab states—Syria and Iraq—consider these dams a threat.

If the set of relations among the three states changed, and trust were created, it would be possible to institute a fair distribution of water among them, with optimal use of the other resources of each of them (see Chapter 3). It would also be possible to carry water from the Euphrates in Iraq to Jordan, and from Turkey to Israel, Jordan, the Palestinian entity, and even to the Arabian Peninsula (in accordance with the Turkish Peace Pipeline plan).

### The Jordan Drainage Basin

Full cooperation in the Jordan basin would promote the revival of the Lowdermilk-Hayes plan: transfer of water from the Litani to the Jordan, joint storage in the Maqarin (al Wahda) region, joint management of Lake Kinneret and the Yarmuk basin, and cooperation over the reservoirs on the Judean and Samarian highlands. Such cooperation would permit transfer of water surpluses from the rivers in Lebanon to the thirsty Damascus basin and other parts of southern Syria, and would also allow the transfer of more water from the Yarmuk to the Jordanian kingdom.

In sum, cooperation among the states of the region over water issues would undoubtedly bring great benefit to all of them.

Is such cooperation feasible? The peoples of the region have no experience in cooperation. In the last seven millennia there was never cooperation in the Middle East among states or regions, or even among clans and families. Prior to 1995, not even economic distress moved the leaders of the region to talks and cooperation. In conditions of political instability, of dictatorial, quasi-feudal regimes, of deep residues of bitterness and suspicion, is it possible to plan for cooperation without endangering national existence? Could Egypt, for example, in the coming decades, trust Uganda, Sudan, and Ethiopia to the point of placing control of its precious water in their hands?

In this survey I have shown that even in democratic, advanced, and rich states very little has been done in the field of cooperation. It is difficult to believe, however, that even such slight cooperation as this is actually possible in the Middle East, between Jews and Arabs, between Christians and Muslims, and between personal rivals (such as Assad and Saddam Hussein). It is premature to conceive that in the Middle East a fresh wind has been blowing since the Madrid Conference, the Oslo agreements and the Arava accord.

It transpires that the only state in the region that speaks of a new Middle East and a new era is the state of Israel. The responses of the neighboring countries are cold. Moreover, the Arab development plans submitted to the Casablanca Conference by Jordan, Egypt, and the Palestinians contain no reference to cooperation with Israel, and in most of them Israel does not figure even on the maps. The only cooperation mentioned in these plans is among the Arab states, but even this is rare. For the most part they are internal plans, separate for each state (World Bank, 1994; Jordan, 1994).

It may be said, of course, that the agreements on the transfer of water from Lake Kinneret to the Jordanian kingdom, and permission for Israel to use Jordanian groundwater in the Arava region, constitute proof of the possibility of regional cooperation over water. It must be borne in mind that both these cases involve relatively small quantities of water and that this cooperation is more a humane gesture than a genuine common cause.

The Palestinians as well as the Jordanians constantly repeat their fears of Israel's economic power. They are also concerned that Israel will replace physical occupation by economic occupation. Israel's leaders and economists are obviously aware of this mood, and draw conclusions from it regarding future modes of action. They must take care to avoid sacrificing Israel's resources to economic considerations.

## Conclusion

From various considerations enumerated in this chapter, I am forced to delete from the list of practical nonconventional means for solving the water problems of the Middle East the methods of trapping flood water, cloud seeding, import of water from remote places, and warfare over water. We are left with the following three means, which any state may apply in its own territory: recycling of water, desalination, and saving water at various levels. If the states of the region approach these solutions seriously, the amount of water available will supply the domestic needs of the entire population, even if this doubles from 200 to 400 million, as forecast for 2020. The order of preference for the states is this: first, an effort must be made to recycle sewage water, and then to save water by all the means outlined here. Desalination should be initiated only after the other means have been exhausted. If progress along these lines is too slow, supply of water will lag behind demand. In such a case the countries will be obliged to adjust demand to supply, with all the hardships this will involve.

# Conclusion

In *Rivers of Fire* I have discussed in depth the great international rivers and the groundwater in the Middle East, the Nile, the Tigris and the Euphrates; the smaller international rivers, the Jordan and its tributaries and the Orontes; and the aquifers of the West Bank, Libya, and the Jordanian kingdom. The lack of water is forcing the countries of the region to search for alternative water sources. The likelihood of structural changes, saving water, importing water, desalinating water, or going to war have also been discussed.

From the previous chapters, several common features of international water in the Middle East can be discerned.

### Historical Rights of Downstream Countries

Exploitation of the water of Middle Eastern rivers is as ancient as time. It began in the cradles of human civilization: the Nile valley in Egypt; the Tigris and Euphrates valley in Mesopotamia; and the kingdoms of Sumer and Akkad, Babylonia and Assyria, parts of Persia and Media and the Arab civilization. On the Jordan and its tributaries flourished Jericho and Karak, Dan and Avel-Bet-Macha, the cities of Adam and Kinnarot, and later, some marvelous corners of the Roman Empire. Christianity also developed there. On the Orontes river, Antilles water has been used since time immemorial, and along its course rose and flourished the cities of Hama (Hamath), Homs (Emesa), Antakya (Antioch), Baalbeck, and others.

The populations that shared the lower stretches of these rivers have used their waters since the dawn of history, and therefore the downstream countries—Egypt in the Nile basin, Iraq in the Tigris–Euphrates basin, and Palestine in the Jordan basin—have historical rights to these rivers. The exception is the Orontes basin, all of whose inhabitants used its water. The settlers of the upper sections of these rivers hardly used the water, either because they did not need it, because in mountainous

261

terrain they were not able to cultivate wide tracks of land for agriculture, or because they did not possess the technical knowledge needed to elevate water to high areas.

Today it is possible to build dams, to raise the level of the water, and to divert it to the high plateaus; therefore, upstream countries now demand their share of the water without considering the historical rights of downstream countries. Turkey demands recognition of its rights to the Tigris and Euphrates, Syria demands recognition of its rights to the Yarmuk, and Ethiopia and Sudan demand recognition of their rights to the Nile.

### Dependency on the Water of the River

All the rivers of the Middle East flow in arid or semiarid areas, and therefore, their water is vital for the inhabitants of their basins. Because agriculture is an important economic activity in all the riparian countries, they all need large volumes of water to irrigate the fields. Dependency on agriculture and water has deep psychological roots. From the dawn of time, populations on the banks of these rivers lived by agriculture. It is thus most difficult for the people in these regions to acknowledge the reality that they have to limit the agricultural sector.

### Population Explosion

All the countries in the international basins in the Middle East are caught in the Malthusian trap—they all face the danger of a population explosion. In most Middle Eastern countries the doubling time of population is 20–25 years, and it is obvious that they will face shortages of food and water.

### The Rush for Development of Water Plants and Full Exploitation of the Water

Because of their dependency on agriculture and the rapid growth of their populations—which exceeds the increase in food production—all the countries are obsessed with developing water projects to increase food production. This frenzy has common characteristics in all countries: building of multiple dams, ignoring neighboring countries, and inflicting harm on water quality. Because of hasty development, the water of the Nile, Jordan, and Orontes Rivers has been fully exploited, and it is impossible to add water to one country without affecting the other riparian countries. In other words, these rivers have no surplus water; the water that runs to the sea is used to flush the river course to preserve the ecological system, or it is so polluted as to be unusable. The Euphrates water is almost entirely used. If the GAP Project in Turkey and the development of the Euphrates valley in Syria continue as planned, in the decade 2005–2015 this river too will be fully exploited. Iraq may cease using Euphrates water even earlier because of its poor quality.

The Tigris is the only international river in the region that still has an abundance of water running to the sea, and not all the possibilities of using its water have been exhausted. Its exploitation will apparently be complete only after 2015. By then Turkey will have implemented all its GAP Project, Syria will pump as much water as possible from the sections of the river flowing through its territory, and Iraq will have completed the series of dams being built on the river and its tributaries. All this assumes that political developments in an area with a Kurdish majority allow the project to be finished. The countries of the region are also reaching the "red line" in their pumping of groundwater. Due to overpumping in the coastal areas in Lebanon, Syria, Israel, Egypt, and Libya, the dangers of salinity are becoming increasingly grave. In Saudi Arabia and Jordan, and even in Egypt and Libya, fossil water is being pumped, and it will evidently not be possible to continue this pumping indefinitely.

The rush to development will certainly end in abysmal failure; evaporation and seepage will decrease the amounts of water and will lower its quality. Regardless of the plethora of water projects, the rivers and groundwater will not be able to satisfy the food and energy needs of the growing population. Population growth will not abate owing to various factors, including religion, which affects the birthrate directly and indirectly. Even if the high birthrate halted immediately, the effect would be felt only 20 years from now owing to demographic momentum.

The water shortage in the Middle East is worsening, and there are also forecasts (which have not yet been validated) that the amount of precipitation in the area will continue to decrease, and the drought that struck the area in the 1980s is not transient. This shortage excites great anxiety and sensitivity regarding everything related to water. One of the ways this anxiety is expressed is the complaint lodged by Arab countries that Israel is planning to use or is already using the waters of the Litani for its needs. Egypt fears that Israel may help Ethiopia exploit the Nile or that Libya is damaging Egypt's groundwater, even though it is quite unclear whether Egypt and Libya in fact share groundwater reservoirs at all; Syria and Iraq fear that Turkey will exploit the Euphrates. Great sensitivity also exists about the connected groundwater reservoirs between Israel and the Gaza Strip and between Israel and the West Bank (Judea and Samaria). Sensitivity about groundwater also exists between Jordan and Saudi Arabia, and between Tunisia and Algeria.

## *Alternatives to the Present Conventional Use of Water*

It may be argued that in the Middle East there is no problem of water, but it is one of politics, society, and culture. The leaders of the region are not aware of the gravity of the condition of the water regimes in their countries. It may be that they hope to solve their water problems by conventional water projects or by adding more dams. They perhaps do not know or do not believe that it is possible to approach the problem differently. In each of the basins analyzed here there are nonroutine ways for achieving an addition of water. If the countries of the Middle East wish to prevent national disasters or a regional disaster they must make agriculture more efficient; cease growing crops that demand large amounts of water such as rice, cotton, sugarcane, mango, and avocado; and move to water-saving crops, such as wheat and barley, and to water-saving irrigation systems such as drip irrigation instead of the existing methods. It is estimated that Egypt loses about 18 billion $m^3$ of water a year, mainly through wasteful irrigation in a water-transfer system in earth canals, the same as existed five millennia ago. With this system the greatest waste is through seepage, evaporation, and water plants growing in the canals and along their banks.

In most countries of the region it is difficult to introduce recycled water for use in the national water cycle; this is due to cultural and psychological factors as well as neglect. An additional way of saving is to set a price for water. As of 1997 water in Egypt is still free; the populations of Jordan, Syria, and Iraq regard water as a national staple that will never run out, as has been the case for the last 4,000–6,000 years! But these saving methods are not enough either, and the countries of the region will be forced to make a revolutionary change in their economic structures and move from agriculture-based to industry- and services-based economies.

In parallel with the direct operations on the water itself, there is an immediate need to reduce birthrate and raise the level of education. The latter, in turn, will be conducive toward limiting childbirth. There is a need for intelligent exploitation of water and reduction of the number of workers dependent on agriculture.

Similarly, it is possible to apply various technological means that exist in the world. Desalination can be an effective solution for the water shortage in a few cities, and today desalinated water is used in cities such as Eilat, Aqaba, Abu Dhabi, Manama, Dhahran, Riyadh, Jedda, and Yanbu, for industrial purposes as well as in greenhouses, but it cannot provide irrigation water. Plants able to desalinate 0.25 billion $m^3$ of water would offer a solution to the problem of water for agriculture in small countries such as Israel and Jordan, in the West Bank and the Gaza Strip, which would be able to receive international aid for that purpose. Such is not the case with Egypt, Sudan, Iraq, and Syria, whose water needs are measured in billions of cubic meters. In 1997, throughout the world 6–7 billion m³ of water were desalinated, a volume less than the water demand in Egypt for one month! In these countries desalination would aim at solving the water problem of the cities, but it would be incapable of providing enough for agriculture.

Are the countries of the region able to realize this revolution? Their agricultural tradition makes it very difficult for the river basin populations to adapt to the thought that they must abandon their ancient agricultural culture, so deep-rooted in their consciousness and in their way of life, and look for other economic opportunities. The leaders will find it difficult to do this. They too have grown up in villages and close to the soil and farming, and they will be hard-pressed to take steps to change their peoples from farmers to industrial and service workers. An additional difficulty arises from the fact that such a change will require cooperation with foreigners, who are suspect in their eyes. For these reasons and others, the path to endorsing such a plan is long and difficult, and the leaders who will have to make key decisions will not be able to reap the fruit of their work.

At the same time, here and there encouraging signs appear. Some of these are large investments and aid from the World Bank and other economic bodies concerned to help the countries of the region to prevent the approaching crisis. This aid will increase in the future.

In Egypt efforts are under way to improve the efficiency of the water regime; this is the case in Turkey and Jordan also. Success is more limited in Iraq, Sudan, and Syria.

If and when the Arab–Israeli conflict comes to an end, much money will be invested in the Palestinians. It will be fairly easy to deal with the hardships of the Palestinians because the territory and the population are not particularly large.

A further solution that reappears from time to time as a panacea for all the ills of the region is international cooperation. Four fundamental questions arise in this respect: Can cooperation enlarge the supply of water in the region? Is voluntary cooperation possible in the Middle East? Is it possible to impose cooperation as a final resort before catastrophe or before confrontation? If, despite all, steps are not taken to improve the water regimes of all the states of the Middle East, and there is no cooperation, what then?

### Can Cooperation Enlarge the Supply of Water?

Many advantages would accrue from such cooperation. First, it would increase the amount of water available for use. Nile basin cooperation would allow Lake Victoria, Lake Tana, and the drainage system in Ethiopia to be transformed into multiyear reservoirs, instead of Lake Nasser at the Aswan Dam and Jabel Awliya Dam being used for this purpose. Evaporation losses from these lakes would be much lower than from Lake Nasser and the Jabel Awliya Dam reservoir in their desert setting, thus saving more than 12 billion m³ of water. In addition, the energy potential of the lakes is enormous, and they will be able to increase the overall discharge of the Nile in dry years. If Lake Victoria were transformed into a reservoir, water could be allocated to Uganda, Kenya, and Tanzania to satisfy all their needs. (Raising the lake's level by only three feet would increase its supply by 60 billion m³ of water!) Cooperation in the Nile basin would permit renewal of the Jonglei Canal project and the other projects in the Sudd swamp area, and an additional 5–10 billion m³ of water could be added to the Nile's discharge in north Sudan and in Egypt. Altogether, 20 billion m³ could be added to the Nile. If the flow of the Nile were expanded, it would be possible to allocate to Ethiopia and Eritrea 6–12 billion m³ of water and to add more water to Sudan and Egypt.

In the Jordan basin regional cooperation would make it possible to construct the al Wahda Dam; it would then be possible to prevent the waste of the Yarmuk floodwater in winter. The Yarmuk water could be diverted to the Kinneret when its water level falls. A series of dams could be erected on the Jordan River between Israel and the Jordanian kingdom to be used for desalination, recreation, and tourism. It would be possible to cut two canals from the Kinneret that would irrigate the eastern and western Jordan valley. This would prevent wastage of floodwater, which now streams, unused, to the Dead Sea.

Regional cooperation would allow surplus water from the Litani to be taken to the Jordan basin, water that today runs from the Awali and pours into the sea. This diversion would add another 50–200 million m³ of water to the region and would also permit production of electricity.

Regional cooperation could also contribute greatly in the Tigris and Euphrates basins. If Syria did not fear unilateral construction by Turkey of more water projects on the Euphrates, it could cancel building several of the dams it has planned to protect itself from Turkey's programs. For the same reasons, Iraq would not need the Haditha Dam (Kadisiya). If these dams are not built, much water can be saved that would otherwise be lost through seepage and evaporation. Regional cooperation would also allow a fair distribution of the rivers' water: Turkey and Syria would use the Euphrates and Iraq would use the Tigris.

In the Orontes basin regional cooperation would make it possible to bring surplus water that flows from the rivers of western Lebanon to the Orontes, and even to the Zabdani, to irrigate the thirsty Damascus basin.

Regional cooperation on water use issues could help to solve political disputes. With regional cooperation, Turkey could offer to release significant amounts of water from the Tigris and the Euphrates. In return, Iraq could sell oil cheaply to Turkey, and Syria could recognize the annexation of the Hatay region, terminate its assistance to the Kurds and the Armenians, and settle disputes with Turkey over borderlands.

However, for all its advantages it should be emphasized that cooperation will not solve the region's water problems but only postpone them briefly. Even given the importance of regional cooperation and a fair distribution of water, if the population increase continues at today's rate of about 3 percent, and if there is no technological breakthrough in the countries of the region to reduce dependency on water for irrigation, in the very near future all the rivers' water will be completely utilized, and it will not matter whether cooperation occurs. Cooperation can put off catastrophe but cannot prevent it.

## *Is Regional Cooperation in the Middle East Possible?*

To answer this question we can infer only from past experience and from the current situation. Past experience teaches us about the lack of cooperation among the countries of the region on water issues. For example, an agreement exists between Egypt and Sudan on the division of Nile water, but it does not diminish the suspicions between the two countries. And agreements dating from the colonial period do not provide examples of cooperation, because they were forced on the countries of the region by the colonial powers.

Relations among neighbors in this part of the world are linked to grim memories of violent conquest, exploitation, deception, and corrupt and predatory rulers. It is difficult to break free of these residues, especially when at issue is the defense of a resource as precious as water. And because of mutual suspicion based to some degree on bitter experience from the past, every country in the region, out of concern for its national security, formulates its own development plans and seeks to realize them itself.

These countries, therefore, are afraid of depending on each other. It is unthinkable for Egypt to rely on Ethiopia, Sudan, Tanzania, and Uganda, in all of which political instability is rife. Already in 1952 Nasser decided on building the Aswan Dam so that it could provide Egypt with national security within its borders; he said, "It is not possible to leave Egypt's fate in the hands of the countries of the upper Nile basin" (Little, 1965: 40). I assume that the positions of the rulers of Egypt, Iraq, and Syria today are not very different from that of Nasser in 1952. In the intervening forty years, the atmosphere in this region has hardly changed in a way that would justify a more optimistic attitude. Iraq can barely rely on Turkey and Syria, and the honesty of their wish for cooperation.

Furthermore, cooperation requires strong countries to yield some of their water and some of their plans to develop their water resources, and they will not agree to this. That is why it seems likely that Turkey and Egypt will reject the notion of cooperation.

An additional obstacle to cooperation is the inability to admit mistakes and to repair the damage done. As time passes, dams are built and reservoirs fill up, and things cannot be restored to the way they were. It is inconceivable that Egypt will tear down the Aswan High Dam and Sudan and Egypt the Jabel Awliya Dam to create reservoirs in Lake Tana and in Lake Victoria instead. It is unthinkable that Turkey will acquiesce to emptying the Ataturk Dam and cease using it for irrigation. It is an impossibility that the very leaders who envisaged and raised the Ataturk Dam, the Saddam Dam, the Tabqa Dam, and the dams of the Nile will declare before their people and the world that they erred, that the enterprises they erected are unnecessary, and that now they have decided to cooperate with foreigners.

In discussions on water issues among countries, the issue of each country's general economic potential and its ability to make a transition from agriculture to industry or tourism will arise (in keeping with United Nations agreements and the Helsinki Accords on considerations for fair distribution of water). Turkey is unlikely to be willing to abandon water development and to concentrate on industry and tourism alone. Iraq will project such a demand on the basis of its oil reserves. Israel will probably be willing to forego agriculture for the sake of the Jordanian kingdom, and focus instead on high technology.

Cooperation raises technical problems, and not everywhere will the geographical structure of the basin allow an equal distribution of water to all the riparians. In the Nile basin, for example, an improvement in the drainage system of the Sudd and the streaming of excess water northward has to be accompanied by the retention of White Nile water in Lake Victoria. This, in turn, will cause the level of the lake to rise, flooding wide areas in the three countries located around its shores (Uganda, Kenya, and Tanzania). By contrast, lowering the water level of the lake where there is heavy rainfall will cause overflowing in the Sudd region, as has already happened in the past with disastrous consequences for the inhabitants of the Sudd swamps.

Facts from 1994–1995 may justify this pessimistic approach: In the peace talks between Israel and its neighbors, and also at the Casablanca Conference (October 1994), Egypt and Jordan, suggested programs of their own. These were almost all national plans, within each country itself. Only very few of them involved cooperation. Even at a time of great goodwill such as existed at the Casablanca Conference the large Middle Eastern states were found to lack the spirit of striding forward toward cooperation.

In 1997 the overall political map of the Middle East is remote from encouraging cooperation. The opposite is the case: it seems that division and hostility are greater than before. Sudan is in a state of civil war, south Sudan wishing to become detached from the state, and the few projects created in the past in the Sudd region have been destroyed. Eritrea has separated from Ethiopia and will certainly claim its share of Nile water. Iraq has at least three divisions: the Kurdish part in the north, the Shi'ite Arab part in the south, and the Sunni Arab part in the center. Turkey is locked in a severe and seemingly intractable struggle with its Kurdish population. Egypt is beset by Muslim extremists and its relations with Sudan are tense. Terrorist groups strike at all parts of the region, including Saudi Arabia. The peace negotiations between Israel and its neighbors, the sole ray of light in the region in 1993–1996, have been derailed by conservative or extremist factions on both sides. In any event, the hopes for a New Middle East and cooperation have no firm grounds.

### Is it Possible to Impose Cooperation?

We live in an age in which the United States is the only superpower in the world, and it has the strength and the means to force states to implement measures that are clearly US interests even if they are unpopular with the states concerned. Since the United States has obvious interests in the Middle East (including principally oil, the Suez Canal, and restraining Iran and extremist Islam, which even threatens the United States at home), it clearly seeks the greatest possible calm in this region of the world. The problem of water shortage is but a small detail in the plethora of serious problems in need of solutions. Imposition of cooperation on water issues alone is unlikely to bring about the desired calm. Nor is it clear whether the United States and its powerful friends can solve the water problems in this region over a protracted period.

I have already noted that imposed cooperation has many disadvantages. The chances for imposed cooperation are likely to increase if the United States and other economic powers, all of which have interests in this region, were willing to assist in the creation of additional water by desalination plants, a water infrastructure, changes in the economic structure of the Middle Eastern countries, and aid in import of food as an alternative to producing it by means of local water.

Regarding assistance to the approximately 14 million inhabitants of the Jordan basin alone (Israel, the West Bank, the Jordanian kingdom, and southern Syria), with overall international aid it would be possible to "create water" for them (through water-saving methods, desalination, food aid, etc.). But matters are otherwise regarding the Nile basin, where about 138 million people live (in 1997, and not including the equatorial countries), or regarding the Euphrates and the Tigris basin, where 53 million people live. These figures make the solution expensive almost to the point of being impossible.

There is yet a further consideration: it is difficult to envisage that the United States will agree to harm its friendship with Egypt by forcing it to make concessions in favor of Ethiopia and Sudan or its friendship with Turkey by offering aid to Iraq.

As already stated, some of the problems are solvable by increasing food exports from the United States to the countries of the region. However, the United States may not be willing to shoulder aid of such dimensions for a lengthy period of time, and the states of the region may not agree to become dependent on the United States. Furthermore, the United States has not proved that it has the power, the ability, and the desire to impose its will on Iran, Iraq, Syria, Sudan, and even Somalia. Although some of these countries are very weak, there have been instances in the past where they refused to comply with American wishes.

To sum up, the United States cannot impose a solution in the Nile basin and the Euphrates and Tigris basin. The reasons for this are historical, political, and economic. In the Jordan basin the United States can exert influence, because this basin is relatively small. It is Israel that is being asked to donate water to its neighbors, and the United States will undoubtedly compensate it. This is not genuine cooperation but the imposition of a solution. As we have already stated, the transfers of water from Israel to Jordan are more an exercise in arithmetic than a solution to the water shortage.

From this arises the last question: If there is no cooperation and there are objective problems in adopting nonconventional solutions, what will happen then to the countries of the region?

Tony Allan classifies the states of the region in three groups, distinguished by the economic future they may expect when the problem of water shortage grows worse (Allan, 1991: 190–198). I include Israel in this model.

Group A is the oil states: these have the means to purchase food even though they do not have water. Such are Saudi Arabia, Iran, Kuwait, Iraq, and Libya. These states will overcome the water shortage by means of their money. Group B states will not suffer a shortage because of the abundance of their water or because of their high level of technology. These are Turkey, Lebanon, and Israel. Group C consists of Third

World states, poor in resources and water (some of them are already suffering from water shortage and some will suffer from it in the near future). These states will find it difficult to complement the food that their ever-growing populations lack. The states in this group are divided into two subgroups. The first includes Jordan, Morocco, Tunisia, Eritrea, Egypt, and the Palestinian entity, states located in areas of strategic interest to the United States. These will receive food aid (as a substitute for the production of food themselves with the use of water). The second subgroup includes Syria, Ethiopia, Sudan, and Yemen. American interest in these states is smaller, so they may expect hardships. However, it is possible that the United States will be willing to provide these states with food without charge in return for political quiet.

A further crisis in the oil states is liable to shift several states from group A to group C. A crisis in American food reserves, or an American isolationist policy, may cause group C states economic, social, and political disturbances, and even famine.

The region is running out of water. The rivers are liable to become rivers of fire. We may witness cooperation or noncooperation in the area, peace or war. The key lies in addressing the matter of population growth, on which hangs the future of the planet.

# Appendix: Metric Conversion Table

| Used in the book | Symbol | Multiply by | To find |
|---|---|---|---|
| *Length* | | | |
| Meter | m | 3.3 | feet |
| Kilometer (1,000 m) | km | 0.6214 | miles |
| Millimeter | mm | 0.04 | inches |
| Centimeter | cm | 0.4 | inches |
| *Area* | | | |
| Sq. Kilometer = 100 hectares | km$^2$ | 0.4 | sq. miles |
| Hectare = 10,000 m$^2$ | ha | 2.47 | acres |
| Feddan = 42.1 m$^2$ (in Egypt) | Feddan | 1.038 | acres |
| Dunam = 919 m$^2$ (in the Middle East) | Dunam | 0.23 | acres |
| Acre | Acre | 4.3 | dunams |
| Acre | Acre | 0.96 | Feddans |
| *Volume* | | | |
| cubic meter | m$^3$ | 1.3 | cubic yards |
| cubic meter | m$^3$ | 35.32 | cubic feet |
| million m$^3$ | m/m$^3$ or mm$^3$ | 1.3 | 1.3. m.c.y., or 810 acre feet |
| billion m3 = one cubic kilometer of water | b/m$^3$ or bm$^3$ | 35.32 | 35 b.c.f., or 0.81 million acre feet |
| cubic yard | yd$^3$ | 0.76 | cubic meters |
| cubic feet | ft$^3$ | 0.028 | cubic meters |

# References

Abate, Z. (1990). "The Integrated Development of the Nile Basin Waters," in *The Nile*, P. P. Howell and J. A. Allan (eds.). London: SOAS, 137–152.

Abdel-Mageed, Yahia (1994). "The Central Region: Problems and Perspectives," in *Water in the Arab World*, P. Rogers and P. Lydon (eds.). Cambridge, Massachusetts: Harvard University Press, 101–119.

Abebe, Mesfin (1995). "The Nile—Source of Regional Cooperation or Conflict," *Water International* 20, 32–35.

Adams, E., and James M. Holt (1985). "The Use of Land and Water in Modern Agriculture: An Assessment," in *Agricultural Development in the Middle East*, P. Beaumont and K. McLachlan (eds.). New York: John Wiley, 63–85.

Ahmed, M. E. (1983). "A Quantitave Model to Predict Safe Yield for Well Fields in Kufra and Sarir Basins," *Ground Water* 21(1): 56–64.

Ahmed, S. (1990). "Context and Precedents with Respect for the Development, Division and Management of Nile Waters," in *The Nile*, P. P. Howell and J. A. Allan (eds.). London: SOAS, 225–238.

Al Abed, N. A., H. R Whiteley, R. P. Rudra, and W. James (1993). "Salinity Problem by Irrigation in Jordan and the Middle East," in *Proceedings of the International Symposium on Water Resources in the Middle East: Policy and Institutional Aspects*, Urbana, IL.: University of Illinois, 92–99.

Al Akram, N. (1992). *The Jewish Occupation of Arabic Water*. Beirut: Dar al Nafess.

Al Ansar, N. (1981). "Water Resources in Iraq," *Journal of Geological Society of Iraq* 2: 35–42.

Al Katib, N., and K. Assaf (1994). "Palestinian water supplies and demands," in *Israel-Palestine Water*, J. Issac and H. Shuval (eds.). Amsterdam: Elsevier, 55–68.

Al Kloub, B., and T. T. Al Shemmer (1996). "Application of multi-criteria decision aid to rank the Jordan-Yarmouk basin co-riparians according to the Helsinki and ILC rules," in J. A. Allan (ed.), *Water, Peace and the Middle-East: Negotiating Resources in the Jordan Basin,* . London: Taurus Academic Studies, 185–210.

Ali, H. M. (1955). *Land Reclamation and Settlement in Iraq*, Baghdad: Printing Press.

Allan, J. A. (1985). "Irrigated Agriculture in the Middle East: The Future," in *Agricultural Development in the Middle East*, P. Beaumont and K. McLachlan (eds.). New York: John Wiley, 51–62.

———. (1987). "Syria's Agricultural Options," in *Politics and the Economy in Syria*, J. A. Allen (ed.). London: Center of Near East and Middle Eastern Studies, 22–38.

———. (1988). "The Great Man-Made River: Progress and Prospects of Libya's Great Water Carrier," *Libyan Studies* 19, 141–144.

———. (1988–1989). "Water in the Arab Middle East: The Nile Changing Expectations and Priorities," *Arab Affair* 1 (8; Winter): 44–52.

———. (1989). "Natural Resources: Not So Natural for Ease of Development," in *Libya: State and Region*, J. A. Allan et al. (eds.). London: SOAS, 63–72.

———. (1990). "Review of Evolving Water Demands and National Development Options," in *The Nile*, P. P. Howell and J. A. Allan (eds.). London: SOAS, 181–192.

———. (1991). "Water Resources in the Middle East and North Africa: Managing the Deficit," in *Brismes Conference Proceedings*. London: SOAS, 190–198.

———, (ed.) (1996a). *Water, Peace and the Middle East: Negotiating Resources in the Jordan Basin*. London: Taurus Academic Studies.

———, (1996b). "The Political economy of water: Reasons for optimism but long term caution," in *Water, Peace and the Middle East: Negotiating Resources in the Jordan Basin*, J. A. Allan (ed.). London: Taurus Academic Studies, 75–120.

Allan, J. A., and C. Lantz (eds.) (1990). *Geographical Digest* 1990/1, Oxford: Heineman.

Allan, J. A., K. S. McLachlan, and M. M. Boru (eds.) (1989). *Libya: State and Region*. London: SOAS.

Allan, J. A., and Chibli Mallat (eds.) (1995). *Water in the Middle East*, London: British Academic Press.

Alvi, S. H., and N. A. Elagib (1996). "Study of Hydrology and Drought in the Flood Region of Sudan," *Water International* 21, 76–82.

Amery, Hussein (1993). "The Litani River of Lebanon," *The Geographical Review* 83 (3): 229–237.

Arad, A. (1988). "Underground Water: Potential for Conflicts between Israel and its Neighbours," in *Regional Water Project in the Middle East*, A. Soffer, and N. Kliot (eds.), Haifa: University of Haifa.

Arlosoroff, S. (1996). "Managing scarce water: Recent Israeli experience," in *Water, Peace and the Middle East: Negotiating Resources in the Jordan Basin*, J. A. Allan (ed.). London: Taurus Academic Studies, 21–48.

Assaf, K., N. Khatib, E. Kally, and M. Shuval (1993). *A Proposal for the Development of a Regional Water Master Plan*. Jerusalem: IPCRI.

Avnimelech, Y. et al. (eds.) (1978). *Kinneret, the Lake and the Drainage Basin*. Tiberias: Kinneret Basin Administration.

Badary, M. M. (1980). "Water Resources in Iraq," in *Irrigation of Agriculture Development*, S. S. Johl (ed.). New York: Pergamon Press.

Bakour, Y. and J. Kolars (1994). "The Arab Mashrek: Hydrologic History, Problems and Perspectives," in *Water in the Arab World*, P. Rogers and P. Lydon, (eds.). Cambridge, MA: Harvard University Press, 121–146.

Barberis, J. (1991). "The Development of International Law of Transboundary Groundwater," *Natural Resources Journal* 31: 167–185.

Beaumont, P. (1978). "The Euphrates River: An International Problem of Water Resources Development," *Environmental Conservation* 5 (1; Spring): 35–43.

———— (1985). "The Agricultural Environment: An Overview," in *Agricultural Development in the Middle East*, P. Beaumont and K. McLachlan (eds.). New York: John Wiley, 3–26.

Beaumont, P. and K. McLachlan (eds.) (1985). *Agricultural Development in the Middle East*. New York: John Wiley.

Beaumont, P., G. H. Blake, and J. M. Wagstaff (1988). *The Middle East: A Geographical Study*. London: Halsted Press.

Beecher J. A. (1997). "Water Utility Privatization and Regulation: Lessons from the Global Experiment," *Water International* 20(1): 54–62.

Beeley, Brian W. (1985). "Progress in Turkish Agriculture," in *Agricultural Development in the Middle East* P. Beaumont and K. McLachlan (eds.). New York: John Wiley, 289–302.

Ben Aryeh, Y. (1965). *The Central Jordan Valley*. Israel, Merchavia: Hashomer Hatzair.

Ben Shachar, H., G. Fishelson, and S. Hirsch (1989). *Economic Cooperation and Middle East Peace*. London: Wiedenfeld and Nicolson.

Benvenisti, E. and H. Gvirtzman (1994). "Harnessing International Law to Determine Israel-Palestinian Water Rights: The Mountain Aquifer," *Natural Resources Journal* 33, 671–718.

Benvenisti, M. (1987). *The West Bank Handbook*, Jerusalem: Kame.

Benvenisti, M. (1984). *The West Bank Data Project*. Washington, D.C.: American Enterprise Institute for Public Policy Research.

Benvenisti, M. and S. Khayat (1988). *The West Bank and Gaza Atlas*. Jerusalem: The West Bank Data Base Project.

Berenyi, I. (1994). "The Rise and Fall of the Caspian Sea," *Briefing Review*, 25–27.

Beschorner, Natasha (1992–1993). *Water and Instability in the Middle East*. London: Adelphi Paper 273.

Bilen, O. (1994). "Prospects for Technical Cooperation in the Euphrates-Tigris Basin," in *International Waters of the Middle East*, A. K. Biswas (ed.). Bombay: Oxford University Press, 95–116.

Biswas, A. K. (1989). "Issues and Politics," in *Water Management for Arid Lands in Developing Countries*, A. K. Biswas, (ed.). Oxford: Pergamon Press, 9–27.

Biswas, A. K. (ed.) (1994). *International Water of the Middle East*. Bombay: Oxford University Press.

Biswas, A. K. and J. Kindler (1989). "Sustainable Water Development and Management," *International Journal of Water Resources Development:* 225–251.

Biswas, A. K., J. Kolars, M. Murakami, J. Waterbury, and A. Wolf (1996). *Core and Periphery: A Comprehensive Approach to Middle Eastern Water*. Oxford: Oxford University Press.

Blake, G. H., J. C. Dewdney, and J. K. Mitchell (1987). *The Cambridge Atlas of the Middle East*. Cambridge, UK: Cambridge University Press.

Blass, S. (1973). *Water in Strife and Action*, Tel Aviv: Massada.

Bourgey, A. (1974). "Le Barrage De Tabqa Et L'amenagement Du Bassin De L'euphrate en Syrie," *Revue De Geographie De Lyun*: 343–345.

Braverman A., N. Hasid, S. Drori, J. Schwartz, and J. Maoz (1994). "Water Supply in Israel—Observations towards the Twenty-First Century," *Rivon Le Kalkala (The Economic Quarterly)*, 41(3) 369–399.

Brawer, M. and Y. Karmon (1968). *The Middle East Atlas*, Tel Aviv: Yavneh.

Briggs, H. W. (1952). *The Law of Nations,* 2nd. ed. New York: Appleton-Century Croft.

Brosh, R. (1980). *The Possibilities to Use Solar Energy to Desalinate Water*. Jerusalem: Energy Ministry: 875–902.

Brown, F. Lee (1997). "Water Markets and Traditional Water Values: Merging Commodity and Community Prespectives," *Water International* 20: 2–5.

Burdon, D. J. (1954). "Infiltration Rates in the Yarmouk Basin of Syria-Jordan," *Assemblee General de Rome*: II, 343–355.

———. (1954). "Ground Water in Syria," *Assemblee General de Rome*, vol. II, 377–388.

Caelleigh, A. S. (1983). "Middle East Water: Vital Resource, Conflict, and Cooperation," in *A Shared Destiny*, Joyce Starr and A. S. Caelleigh (eds.). New York: Praeger.

Canaan, F. M. (1990). "Water Resources and Irrigation Perspectives for the Year 2000," *Water and Irrigation Review* 10 (3–4): 18–21.

Cano, G. J. (1989). "The Development of the Law of International Water Resources and the Work of the International Law Commission," *Water International* 14, 167–171.

Caponera, D. (1993). "Legal Aspects of Transboundary River Basins in the Middle East: The Al Asi (Orontes), the Jordan, and the Nile," *Natural Resources Journal* 33 629–649.

Chapman, J. D. (ed.) (1963). *The International River Basins*. Vancouver, Canada: University of British Columbia.

Chesworth, P. (1990). "History of Water Use in Sudan and Egypt," in *The Nile*, P. P. Howell and J. A. Allan (eds.). London: SOAS, 40–58.

Chezawi, Ali (1992). "Jordan's Water Resources and Uses," *Jordan Times*, March 1.

Clark, Robin. (1993). *Water: The International Crisis*. Cambridge MA: The MIT Press, 1993.

Collins, Robert O. (1990a). *The Waters of the Nile, Hydropolitics and the Jongli Canal 1900–1988*. Oxford: Oxford University Press.

———. (1990b). "Historical View of the Development of Nile Water," in *The Nile*, P. P. Howell and J. A. Allan (eds.). London: SOAS, 153–180.

———. (1994). "History, Hydropolitics and the Nile: Myth of Reality," in *The*

*Nile: Sharing a Scarce Resource,* P. P. Howell and J. A. Allan (eds.). Cambridge, UK: Cambridge University Press, 109–136.

Colton, Y., P. Miro, and R. Rosner (1984). *Hydrological Research of the Yarmuk Basin* (Tahal Report 01/84/67), Tel Aviv: Tahal.

Cooley, J. (1983). "The Hydraulic Imperative," *Middle East International,* July 22, 10–11.

Copaken, N., and A. Soffer (1996). *The Perception of Water as Part of Territory in Israel, and Arab Ideologies Between 1964–1993: A Further Understanding of the Arab-Jewish Conflict.* Haifa: University of Haifa.

Cressey, G. B. (1960). *Crossroads.* Chicago: J. P. Lippincott.

Dabbagh, T., P. Sadler, A. Al Saqabi, and M. Sadeqi (1994). "Desalination, an Emergent Option," in *Water in the Arab World,* P. P. Rogers and P. Lydon (eds.). Cambridge, MA: Harvard University Press, 203–242.

Derrick, J. (1987). "Is the Nile Drying Up?" *The Middle East,* October: 28.

Dethier, J. J., and K. Funk (1987). "The Language of Food." *Middle East Report* (March-April): 22–27.

Dewdney, J. C. (1981). "Agricultural Development in Turkey," in *Change and Development in the Middle East,* J. I. Clark and H. B. Jones (eds.). New York: Methuen, 213–223.

De Vaumas, E. (1954). *Le Liban: Etude de géographie physique.* Paris: Firmin-Didot.

Dinar, A., and E. Tusak Loehman (eds.) (1995). *Water Quantity/Quality Management and Conflict Resolution.* London: Praeger.

Doherty, K. B. (1965). *Jordan Waters Conflict.* New York: The Carnegie Endowment for International Peace.

Drezon-Tepler, M. (1994). "Contested Waters and the Prospects for Arab-Israeli Peace," *Middle Eastern Studies* 30: 284–303.

Duna, C. (1988). "Turkey Peace Pipeline," in *The Politics of Scarcity, Water in the Middle East,* J. R. Starr and D. C. Stoll (eds.). Boulder, CO: Westview, 119–124.

Earle, Sylvia A. (1992). "Persian Gulf Pollution: Assessing the Damage, One Year Later," *National Geographic* 181 (2): 122–134.

Eckstein, Z., D. Zakai, Y. Nachum and G. Fishelson (1994). "The Allocation of Water Sources Among Israel, the West Bank, and Gaza: An Economic Analysis," *Rivon Le Kalkala* (*Economic Quarterly*) 41, 331–368.

Ehlers, E. (1979). "Population Growth and Food Supply Margin in Egypt," *Applied Sciences and Development* 14: 65–87.

Eitan, G. (1995). *Sewage Treatment and Use—Survey.* Jerusalem: Water Commissioner.

El Baz, F. (1979). "The Western Desert in Egypt, Its Problems and Potentials." *Desert and Arid Lands,* 1.

El-Hindi, J. L. (1990). "The West Bank Aquifer and Conventions Regarding Laws of Belligerent Occupation," *Michigan Journal of International Law* 11: 1400–1423.

Elmusa, S. S. (1993). "Dividing the Common Palestinian-Israeli Waters: An International Water Law Approach," *Journal of Palestine Studies* 22(3): 87–97.

———— (1995). "The Jordan-Israel Water Agreement: A Model or an Exception?" *Journal of Palestine Studies* 24(3): 68–73.

El Saman, N. (1993). *The Water Wars from the Euphrates up to Nile*. Damascus: Dar el Knahan.

Evans, T. (1990). "History of the Nile Flows," in *The Nile*, P. P. Howell and J. A. Allan (eds.). London: SOAS, 4–39.

Fahim, H. M. (1981). *Dams, People and Development: the Aswan High Dam Case*. New York: Pergamon Press.

Fahmy, H. (1996). "Comparative Analysis of Egyptian Water Policies," *Water International* 21: 35–45.

FAO, Yearbook (1996). *Commerce*. Rome: Food and Agriculture Organization of United Nations.

Feitelson, E. (1995). "Institutional Perspectives for Common Management of the Mountain Aquifer," Lecture in a Colloquim on *Water in Israel and the Peace Process*, Feb. 15, Beersheba, Israel.

Feitelson, E., and M. Haddad (1994). *Joint Management of Shared Aquifers: Final Report—1995*. Jerusalem: The H. S. Truman Institute for Advancement of Peace and the Palestine Consultancy Group.

———— (eds.) (1994). *Joint Management of Shared Aquifers: The Second Workshop*, Jerusalem: The H. S. Truman Institute for Advancement of Peace and the Palestine Consultancy Group.

———— (eds.) (1996). *Joint Management of Shared Aquifers: The Third Workshop*, Jerusalem: The H. S. Truman Institute for Advancement of Peace, the Palestine Consultancy Group, and the International Development Research Centre, Canada.

Fisher, A. (1993). "Desalination Process." *Teka Mazdiya* 53: 32–37.

Fisher, W. B. (1979). *The Middle East*. London: Methuen.

Foreign Broadcast Information Service (1964). *Daily Reports*, Washington, D.C.: United States Information Agency.

Frankel, Norman (1992). "Water and Politics: The Turkish Perspective." *Middle East Focus* 14: 4–17.

Frey, F. W., and T. Naff (1985). "Water: An Emerging Issue in the Middle East?" *Annals of the American Academy of Political and Social Sciences* 42: 65–81.

Gabar B. (1994). "Water Problems in Lebanon," in *Water Problems in the Middle East*, N. Issa (ed.). Beirut: Center of Strategic Studies, 19–63.

Gal, Y. (1987). "Introduction," in *The Kinneret*, Y. Gal and E. Shiller (eds.). Tiberias and Jerusalem: The Kinneret Basin Administration.

Gal, Y., and E. Shiller (eds.) (1987). *The Kinneret—Source of Life for Israel*, Jerusalem: Ariel.

Garbell, M. A. (1965). "The Jordan Valley Plan." *Scientific American* 212(3): 23–71.

Garstin, W. (1901). *Report as to Irrigation Projects on the Upper Nile*, London.

———— (1904). *Report upon the Basin of the Upper Nile*, London.

*Gaza-Jericho Agreement*, May 4, 1994, signed at Cairo. (Reprinted in 33 International Legal Materials 622 (1994).

Geffen, M. (1987). "Changes in the System of the Kinneret," *Biosphera* 17(1): 6–9.

Gilad, D. (1988). "Mount Hermon—the Main Water Source for the Golan and Kinneret Basin," *Horizons in Geography* 25–26: 51–70.

Gischler, C. (1979). *Water Resources in the Arab Middle East and North Africa*, Cambridge, UK: Menas.

Glickstern P. (1996). "Desalination 1996—Processes—Technology—Cost," *Water and Irrigation* 361: 4–41.

Glickstern, P., and Priel M. (1996). "Optimized Brakish Water Desalination Plants with Minimum Impact on the Environment," *Desalination* 108: 19–26.

Glick, P. H. (1993). *Water in Crisis: A Guide to the World's Fresh Water Resources*. New York: Oxford University Press.

——— (1994). "Reducing the Risks of Conflict over Fresh Water Resources in the Middle East," in *Water and Peace in the Middle East*, J. Isaac and H. Shuval (eds.). Amsterdam: Elsevier: 41–54.

Golan, S. (1983). "The Struggles over the Jordan Waters," in *The Lands of Galilee*, A. Shmueli, A. Soffer, and N. Kliot (eds.). Haifa: University of Haifa: 853–862.

Gross, D. and A. Soffer (1996). *International Groundwater and International Rules—The Case of the Middle East, and the Agreements Between Israel and Jordan and Between Israel and Palestinians about Gaza Strip*. Haifa: University of Haifa.

Gruen, George (1964). "Water and Politics in the Middle East," *American Jewish Committee. Report on the Foreign Scene*, no. 5, December.

Gur, Shlomo (1992). "Water and the Peace Process: A View from Israel," *Policy Focus* 20: 1–20.

Gvirtzman, H. (1990). "The Water Supply of Israel Where Does It Turn?" *Mada* 28: 875–902.

——— (1994). "The Implications of the Peace Agreements on Water Supply to Central Israel," *Ecology and Environment* 1–2: 85–93.

——— (1995). *Geo-Hydrological Consideration to Divide Between Jews and Arabs in Judea and Samaria*, Special Report to the Israeli Water Commissoner (Unpublished).

Gvirtzman, H. and E. Benvenisti (1993). "The Jewish-Arab Water Conflict — Hydrological and Jurisdictional Perspectives," *Water* 10: 32–40.

Halawani, S. (1985). "Lebanese Development Projects and Israel Pursuit of the Litani and Hasbani Waters," in *Israel and Arab Water*, A. M. Farid and H. Sirriyeh (eds.). London: The Arab Research Center: 51–56.

Hamdy, A., M. Abuzzeid, and C. Lacirignola (1995). "Water Crisis in the Mediterranean: Agricultural Water Demand Management," *Water International* 20: 176–181.

Haynes, K. E., and D. Whittington (1981). "International Management of the Nile: Stage Three?" *Geographical Review* 71: 17–32.

Hayton, R. D. (1981). "International Aquifiers and International Law," *Water International* 6: 158–165.

———— (1982). "Law of International Aquifiers," *Natural Resources Journal* 22: 71–80.

Hayton, R. D., and A. E. Utton (1989). "Transboundary Groundwater: The Bellagio Draft Treaty." *Nature Resources Journal* 29: 663–721.

*Hebrew Encyclopedia* (1957). Jerusalem: Encyclopedia Publishing Company, 6: 524–528.

Henkin, L. R., C. Pugh, O. Schaehter, and H. Smit (1987). *International Law, Cases and Materials.* St. Paul: West Publishing.

Hirsch, A. (1956). "From the Indus to the Jordan: Characteristics of the Middle East International River Disputes," *Political Science Quarterly* LXXI: 203–222.

Hof, Fred (1994). "The Yarmouk and Jordan Rivers in the Israel-Jordan Peace Treaty." *Middle East Policy* 3(4): 47–56.

Homer-Dixon, T. F., J. H. Boutwell, and G. W. Rothjens (1993). "Environmental Change and Violent Conflict," *Scientific American*: 268(2): 16–23.

Hopner, T., and J. Windelberg (1996). "Elements of Environmental Impact Studies on Coastral Desalination Plants," *Desalination* 108: 11–18.

Howell, P., M. Lock and S. Cobb (eds.) (1988). *The Jonglei Canal.* Cambridge, UK: Cambridge University Press.

Howell, P. P., and J. A. Allan (eds.) (1990). *The Nile.* London: SOAS.

———— (eds.) (1994). *The Nile, Sharing a Scarce Resource.* Cambridge, UK: Cambridge University Press.

Hulme, M. (1994). "Global Climate Change and the Nile Basin," in *The Nile, Sharing a Scarce Resource*, P. P. Howell and J. A. Allan (eds.). Cambridge, UK: Cambridge University, 1994: 139–162.

Hulme, M., and A. Trilbach (1989). "The August 1988 Storm over Khartoum: Its Climatology and Impact," *Weather* 44: 82–90.

Hurst, H. E. (1965). *The Nile.* London: Constable Publishers.

Hurst, H. E. et al. (1966). *Long-Term Storage: An Experimental Study.* London: Constable Publishers.

Ionides, M. G. (1937). *The Regime of the Rivers Euphrates and Tigris.* New York: The Chemical Publishing Company.

———— (1953). "The Disputed Water of the Jordan," *Middle East Tributary* 7(2): 153–164.

Inbar, M., and J. Maoz (1984). "The Struggle over Water and the Development of the Jordan River Sources," *Horizons in Geography* 9–10: 45–56.

Irbec, Y. Z. (1993). "Water Issues and Turkey," *Tercüman* (Istanbul, daily), June 27.

Isaac, J. and H. Shuval (eds.) (1994). *Water and Peace in the Middle East.* Amsterdam: Elsevier Press.

Israel, State Comptroller Office (1990, 1991). *Report on the Water Management in Israel.* Jerusalem.

Israel, State of (1993). *Statistical Abstracts of Israel, 1993.* Jerusalem: Central Bureau of Statistics.

Israel, State of, Civil Administration (1993). *Data.* Tel Aviv: Ministry of Defence.

————. Civil Administration (1996). *Data*. Tel Aviv: Ministry of Defence.

Israel, State of. (1994). *Development Options for Regional Cooperation, 1994*. Jerusalem: Ministry of Foreign Affairs.

Israel, State of (1996). *Development Options for Middle East Cooperation*, chap. 4, *Water Development Options, 1996. Jerusalem:* Ministry of Foreign Affairs.

Israel, State of, Water Commissioner (1994, 1995). *Data*. Tel Aviv.

Israeli, State of, Hydrological Service (1993). *Data*. Tel Aviv.

*Israeli-Palestinian Interim Agreement on the West Bank and Gaza Strip*, September 28, 1995. Jerusalem: Ministry of Foreign Affairs.

Istanbul Chamber of Commerce (1989). *Southeastern Anatolia Project* (GAP). Istanbul: Chamber of Commerce.

Jansen, G. (1990). "Tussle over the Euphrates," *Middle East International*, February 16: 12–13.

Jerusalem Media and Communication Centre (1994). *Water, the Red Liner*. East Jerusalem: JMCC.

Jordan, State of (1986). *The National Atlas of Jordan 1984*, Part 1: "Climate and Agro-Climatology"; Part 2: "Hydrology." Amman: Royal Jordanian Geographic Center.

Jordan, The State of (1994). *Jordan: Tomorrow has Arrived: Investing in People*. Amman: Ministry of Planning.

Jovanovic, D. (1985). "Ethiopian Interests in the Division of the Nile River," *Water International* 10: 82–85.

Kahan, David (1987). *Agriculture and Water Resources in the West Bank and Gaza (1967–1987)*. Jerusalem: The West Bank Data Base Project.

Kally, Elisha (1965). *The Struggle for Water: History, Structure and Functions of the National Water Project*. Tel Aviv: Hakibbutz Hameuchad.

———— (1978). "The Kinneret as the Water Source of the Israeli Water Carrier," in *Kinneret the Lake and the Drainage Basin*, N. Avnimelech and M. Lecher (eds.). Tiberias: Kinneret Basin Administration, 31–36.

———— (1990a). *A Middle East Water Plan Under Peace*. Tel Aviv: Tel Aviv University, the Armand Hammer Fund for Economic Cooperation in the Middle East.

———— (1990b). *Water in Peace*. Tel Aviv: Tel Aviv University.

———— (1996). *The National Water Economy: Development and Management Problems*. Jerusalem: Ministry of Economy and Planning.

Kanovsky, Eliyahu (1985a). *What's Behind Syria's Current Economic Problems?* Tel Aviv: Tel Aviv University, Moshe Dayan Center for Middle Eastern Studies.

———— (1985b). *Jordan's Economy: From Prosperity to Crisis*. Tel Aviv: Tel Aviv University, Moshe Dayan Center for Middle Eastern Studies.

Karmon, Yehuda (1956). *The Northern Hula Valley*. Jerusalem: I. L. Magnes.

Khader, B. (1984). *La Question Agrare Dans Le Pays Arabes: Le Cas de la Syrie*, Louvain: University Catholique de Louvain.

Khourie, R. G. (1981). *The Jordan Valley: Life and Society Below Sea Level*. London: Longman.

Kinneret Administration (1994–1995). *Data*. Israel, Zemach.

Kliot, Nurit (1994). *Water Resources and Conflict in the Middle East*. London: Routledge.

Knott, D., and R. G. M. Hewett (1990). "Future Water Development Planning in Sudan," in *The Nile*, P. P. Howell and J. A. Allan (eds.). London: SOAS: 93–106.

Kolars, J. (1986). "The Hydro Imperative of Turkey's Search for Energy," *Middle East Journal* 40: 53–67.

——— (1990). "Testimony on the Euphrates, before the Committee on Foreign Affairs." U.S. House of Representatives, Washington, D.C., June 26.

——— (1994). "Problems of International River Management: The Case of the Euphrates," in *International Waters of the Middle East from Euphrates-Tigris to Nile*, A. K. Biswas (ed.). Bombay: Oxford University Press: 44–94.

Kolars, Y. F., and W. A. Mitchell (1991). *The Euphrates River and the Southeast Anatolia Development Project*. Carbondale: Southern Illinois University Press.

Krishna, R. (1988). "The Legal Regime of the Nile River Basin," in *The Politics of Scarcity of Water in the Middle East*, J. R. Starr and D. C. Stoll (eds.). Boulder, CO: Westview: 23–40.

"The Law of Non-Navigational Uses of International Watercourses." (1991). *Environmental Policy and Law*, 21.5.6.

Le Marquand, D. (1977). "Politics of International River Basin Cooperation and Management," in *Water in a Developing World*, A. E. Utton and L. Teclaff (eds.). Boulder, Colorado: Westview Press, 147–165.

——— (1981). "International Action for International River," *Water International* 6: 147–151.

Libiszewski, Stephan (1995). *Water Disputes in the Jordan Basin Region and Their Role in the Resolution of the Arab-Israeli Conflict*. Bern: Swiss Peace Foundation.

——— (1997). "Integrating High and Low Politics: Lessons from the Israeli-Jordanian Water Regime," *Water International*, 22: 6–14.

Little, T. (1965). *High Dam at Aswan*. London: Methuen.

Lonergan, S. C., and D. B. Brooks (1995). *Watershed, The Role of Fresh Water in the Israeli-Palestiian Conflict*. Ottawa: International Development Research Centre.

Lowdermilk, W. C. (1944). *Palestine: Land of Promise*. London: Victor Gollancz.

Lowi, M. (1993). *Water and Power, The Politics of a Scarce Resource in the Jordan River Basin*. Cambridge, UK: Cambridge University Press.

Main, C. T. Inc. (1953). *The Unified Development of the Water Resources of the Jordan Valley Region*. Knoxville, TN: Tennessee Valley Authority.

Manner, I. R., and T. Sagafi-Nejad (1985). "Agricultural Development in Syria," in *Agricultural Development in the Middle East*, P. Beaumont and K. McLachlan (eds.). New York: John Wiley, 255–278.

McLachlan, K. (1987). "The Libyan South: Background to Current Development and Future Outlook," in *The Economic Development of Libya*. B. Khader, and B. M. Elwafat (eds.). London: Croom Helm, 37–57.

McLachlan, K., and M. Nassar (1986). "Iraq," *Arab Agriculture*. London: Fulcan.

Mekorot Water Company Ltd. (1991). *Dan Region Sewage Treatment and Reclamation Project*. Tel Aviv: Mekorot Water Co. Ltd. (Report).

Mekorot Water Company Ltd. (1996). *Annual Report 1996*. Tel Aviv: Mekorot Water Co. Ltd.

*Middle East and North Africa Yearbook*. London: Europa Publication, various years.

Morton, A. Y., I. K. Collister, and N. M. Wade (1996). "Environmental Impacts of Sea Water Desalination Reverse Osmosis Processes," *Desalination* 108: 1–10.

Murakami, Masahiro (1995). *Managing Water for Peace in the Middle East: Alternative Strategies*. Tokyo: United Nations University Press.

Murray, G. W. (1952). "The Water Beneath the Egyptian Western Desert," *Geographical Journal* 118 (4): 443–452.

Musallam, R. (1989). "Water: The Middle East Problem in the 1990s," *Gulf Report*, 18: 3–18.

Naff, D. (1994). "Israel-Syria: Conflict at the Jordan River 1949–1967," *Journal of Palestine Studies* 23(4): 26–40.

Naff, T. (1990). "Testimony on the Jordan River before the Committee on Foreign Affairs." U.S. House of Representatives, Washington, D.C., June 26.

——— (1991). "Israel and the Waters of South Lebanon," paper presented at the Peacekeeping Water and Security in South Lebanon Conference, Center for Lebanese Studies, Oct. 4.

——— (1993). "Israel and the Waters of South Lebanon." *Prospects for Lebanon*, J. Kolars and T. Naff (eds). Oxford: Center for Lebanese Studies.

——— (1994). "Conflict and Water Use in the Middle East," in *Water in the Arab World*. Cambridge, MA: Harvard University Press: 253–284.

Naff, T., and R. Matson (eds.) (1984). *Water in the Middle East: Conflict or Cooperation*. Boulder, CO: Westview.

Nimrod, Yoram (1966). *Angry Waters: Controversy over the Jordan River*. Givat Haviva: Center for Arabic and Afro-Asian Studies.

North, Andrew (1993). "Saddam's Water War," *Geographical Magazine*: LXV(7) 10–14.

Ockerman, H. W., and S. G. Samano (1985). "The Agricultural Development of Iraq," in *Agricultural Development in the Middle East*, P. Beaumont and K. McLachlan (eds.). New York: John Wiley: 189–208.

Ohlsson, L. (ed.) (1995). *Hydropolitics*. London: Zed Books.

Okidi, Odidi (1990). "A Review of Treaties on Consumptive Utilization of Water of Lake Victoria and Nile Drainage Basins" in *The Nile*, P. P. Howell and J. A. Allan (eds.). London: SOAS, 193–224.

Paldi, Chaim (1987). "The Water Balance in the Upper Basin," in *The Kinneret—Source of Life for Israel*, Y. Gal, and E. Shiller (eds.). Jerusalem: Ariel, 21–30.

Pallas, P. (1980). "Water Resources in the Socialist People's Libyan Arab Jamahiriya," in *The Geography of Libya*, M. J. Salem and M. T. Busrewil (eds.). London: Academic Press, 539–594.

Peres, S. (1993). *The New Middle East*. New York: Henry Holt.

Pope, H. (1990). "Water in a Bag," *Middle East International,* June 8: 14.

Population Reference Bureau (1996). *World Population Data Sheet*. Washington, D.C.: Population Reference Bureau.

Postel, Sandra (1992). *Last Oasis: Facing Water Scarcity*. New York: W. W. Norton and Company.

Preul, H. C. (1994). "Rainfall-Runoff Water Harvesting Prospects for Greater Amman and Jordan," *Water International* 19: 82–95.

Rabinovitz, I. (1983). "The Conflict of Water as a Factor in the Israeli-Arab Conflict," in *The Lands of Galilee*, A. Shemueli, A. Soffer, and N. Kliot (eds.). Haifa: University of Haifa: 863–868.

Reguer, Sara (1993). "Controversial Waters: Exploitation of the Jordan River," *Middle Eastern Studies* 29: 53–90.

—— (1995). "Rutenberg and the Jordan River: A Revolution in Hydro-Electricity," *Middle Eastern Studies* 31: 695–729.

Reisner, Marc (1993). *Cadillac Desert*. New York: Penguin Books.

Rhodes, S. (1993). "Groundwater Rights in an Uncertain Environment: Theoretical Perspectives on the San Luis Valley," *Natural Resources Journal* 32: 727–758.

Richards, A. (1980). "Egypt's Agriculture in Trouble," *Middle East Research and Information Project*, 84: 3–13.

Rogers, P. and P. Lydon (eds.) (1994). *Water in the Arab World*. Cambridge, MA: Harvard University Press.

Ron, Z. (1982). "The Litani River." *Kardom* 5(26–27): 52–66.

Rutenberg, P. (1920). *Water Resources of Palestine and Jordan Valley*. Jerusalem.

Sadik, A., and S. Barghouti (1994). "The Water Problem of the Arab World: Management of Scarce Resources," in *Water in the Arab World*, P. Rogers and P. Lydon (eds.). Cambridge, MA: Harvard University Press, 1–38.

Said, Rushdi (1993). *The River Nile: Geology, Hydrology, and Utilization*. Oxford: Pergamon Press.

Saleh, W. A. (1985). "Development Projects on the Euphrates," in *Israel and Arab Water*, A. M. Farid and H. Sirriyeh (eds.). London: The Arab Research Center, 69–74.

Saliba, S. N. (1968). *The Jordan River Dispute*. The Hague: Martinus Nijhoff.

Salik, David (1988). "The Lower Jordan River," *Horizons in Geography* 25–26: 111–120.

Sasson, J. M. (ed.) (1995). *Civilizations of the Ancient Near East*. New York: Simon and Schuster.

Sayed, B.A. (1960). *Sudanese Egyptian Relations*. The Hague: Martinus Nijhoff.

Schiller, Eric J. (1996). "Water Resources in the Middle East, Engineering Options with a Scarce Commodity," paper presented at the conference "Water Triggers for War," Indiana University.

Schofield, Clive (1993). "Elusive Security: The Military and Political Geography of South Lebanon," *Geojournal* 31(2): 149–161.

Schwartz, Yehoshua (1986). "The Water in Israel," *Skira Hodshit* 51: 24–34.

—— (1988). *The Water Master Plan for Israel* (Tahal Publication No. 01/88/70), Tel Aviv: Tahal.

—— (1996). "The Master Plan No. 34—The Recycled Water," Lecture presented at a conference organized by the Ministry of Health, Tel Aviv, November 6.

Sexton, R. (1990). *Perspectives on the Middle East Water Crisis: Analyzing Water Scarcity Problems in Jordan and Israel.* London: Overseas Development Institute.

Shady, A. M., A. M. Adam, and K. A. Mohamed (1994). "The Nile 2002: The Vision Toward Cooperation in the Nile Basin," *Water International* 19: 77–80.

Shahin, M. (1985). *Hydrology of the Nile Basin.* Amsterdam: Elsevier.

—— (1986). "Ethiopian Water Interests in the Division of the Nile River: Discussion," *Water International* 11: 16–20.

—— (1989). "Review and Assessment of Water Resources in the Arab Region," *Water International* 14: 206–219.

Shamir, Uri, J. Bear, and N. Arad (1985). *Water Policy for Israel.* Haifa: The Technion Institute of Technology.

Shatanawi, M. R., and O. al Jayousi (1995). "Evaluating Market-Oriented Water Policies in Jordan: A Comparative Study," *Water International* 20: 88–97.

Shuval, H. I. (1992). "Approaches to Resolving The Water Conflict Between Israel and Her Neighbors—A Regional Water for Peace Plan," *Water International* 17: 133–143.

Soffer, A. (1992). *Changes in the Geography of the Middle East.* Tel Aviv: Am Oved.

Soffer, A. (1994). "The Litani River—Fact and Fiction," *Middle Eastern Studies* 30: 963–974.

Solanes, M. (1994). "Legal and International Aspects of River Basin Development," *Water International* 17: 116–123.

Stanley, D. I. (1988). "Subsidence in the Northeastern Nile Delta: Rapid Rates, Possible Causes and Consequences," *Science* 240(4851): 497–500.

Starr, J. R., and D. C. S. Stoll (1987). *Foreign Policy of Water Resources in the Middle East.* Washington, D.C.: The Center for Strategic and International Studies.

Stevens, G. G. (1965). *Jordan River Partition.* Stanford, CA: Hoover Institution Studies, no. 6.

Stoner, R. R. (1990). "Future Irrigation Planning in Egypt," in *The Nile*, P. P. Howell and J. A. Allan (eds.). London: SOAS: 83–92.

Stork, J. (1983). "Water and Israel's Occupation Strategy," *Middle East Research and Information Project* 13(6): 19–24.

Stork, J., and K. Pfeifer (1987). "Bullets, Banks and Bushels: The Struggle for Food in the Middle East." *Middle East Report* March: 3–6.

Sutcliff, J. V., and Y. P. Parks (1987). "Hydrological Modeling of the Sudd and Jonglei Canal." *Hydrological Science Journal* 32: 143–159.

Sutcliff, J. V., and J. B. C. Lazenby (1990). "Hydrological Data Requirements for Planning Nile Management," in *The Nile*, P. P. Howell and J. A. Allan (eds.). London: SOAS, 107–126.

Syria, Government of (1988). *Raport, Economique Syrien 1986/7*, Damas, Syrie: L'office Arabe de Presso et de Documentation.

Syria, Government of (1990). *Statistical Abstract*, Damascus: Government of Syria.

Tahal (1988). *Basic Data on the Jordan Basin*. Tel Aviv: Tahal.

Taubenblatt, S. A.(1988). "Jordan River Basin Water: A Challenge in the 1990s," in *The Politics of Scarcity, Water in the Middle East*, J. R. Starr and D. C. Stoll (eds.). Boulder, CO: Westview, 41–52.

Teclaff, L. A. (1967). *The River Basin in History and Law*. The Hague: Martinus Nijhoff.

Tekeli, Shahim (1990). "Turkey Seeks Reconciliation for the Water Issue Endured by the Southeastern Anatolia Project," *Water International* 15: 206–216.

Toepfer, H. (1991). "The South East Anatolia Project: Objectives and Problems of an Integration Development Project in Turkey," paper presented at Brismes Annual Conference at SOAS, July.

Turkey, Government of (1989). *GAP Project*. Ankara: Southeastern Anatolia Project Management Unit.

——— (1990). *Official Announcement Concerning Ataturk Dam*. Ankara: Ministry of Information.

——— (1995). *Water Issues Between Turkey, Syria and Iraq*. Ankara: Ministry of Foreign Affairs.

Ubell, K. (1971). "Iraq's Water Resources," *Nature and Resources* 7(2): 3–9.

United Nations, Department of Economic and Social Affairs (1970). *Integrated River Basin Development* (Rev. Ed.). New York: United Nations.

——— (1972). *Abstraction and Use of Water: A Comparison of Legal Regimes*. New York: United Nations.

——— (1977). *Report of the United Nations Water Conference, Mar del Plata*, New York: United Nations.

——— (1978). *Register of International Rivers*. Oxford: Pergamon Press.

——— (1991). International Law Commission, *Report of the International Law Commission on the Work of its Forty-Third Session*. New York: United Nations.

U.S. Army Corps of Engineers (1991). *Water in the Sand*.

Utton, A. (1973). "International Water Quality Laws," *Natural Reserve Journal* 13: 279–296.

Utton, A., and L. Teclaff (1987). *Transboundary Resource Law*. Boulder, CO: Westview.

Vestal, T. M. (1985). "Famine in Ethiopia: Crisis of Many Dimensions," *Africa Today* 4th Quarter: 7–19.

Voll, S. P. (1980). "Egyptian Land Reclamation Since the Revolution," *The Middle East Journal* 34(2): 127–140.

Wachtal, B. (1993). "The 'Peace Canal' Plan," *Proceedings of the International Symposium on Water Resources in the Middle East: Policy and Institutional Aspects*. Urbana, IL: University of Illinois, 137–146.

———— (1994). "The Peace Canal Project: A Multiple Conflict Resolution Perspective for the Middle East," in *Water and Peace in the Middle East*, J. Isaac and H. Shuval (eds.). Amsterdam: Elsevier: 363–374.

Waterbury, J. (1978). *Egypt*. Bloomington: Indiana University Press.

———— (1979). *Hydropolitics of the Nile Valley*. New York: Syracuse University Press.

———— (1990). "Testimony on the Nile, before the Committee on Foreign Affairs," U.S. House of Representatives, Washington, D.C., June 26.

———— (1994). "Transboundary Water and the Challenges of International Cooperation in the Middle East," in *Water in the Arab World*, P. Rogers and P. Lydon (eds). Cambridge, MA: Harvard University Press, 39–64.

White, G. F. (1988). "The Environmental Effects of the Aswan High Dam," *Environment* 30: 5–40.

Whittington, D., and K. E. Haynes (1985). "Nile Water for Whom? Emerging Conflicts in Water Allocation for Agricultural Expansion in Egypt and Sudan," in *Agricultural Development in the Middle East*, P. Beaumont and K. McLachlan (eds.). New York: John Wiley, 125–150.

Whittington, D., and E. McClelland. "Opportunities for Regional and International Cooperation in the Nile Basin," *Water International* 17: 144–184.

Whittington, D., J. Waterbury, and E. McClelland (1995). "Toward New Nile Waters Agreement," in *Water Quantity/Quality Management and Conflict Resolution*, A. Dinar and E. Tusak Loeman (eds.). London: Praeger, 167–178.

Wilcocks, W. (1904). *The Nile in 1904*, Cairo: National Printing, Department of Egypt.

Wolf, A. T. (1994). "A Hydropolitical History of the Nile, Jordan, and Euphrates River Basins," in *International Waters of the Middle East*, A. K. Biswas, (ed.). Bombay: Oxford University Press: 5–43.

———— (1995a). *Hydropolitics Along the Jordan River*. United Nations University Press.

———— (1995b). "International Water Dispute Resolution: The Middle East Multilateral Working Group on Water Resources," *International Water* 20(3): 141–150.

Wolf, A. T., and S. Lonergan (1995). "Resolving Conflict over Water Disputes in the Jordan River Basin," in *Water Quantity/Quality Management and Conflict Resolution*, A. Dinar and E. Tusak Loeman (eds.). London: Praeger: 179–188.

Wood, A. P. (1995). "Population Redistribution and Agricultural Settlement Schemes in Ethiopia 1958–1980," in *Population and Development Projects in Africa*, J. I. Clark, M. Khogali, and L. A. Kosinsky (eds.). Cambridge, UK: Cambridge University Press, 84–111.

World Bank (1989). *World Development Report, 1989*. New York: Oxford University Press.

———— (1993). *World Tables 1993*. Baltimore: Johns Hopkins University Press.

———— (1994). *Integrated Development of the Jordan Rift Valley*, Washington, D.C.: The World Bank.

———— (1994). *World Development Report, 1994*. New York: Oxford University Press.

———— (1996). *World Development Report, 1996.* New York: Oxford University Press.

———— (1997). *Atlas.* Washington, D.C.: The World Bank.

———— (1997). *World Development Report,* 1997. New York: Oxford University Press.

World Resources Institute (1989). *World Resources 1988/9,* New York: Basic Books.

———— (1995). *World Resources 1994/5.* New York: Basic Books.

———— (1997). *World Resources 1996/7.* New York: Basic Books.

Young, G. Y., J. C. I. Dooge, and J. C. Rodda (1994). *The Global Water Resources Issues.* Cambridge, UK: Cambridge University Press.

Zarour, H., and Isaac, J. (1991). "The Water Crisis in the Occupied Territories," paper presented at The 7th World Congress on Water, Rabat, Morocco, May, 16.

Zohar, A., and Schwartz, Y. (1991). *The Water Problem in the Framework of Arrangements Between Israel and the Arab Countries.* Tel Aviv: Tahal.

## Newspapers and Journals

### Hebrew

*Biosphera* (Israel) vol. 18, No. 10–11, 1989

*Ha'aretz* (Israel) July 18, 1990; July 26, 1990; Sept. 14, 1990; Oct. 17, 1991; Nov. 15, 1993; May 2, 1995; May 25, 1997; June 13, 1997; Aug. 21, 1998

*Ha'ir* (Israel) Feb. 11, 1994

*Yediot Aharonot* (Israel) Oct. 2, 1990; Sept. 1, 1995; May 16, 1995

*Ma'ariv* (Israel) Jan. 7, 1990

### Arabic

*Achbar al Asbua* Sept. 10, 1987

*Al Maged* (Jordan) Feb. 25, 1995

*al Qabas* (Kuwait) March 12, 1990; Jan. 29, 1990

*al Rai* (Jordan) Nov. 1, 1989; Jan. 8, 1990; Feb. 11, 1990

*al Yawm al Usbu'a* (Syria) Dec. 18, 1989

*al Hayat* July 1990

*al Ba'ath* (Syria) Dec. 14, 1987; Dec. 9, 1987; May 9, 1988; March 9, 1990; June 24, 1990; Oct. 28, 1991; Jan. 8, 95

*Sawt al Sha'b* (Jordan) Dec. 4, 1987; June 6, 1989; June 27, 1989; Nov. 1, 1989

*Tishrein* (Syria) Sept. 22, 1987; April 30, 1988; Nov. 12, 1989; Oct. 15, 1990; March 9, 1991; March 8, 1995

*October* (Egypt) May 3, 1993

**English and French**

*Briefing* Feb. 27, 1982
*Economist* Dec. 16, 1989, Sept. 8, 1990
*Independent on Sunday* May 15, 1990
*Jordan Times* Sept. 5, 1987; Feb. 7, 1991
*MEED (Middle East Economic Digest)*, July 17, 1981; Jan. 19, 1990;
    July 2, 1990; July 10, 1990; Oct. 13, 1989; March 26, 1988; March
    13, 1988
*Middle East* October 1987; July 22, 1983
*Middle East International* July 22, 1983; Feb. 16, 1990
*Monday Morning* (Beirut) Aug. 16, 1984
*Newspot* Jan. 18, 1990; May 31, 1990; June 28, 1990
*South* June 1988
*Syrie et le Monde Arabe (Syria)* March 1982; October, 1987
*The Mideast Market* June 27, 1983; Nov. 9, 1987; Feb. 8, 1988; May
    16, 1988
*Time* Nov. 5, 1990


**Conversations, Interviews, Conferences**

Al Bian, July 7, 1991, Cairo
Gur, S., Jan. 3, 1995; Sept. 1, 1995, Tel Aviv
Kolars, J., Oct. 26, 1995, Portland, Oregon
Nativ, Feb. 15, 1995, Beer-Sheva
Rozental, E., Feb. 15, 1995, Beer-Sheva
Sagi, U., Sept. 9, 1995, Tel Aviv
Shamir, U., Feb. 15, 1995, Beer-Sheva
Shalev, Z., May 26, 1994, Tel Aviv
Zur, G., Israel Water Commissioner, February 1995, Tel Aviv

# Index

# About the Author

**Arnon Soffer** is professor of geography at the University of Haifa, Israel. He is chairman of the Geostrategy Institute and vice-chairman of the National Security Study Center at the University of Haifa.

He has served as an adviser in the fields of Jewish-Arab relations, water, demography, and Middle Eastern issues for most of the Israeli government ministries in the past three decades.

He has been a visiting scholar at the universities of London, Utah, Portland, and Jerusalem, and at the Israeli National Defense College and at West Point.

Among the books he has authored and coauthored are *Changes in the Geography of the Middle East, The Lands of Galilee,* and *Atlas of Haifa and Mount Carmel.* His most recent monographs are *International Groundwater and International Rules: The Case of the Middle East,* coauthored with D. Gross, and *The Perception of Water as Part of Territory in Israeli and Arab Ideologies Between 1964–1993,* coauthored with Nina Copaken.